MW01273926

1st ENGLISH DICTIONARY

F. R. Witty

Nelson

To the teacher

The Nelson First English Dictionary is intended as a first dictionary for 7 to 9 year olds. It includes the following distinctive features:

- 5200 headwords carefully selected from the vocabulary commonly used by this age group
- parts of speech
- tenses of verbs (present and past participles)
- irregular plurals of nouns
- comparatives and superlatives of adjectives where the final consonant is doubled (fat, fatter, fattest), or where they are irregular (bad, worse, worst)
- pronunciation where two words of the same spelling are pronounced differently
- a number of useful idioms
- a special illustrated section of useful information to help children with their writing. This comprises lists of useful words (days of the week, months, and special days), mathematical words (shapes, solids, fractions, numbers, and signs), and five pages of geographical information (maps of the British Isles, Europe and the World, and a list of countries and their people).

On pages 3, 4 and 5 there is a simple step-by-step guide to using the dictionary. It is suggested that children should be given plenty of practice at finding words by this method and understanding the information. In addition, The Nelson First English Dictionary Workbook, which provides a carefully structured introduction to dictionary skills, is an invaluable aid to the use of this dictionary.

Thomas Nelson and Sons Ltd.
Nelson House Mayfield Road
Walton-on-Thames Surrey
KT12 5PL UK

51 York Place
Edinburgh
EH1 3JD UK

Thomas Nelson (Hong Kong) Ltd.
Toppan Building 10/F
22A Westlands Road
Quarry Bay Hong Kong

Distributed in Australia by

Thomas Nelson Australia
102 Dodds Street
South Melbourne
Victoria 3205 Australia

Nelson Canada
1120 Birchmount Road
Scarborough Ontario
M1K 5G4 Canada

© F.R. Witty 1981
First published 1981
ISBN 0-17-424393-6
NPN 20 19 18 17 16 15 14

All rights reserved. No paragraph of this publication may be reproduced, copied or transmitted save with written permission or in accordance with the provisions of the Copyright, Design and Patents Act 1988, or under the terms of any licence permitting limited copying issued by the Copyright Licensing Agency, 90 Tottenham Court Road, London, W1P 9HE. Any person who does any unauthorised act in relation to this publication may be liable to criminal prosecution and civil claims for damages.

Illustrations by Margaret Kaufhold and Gary Rees

Filmset in Nelsons Teaching Alphabet by Mouldtype Foundry Ltd
Preston England

Printed in Hong Kong

CONTENTS

HOW TO FIND A WORD

To find the word **jealous**, you need to follow three steps.

1. Try to open the dictionary near the right letter.

The word **jealous** begins with **j**, so you need to find the **j** pages. Remember that the dictionary is in alphabetical order. It helps to think of it in three parts like this:

Front	Middle	End
abcdefghi	jklmnopq	rstuvwxyz

So to find **j** you need to open it near the middle.

2. Now use the guidewords to find the right letter.

The guidewords are printed at the top of the page like this:

> **marrow-merit**

They tell you the first and last words on that page. If you did not open the book at **j** first time, use the guidewords to turn back and forward until you come to the **j** words.

3. Now use the guidewords again to find the right word.

You must look at the first two letters of **jealous**: **je**. Turn the **j** pages back or forward until you come to the page with the guidewords that include **je** words. It will be the page with the guidewords

> **jab-jumper**

Run your finger down the columns until you come to words starting **je**, and then **jea**. Then you will come to **jealous**.

Now try to find **jealous** by yourself.

WHAT THE DICTIONARY CAN TELL YOU

This dictionary can tell you:

1. **what a word means.**

   If there is more than one meaning these are numbered.

   ascent *n* |1.| a climb |2.| a slope upwards:

   Sometimes an example is given to make the meaning clearer.

   | *a steep ascent on a hillside.* |

2. **how to say some words.**

   When you find two words that are spelled the same, it will tell you how to say them.

   minute¹ |(min it)| *n* sixty seconds of time.

3. **about different kinds of words.**

   After every word in the dictionary there are letters that tell you what kind of word it is. (See below.)

   breeze |n| a gentle wind.

4. **about different forms of words.**

   - You can find out how to spell unusual plurals. When you have more than one of something it becomes a plural. Usually this is done by adding 's': 'cat' becomes 'cats'. If the word already ends in 's', or in 'sh', 'x', 'ch' or 'z', it adds 'es': 'bus' becomes 'buses'; 'bush', 'bushes'; 'fox', 'foxes'. But some nouns do not just add 's' or 'es'. The dictionary tells you about these.

     cod *n* a sea fish that we eat. | *pl* **cod.** |

   - You can find out the opposite of many words.

     pleasant *adj* pleasing. | *opp* **unpleasant.** |

   - You can find out the masculine and feminine of many words.

     husband *n* a married man. | *fem* **wife.** |

   - You can find out how to add 'ed' and 'ing' to verbs.

     harm *v* to hurt. | **harming, harmed.** |

- You can find out how to add 'er' and 'est' to adjectives. Usually you just put these endings onto the word: black, blacker, blackest. But some adjectives are different. The dictionary tells you about these.

lowly *adj* humble. **lowlier, lowliest.**

Here is a list of the special letters in the dictionary, and what they stand for:

n   noun, the name of something, as **cat, faith**.

pron pronoun, a word in place of a noun, as **he**, **they**.

adj   adjective, which describes a noun or pronoun, as **red**, **many**.

v   verb, the active doing word, as **go**.

adv   adverb, which tells you more about a verb or adjective, as **badly**, **slowly**, **very**.

prep preposition, which tells you the position between two nouns or pronouns, as **on**, **beside**.

conj conjunction, a word used to join words and sentences, as **and**, **but**.

fem   feminine, having to do with women.

masc masculine, having to do with men.

opp   opposite

sing singular, one of something, as **cow**.

pl   plural, more than one, as **cows**.

Aa

abandon *v* to leave someone or something, and never return. **abandoning, abandoned.**

abbey *n* I. a building in which monks or nuns live, or used to live. 2. a great church.

able *adj* I. having the power or skill to do something: *Most birds are able to fly.* 2. clever. *opp* **unable.**

aboard *prep* or *adv* on or into a ship, plane, bus, or train.

abolish *v* to bring something to an end. **abolishing, abolished.**

about I. *prep* to do with: *Ann's book is about games.* 2. somewhere near: *about two o'clock.* 3. *adv* in all directions: *The boys were running about.*
  about to just going to: *Sue was about to go out when Mary came.*
  about turn to turn round to face the opposite direction.

above I. *prep* higher than: *The picture hangs above the table.* 2. *adv* overhead. *opp* **below.**

abreast *adv* side by side: *The soldiers marched four abreast. opp* **in single file.**

abroad *adv* in or to a foreign country.

absent *adj* not present: *Pam was absent from school.*
  absent-minded I. forgetful. 2. not paying attention.

absurd *adj* silly.

accent *n* a way of speaking: *a foreign accent.*

accept *v* to take something that is offered: *to accept a gift.* **accepting, accepted.**

accident *n* something that happens by mistake or by chance and is harmful.
  by accident by chance.

according (to) *prep* from what someone says: *According to Bob it is now one o'clock.*

accurate *adj* exact: *My watch is accurate. opp* **inaccurate.**

accuse *v* to say that someone has done something wrong. **accusing, accused.**

ace *n* a playing-card with one spot.

ache I. *n* a continuous pain: *a headache.* 2. *v* to have a continuous pain. **aching, ached.**

acid I. *n* a very sour liquid that can sometimes burn your skin. 2. *adj* sour.

acorn *n* the nut-like fruit of the oak tree.

acrobat *n* a person who can do daring leaps, jumps, and balancing tricks, often in a circus.

across I. *prep* or *adv* from one side to the other: *They walked across the road.* 2. *prep* on the other side of: *Their house is across the road.*

act I. *v* to take part in a stage play or a film. 2. to pretend: *Clive acted as if he was ill.* 3. to do something: *Act now!* **acting, acted.** 4. *n* a deed: *an act of bravery.* 5. a part of a play. 6. a law made by a parliament.

active *adj* lively. *opp* **inactive.**

activity *n* I. busy movement. 2. something for you to do. *pl* **activities.**

actor *n* someone appearing on stage, in a film, or on television. *fem* **actress,** *pl* **actresses.**

add *v* I. to find the total of two or more numbers. 2. to put one thing to another: *to add milk to tea.* **adding, added.** *opp* **subtract.**

adder *n* the only poisonous snake living wild in Britain.

addition *n* I. the act of adding numbers. 2. the adding of one thing to another.

address I. *n* the house, street, and town where a person lives. *pl* **addresses.** 2. *v* to write on a letter or parcel where it is to go. **addressing, addressed.**

adjective *n* a word that tells you more about somebody or something: in 'a red rose', the word 'red' is an adjective.

admiral *n* a naval officer who commands a fleet of ships.

admire *v* I. to think highly of something or someone. 2. to look at something with pleasure. **admiring, admired.**

admission *n* the cost of going in: *Admission to the fair is free.*

admit *v* I. to let in: *This ticket admits two people.* 2. to confess. **admitting, admitted.**

adopt *v* to care for someone else's child or pet as your own. **adopting, adopted.**

adore *v* to love very much. **adoring, adored.**

adrift *adv* floating loose.

adult *n* a grown-up person.

advance *v* to move forward. **advancing, advanced.** *opp* **retreat.**

advantage *n* something that makes you better or more capable than others.

adventure *n* an exciting experience: *I read about an adventure in the jungle.*

adverb *n* a word that tells you more about a verb, adjective, or another adverb: in 'Denis walked slowly', the word 'slowly' is an adverb.

advertise *v* to make widely known, for example by posters. **advertising, advertised.**

advertisement *n* a notice, usually of something on sale.

advice *n* helpful suggestions.

advise *v* to give advice. **advising, advised.**

aerial *n* a metal rod that receives or sends out radio or television programmes.

aerodrome *n* a place where aeroplanes take off or land.

aeroplane *n* a flying machine with wings and an engine.

affect *v* to cause a change in something or someone: *Jean's illness will affect her holiday plans.* **affecting, affected.**
Note: do not mix up **affect** with **effect**, which is the result of a change.

affection *n* a feeling you have for someone or something you are fond of.

affectionate *adj* loving.

afford *v* to spare money or time for something. **affording, afforded.**

afloat *adj* or *adv* floating.

afraid *adj* frightened.

after 1. *conj* later than: *after lunch.* 2. *prep* behind: *The soldiers marched after the band.* *opp* **before.**

afternoon *n* the time between midday and evening.

afterwards *adv* later.

again *adv* once more.

against *prep* 1. touching: *Colin leaned against the fence.* 2. facing: *to walk against the wind.*

age *n* 1. the number of years a thing has lasted or a person has lived. 2. a time in history: *the Stone Age.*

ago *adj* or *adv* in the past: *ten years ago.*
long ago many years past.

agony *n* very great pain. *pl* **agonies.**

agree *v* 1. to be willing: *Ruth agreed to go shopping.* 2. to think the same as someone and not to quarrel. **agreeing, agreed.** *opp* **disagree.**

agreeable *adj* pleasant: *an agreeable surprise.* *opp* **disagreeable.**

aground *adv* or *adj* held fast on sand or rocks in shallow water.

ahead *adv* in front.

aid 1. *n* help. 2. something that helps. 3. *v* to help. **aiding, aided.**

aim *v* 1. to point a gun or other weapon at something. 2. to try to do something: *Clive aimed at passing his swimming test.* **aiming, aimed.**

air *n* 1. the atmosphere all around us. 2. an appearance.
Air Force all the military aircraft of one nation, and their airmen.
air mail mail carried by air.

aircraft *n* any flying machine. *pl* **aircraft.**

air-hostess *n* a woman who looks after passengers travelling in an aeroplane.

airport *n* a place where aeroplanes land and take off.

ajar *adv* and *adj* partly open.

alarm *n* 1. a warning of danger. 2. sudden fear. 3. a warning bell, as on an alarm clock.

album *n* a book to hold a collection of stamps or photographs.

alert *adj* ready to act quickly.

alight *adj* on fire.

alike *adj* nearly the same: *The sisters are alike.* *opp* **unalike.**

alive *adj* 1. living. 2. lively.

all 1. *adj* or *n* every one: *All the boys and girls were there.* 2. *adj* every part of something: *We can see all the island from here.*
after all in spite of everything said or done.
all right 1. agreed. 2. safe and well.

Allah *n* the Muslim name for God.

alley *n* a narrow passage or lane between buildings. *pl* **alleys.**

alligator *n* a large reptile found in the rivers of some warm countries.

allotment *n* a piece of ground used as an extra garden, often for growing vegetables.

allow *v* to permit: *Allow him to go.* **allowing, allowed.**

ally *n* a country or person who helps you in a war or struggle. *pl* **allies.**

almost *adv* very nearly.

alone *adv* or *adj* by yourself.

along *prep* from one end to the other: *They went along the road.*

aloof *adv* and *adj* keeping apart from others.

aloud *adv* loudly, so that all can hear.

alphabet *n* the letters of a language A, B, C, and so on.

Alps *n pl* high mountains of Switzerland and neighbouring countries.

already *adv* I. by this time: *Sandra was already there when we arrived.* 2. before now: *We have already seen it.*

Alsatian *n* a large breed of dog.

also *adv* as well.

altar *n* the holy table in a church.

alter *v* to change. **altering, altered.**

alteration *n* a change.

although *conj* even if: *I will go out although I do not like the rain.*

altogether *adv* I. including everybody or everything. 2. in every way.

aluminium *n* a very light silver-coloured metal.

always *adv* at all times.

amaze *v* to surprise very much. **amazing, amazed.**

amber *n* a golden-yellow colour.

ambition *n* I. a longing for success or honour. 2. a great wish: *Malcolm's ambition is to be an engineer.*

ambulance *n* a van for carrying ill or injured people to hospital.

ambush *v* to attack an enemy by surprise after lying in wait. **ambushing, ambushed.**

ammunition *n* bullets and shells for guns.

among, amongst *prep* I. surrounded by. 2. between: *Share the sweets among you.*

amount *n* a quantity.

amuse *v* to make someone laugh or smile. **amusing, amused.**

amusing *adj* funny. *opp* **unamusing.**

ancestor *n* a member of the family who lived a long time ago.

anchor *n* a heavy metal hook that digs into the bottom of the sea and stops a ship moving.

ancient *adj* very old.

angel *n* a messenger of God.

anger *n* a strong feeling when you are not pleased about something.

angle *n* the amount of space between two lines that meet.

angler *n* a fisherman with rod and line.

angry *adj* bad-tempered. **angrier, angriest.**

animal *n* any living creature that can move—except man.

ankle *n* the joint between your foot and leg.

anniversary *n* a day that you remember each year because of something important which happened on it: *a wedding anniversary.* *pl* **anniversaries.**

announce *v* to let a lot of people know something. **announcing, announced.**

announcer *n* someone who gives information: *a television announcer.*

annoy *v* to make someone cross. **annoying, annoyed.**

annual I. *n* a book or magazine that appears once a year. 2. *adj* happening once each year.

anorak *n* a waterproof jacket with a hood.

another *adj* I. one more: *Take another cake.* 2. a different (one): *Choose another dress instead of that one.*

answer I. *n* the result of working out a sum in figures. 2. *v* to reply to a question or a letter. **answering, answered.**

ant *n* an insect that lives together with many others in the ground.

antelope *n* an animal like a deer.

anthem *n* a nation's own song: *the National Anthem.*

anti- a prefix meaning 'against': *Anti-rust paint is used to protect iron against rust.*

antique *n* any old and valuable object.

antlers *n pl* the horns of a stag or other deer.

anvil *n* an iron block on which a blacksmith hammers red-hot metal into shape.

anxious *adj* I. worried. 2. wanting something, but not sure whether you will get it.

any *adj* I. one of several: *Come on any day.* 2. some: *Have you any money?*

anybody, anyone *n* any person.

anyhow I. *adv* in any way: *Dress anyhow you like.* 2. *conj* but: *She did not know whether to go or not, anyhow she went at last.*

apart *adv* I. separate: *Leslie stood apart from the others.* 2. in pieces: *He took the lawn-mower apart.*

ape *n* a kind of monkey, but with no tail.

apologise *v* to say you are sorry. **apologising, apologised.**

apostle *n* one of the twelve followers of Jesus.

apparatus *n* special things that you use for doing something with: *P.E. apparatus*.

appeal *v* I. to beg for help. 2. (with **to**) to interest greatly: *Cricket appeals to me*. **appealing, appealed.**

appear *v* I. to come into sight. *opp* **disappear.** 2. to seem: *David appears to be tired*. **appearing, appeared.**

appendix *n* a tube in the body that makes some people ill so that it has to be taken out.

appetite *n* the wish to eat food.

applaud *v* to clap hands. **applauding, applauded.**

applause *n* clapping.

apple *n* a round fruit of the apple-tree.

approach *v* to get near to. **approaching, approached.**

apricot *n* a soft fruit like a peach.

April *n* the fourth month of the year.

apron *n* a piece of clothing worn in front to keep other clothes clean when working.

aquarium *n* a tank with glass sides holding live fish and water plants. *pl* **aquariums** or **aquaria.**

arch *n* the curved top of a doorway, tunnel, or bridge.

archbishop *n* a chief bishop.

archer *n* a person who shoots arrows with a bow.

architect *n* someone who draws plans for buildings.

area *n* I. a flat space. 2. a region. 3. an amount of space, measured in squares.

aren't a short way of writing **are not.**

argue *v* to talk in a noisy way with someone who does not agree with you. **arguing, argued.**

argument *n* talking in a noisy way with someone who does not agree with you.

arithmetic *n* doing sums with numbers.

ark *n* the boat in which Noah and the animals were saved, in the Bible story of the Flood.

arm I. *n* the part of your body from your shoulder to your hand. 2. *v* to supply with weapons. **arming, armed.** *opp* **disarm.**

armchair *n* a chair with an arm on each side of the seat.

armour *n* iron clothing worn by soldiers in olden times.

arms *n pl* weapons.

army *n* a great number of soldiers under the command of a general. *pl* **armies.**

around *prep* and *adv* on all sides.

arrange *v* I. to place in order. 2. to plan. **arranging, arranged.**

arrest *v* to take prisoner. **arresting, arrested.**

arrival *n* coming to a place at the end of a journey.

arrive *v* to reach a place after a journey. **arriving, arrived.**

arrow *n* a pointed stick with feathers at one end, shot from a bow.

art *n* I. making things of beauty, such as pictures and pottery. 2. being able to do something difficult: *the art of weaving*.

article *n* I. a single thing. 2. a piece of writing in a newspaper or magazine.

artificial *adj* not real or natural.

artillery *n* I. cannon or big guns which fire shells. 2. the regiments in the army which use big guns.

artist *n* someone who draws or paints pictures or makes other beautiful things such as pottery or statues.

ascend *v* to go up. **ascending, ascended.** *opp* **descend.**

ascent *n* I. a climb. 2. a slope upwards: *a steep ascent on a hillside*. *opp* **descent.**

ash *n* I. the powder left after a fire. 2. a kind of tree. *pl* **ashes.**

ashamed *adj* I. very sorry for something wrong you have done. 2. feeling people might make fun of you. *opp* **unashamed.**

ashore *adv* on or to the shore.

ask *v* to put a question to someone. **asking, asked.**

asleep *adv* sleeping.

aspirin *n* a medicine that helps to stop a pain such as a headache.

ass *n* a donkey. *pl* **asses.**

assemble *v* to gather together. **assembling, assembled.**

assembly *n* a meeting: *morning assembly at school*. *pl* **assemblies.**

assist *v* to help. **assisting, assisted.**

assistant *n* I. someone who serves in a shop and helps. 2. someone whose job is to help someone else.

astonish *v* to surprise greatly. **astonishing, astonished.**

astray *adv* I. wandering in the wrong place. 2. doing what is wrong: *to lead someone astray*.

astride *adv* with a leg on each side.

astronaut *n* a traveller in a spaceship.

astronomy *n* the study of the stars and planets.

ate see **eat**.

athlete n someone who takes part in sports such as running and jumping.

atlas n a book of maps.

atmosphere n the air around the earth.

atom n a very, very small particle of anything.

attack v to move forward and start a fight. **attacking, attacked.**

attempt v to try to do something. **attempting, attempted.**

attend v 1. to be present at. 2. (with **to**) to listen carefully to. **attending, attended.**

attendance n 1. being present. 2. the number of people in a place.

attention n care and thought: *Pay attention to your work.*
at attention standing perfectly upright with arms by your sides and feet together.

attic n a room inside the roof of a house.

attract v 1. to make something come nearer. 2. to interest: *The puppies always attract our friends.* **attracting, attracted.**

attractive adj very pleasant to look at. *opp* **unattractive.**

audience n people who have come to a play, a concert, or a talk.

August n the eighth month of the year.

aunt, auntie n 1. a sister of your father or mother. 2. your uncle's wife.

author n a writer of books or stories.

authority n the power to make people do as you say.

autograph n your own name written by yourself.

automatic adj working by itself.

autumn n the season after summer.

avalanche n a large amount of snow and rocks falling down a mountain side.

avenue n a road, especially one with trees along both sides.

average adj 1. medium: *George is of average weight for his age.* 2. ordinary.

avoid v to keep away from. **avoiding, avoided.**

awake v to wake up from sleep. **awaking, awoke.**

award v to give a prize, honour, or reward. **awarding, awarded.**

aware adj knowing about something. *opp* **unaware.**

away adv 1. further off: *The man walked away.* 2. absent: *Robert has been away on holiday.*

awful adj dreadful.

awkward adj 1. clumsy. 2. inconvenient. 3. difficult to deal with.

awoke see **awake**.

axe n a sharp tool for cutting wood.

axle n the shaft on which a wheel turns.

Bb

baby n a very young child. *pl* **babies.**

bachelor n a man who has not married. *fem* **spinster.**

back 1. n the opposite side to the front. 2. the part of the body between the neck and the bottom or tail. 3. adv in return: *Jean gave the ticket back.*

backbone n the spine.

backwards adv 1. towards the back. 2. facing the wrong way.

bacon n the meat of a pig.

bad adj 1. not good. 2. rotten. **worse, worst.**

badge n a special sign worn on your hat or clothes to show you belong to some school or club.

badger n an animal with grey fur that lives in a hole in the ground.

bag n a container for holding things.

bagpipes n pl a musical instrument with a bag and pipes, used especially in Scotland.

bait n food put on a hook to tempt a fish, or in a trap to tempt animals.

bake v to cook in an oven. **baking, baked.**

baked beans n pl beans in tomato sauce that you buy in a tin.

bakery n a place where bread and cakes are baked. *pl* **bakeries.**

balance n being steady: *Keith kept his balance when walking on the wall.*

balcony n 1. a platform outside the upper window of a house. 2. an upstairs floor of a theatre or cinema. *pl* **balconies.**

bald adj without hair on the head.

bale n a bundle of straw or cloth tied up.

ball n 1. something round: *a tennis ball.* 2. a big party with dancing.

ballerina n a girl or woman ballet-dancer.

ballet n a story or play told in the form of graceful dancing.

balloon *n* 1. a thin rubber bag that you can blow up. 2. a large bag filled with light gas, carrying passengers in the air.

ballpoint *n* a pen which writes very smoothly, by ink flowing over a tiny ball at the tip.

bamboo *n* a tall grass that grows wild in hot countries and has hollow wooden stems.

banana *n* a long fruit with a thick yellow skin.

band *n* 1. a narrow strip used for holding things together: *a rubber band*. 2. a group of musicians playing together.

bandage *n* a narrow strip of cloth for wrapping round part of your body that you have hurt.

bandit *n* a robber who steals from travellers.

bang *n* a loud noise.

banish *v* to send someone out of a country or a place. **banishing, banished.**

banisters *n pl* the rails and posts down a flight of stairs.

banjo *n* a musical instrument like a small guitar. *pl* **banjos** or **banjoes.**

bank *n* 1. an office where money is kept safe. 2. the side of a river or lake.
   bank holiday a public holiday for everyone to enjoy.

banquet *n* a large feast or dinner-party.

baptise *v* to give a baby a name. **baptising, baptised.**

bar *n* 1. a long rod, especially of metal. 2. a counter where drinks and food are on sale.

barbed wire *n* wire with sharp spikes used for fences round fields.

barber *n* a hairdresser for men and boys.

bare *adj* 1. empty: *a bare room*. 2. uncovered.

bargain *n* something which is bought cheaply, and is good value for money.

barge *n* a flat-bottomed boat used on rivers or canals.

bark *n* 1. the hard covering of a tree trunk or branch. 2. the cry of a dog or wolf.

barley *n* a kind of corn.

barn *n* a farm building used for storing crops.

baron *n* a nobleman. *fem* **baroness.**

barracks *n pl* buildings in which soldiers live.

barrel *n* 1. a wooden container for storing liquids. 2. the tube of a gun.

barrier *n* something that stops you going further.

base *n* the bottom part on which a thing stands.

baseball *n* an American game like rounders.

basement *n* the lowest floor in a building, and usually below ground.

bash *v* to hit very hard. **bashing, bashed.**

basin *n* a round bowl usually fixed in a bathroom.

basket *n* a carrier made of woven cane or straw.

bat *n* 1. a piece of wood used in cricket and other games. 2. an animal with wings that flies at night.

bath *n* a large tub in which you wash your body.

bathe *v* 1. to swim or play in water: *to bathe in the sea*. 2. to wash gently: *to bathe a cut*. **bathing, bathed.**

bathroom *n* the room with the bath in it where you wash.

batter *v* to keep on hitting something using a lot of force. **battering, battered.**

battery *n* a container for storing electricity. *pl* **batteries.**

battle *n* a fight or hard struggle.

battlements *n pl* a low wall on a fort with openings for shooting.

bay *n* a big curve of the sea into the land.

bayonet *n* a long straight knife fixed to the end of a rifle.

bazaar *n* 1. an Eastern market. 2. a sale of goods from stalls for some good purpose.

beach *n* the sea-shore.

beacon *n* a fire lit on a hill-top as a signal.

bead *n* a small round object on a necklace.

beak *n* the hard pointed part of a bird's mouth.

beaker *n* a tall cup, sometimes with no handle.

beam *n* 1. a long piece of wood or metal. 2. a ray of light: *a sunbeam*.

bean *n* a seed from a pod, eaten as a vegetable.

beanbag *n* a bag full of beans that you use for catching.

bear[1] *(bair) n* a large furry animal.

bear[2] *(bair) v* 1. to carry: *The mule can bear heavy loads*. 2. to put up with. **bearing, bore, I have borne.**

beard *(beerd) n* the hair on a man's face and cheeks.

beast *n* a large animal.

beat *v* 1. to keep on hitting. 2. to defeat someone. **beating, beat, I have beaten.**

beautiful *adj* 1. very pretty. 2. very pleasant.

beauty *n* 1. being pleasing to the senses. 2. a lovely thing. *pl* **beauties.**

beaver *n* a furry animal of North America.

became see **become.**

because *conj* for the reason that.

become *v* to come to be. **becoming, became, I have become.**

bed *n* 1. something to sleep in. 2. a part of a garden for flowers or vegetables. 3. the bottom of the sea or a river.

bedroom *n* the room where you sleep.

bee *n* a flying insect with a sting.

beech *n* a tree with smooth grey bark.

beef *n* meat from a cow or bull.

beefburger *n* a fried cake of chopped beef.

beehive *n* a wooden box that bees live in.

beer *n* a strong brown drink.

beet, beetroot *n* a vegetable whose red root is often pickled.

beetle *n* an insect with two hard shiny coverings to protect its wings.

before *prep* 1. earlier than. 2. in front of.

beg *v* to ask in a humble way, sometimes for food or money. **begging, begged.**

began see **begin.**

beggar *n* a poor person who begs for money.

begin *v* to start to do something. **beginning, began, I have begun.**

beginner *n* someone who is just starting to learn something.

beginning *n* the start of something.

behave *v* to show good or bad manners in front of others. **behaving, behaved.** *opp* **misbehave.**

behaviour *n* how someone behaves.

behind *prep* at the back of: *behind the tree.*

being *n* a living creature.

belief *n* something you believe in. *opp* **disbelief.**

believe *v* to think that something is true. **believing, believed.** *opp* **disbelieve.**

bell *n* a piece of metal shaped like a cup, that rings when struck.

bellow *v* to make a loud sound in an angry way. **bellowing, bellowed.**

belong *v* 1. (with **to**) to be owned by. 2. to be a member of. 3. to be in the proper place: *Where does this belong?* **belonging, belonged.**

below *prep* or *adv*. 1. under. 2. lower down than.

belt *n* a leather or plastic strap worn round your waist.

bench *n* a long wooden seat.

bend *v* 1. to make something curved. 2. (with **over**) to lean over. **bending, bent.**

beneath *prep* under.

benefit *v* to do good to: *The swimming lessons benefited Michael.* **benefiting, benefited.**

bent see **bend.**

beret *n* a round soft flat cap.

berry *n* a small fruit full of seeds. *pl* **berries.**

berth *n* a narrow bed in a ship or train.

beside *prep* by the side of.

besides *adv* also.

best *adj* the most pleasing. **best man** the man who is beside the bridegroom at a wedding.

bet *v* to risk money on the result of a race or game. **betting, bet** or **betted.**

betray *v* 1. to act as a traitor and give someone away. 2. to give a secret away to someone, when you shouldn't. **betraying, betrayed.**

better *adj* 1. more pleasing. 2. not as ill as before.

between *prep* 1. in the middle of two people or things. 2. among: *Share the cake between you.*

beware *v* be careful.

bewitched *adj* under a magic spell or charm.

beyond *prep* further than.

bi- a prefix meaning 'two'. A bicycle has two wheels.

Bible *n* the sacred book of the Christian religion.

bicycle *n* a two-wheeled machine with pedals, that you can ride.

bike *n* short for bicycle.

bill *n* a bird's beak.

billiards *n* a game played with coloured balls on a long table.

billy-goat *n* a male goat. *fem* **nanny-goat.**

bin *n* a box for keeping things: *a dustbin.*

bind *v* to tie together. **binding, bound.** *opp* **unbind.**

bingo *n* a game where numbers are called out and marked on a card.

binoculars *n pl* two small telescopes joined side by side, to look through with both eyes.

birch *n* a tree with silver-coloured bark.

bird *n* a flying animal with feathers.

birth *n* being born.

birthday n the day of the year when you were born.

biscuit n a small thin crisp cake.

bishop n a clergyman of high rank.

bison n a wild ox of North America or Europe. pl **bison.**

bit 1. n a small piece of something. 2. the metal part of a horse's bridle, held in its mouth. 3. v see **bite.**

bitch n a female dog.

bite v to take hold of, or cut off, with your teeth. **biting, bit, I have bitten.**

bitter adj 1. having a sour taste. 2. keen: a bitter wind.
　to the bitter end to the very end.

black 1. n the darkest colour, opposite of white. 2. adj very dark.

blackberry n the soft black juicy fruit of bramble bushes. pl **blackberries.**

blackbird n a bird with dark feathers that you often see in gardens.

blackboard n a smooth black board for writing or drawing on with chalk.

blacksmith n a man who makes iron shoes for horses, and other things out of metal.

blade n 1. the flat cutting part of a knife or sword. 2. a long thin leaf: a blade of grass.

blame v to say that it is the fault of a certain person or thing. **blaming, blamed.**

blancmange n a sort of jelly made of flour and milk.

blank adj not written on.

blanket n a woollen bed-cover.

blast n 1. an explosion. 2. a loud sound.

blaze v to burn with a bright light. **blazing, blazed.**

blazer n a jacket, often with a school badge.

bleached adj made white.

bleak adj cold, gloomy, and windy.

bleat v to make a noise like a goat or sheep. **bleating, bleated.**

bleed v to lose blood. **bleeding, bled.**

blend v to mix. **blending, blended.**

bless v 1. to wish happiness on. 2. to ask God's favour on. **blessing, blessed.**

blessing n a good wish.

blew see **blow.**

blind 1. adj unable to see. 2. n a covering that can be drawn down over a window.

blindfold v to cover someone's eyes so that he or she cannot see. **blindfolding, blindfolded.**

blink v to close and open your eyes. **blinking, blinked.**

blister n a sore swelling under your skin with liquid inside.

blizzard n a storm with heavy snow and strong winds.

block 1. n a lump: a block of chocolate. 2. a group of buildings. 3. v to get in the way of. **blocking, blocked.**

blond adj with fair hair. fem **blonde.**

blood n the red liquid moved round your body by the action of your heart.

blossom n a beautiful flower.

blot n a stain, especially an ink stain.

blouse n a garment worn above the waist by women and girls.

blow 1. n a hard knock. 2. sudden bad luck: His accident was a blow to us all. 3. v (of air) to move along. 4. to puff at. 5. to make a musical instrument sound with air from your lungs. **blowing, blew, I have blown.**

blue n the colour of a clear sky. **bluer, bluest.**

bluebell n a plant with flowers like small blue bells.

blunder v to make a stupid mistake. **blundering, blundered.**

blunt adj 1. not sharp. 2. saying what you think and not being polite.

blur v to make something not easy to see. **blurring, blurred.**

blush v to go red in the face because you are shy or ashamed. **blushing, blushed.**

boar n 1. a wild animal like a pig. 2. a male pig. fem **sow.**

board 1. n a thin piece of wood or card. 2. v to enter a ship, train, bus, or aeroplane. **boarding, boarded.**
　boarding school a school where the pupils live in during each term.

boast v to say how good you are and the things that are yours. **boasting, boasted.**

boat n a small open ship.

bob v to move quickly up or down. **bobbing, bobbed.**

body n 1. the whole of any creature. 2. the main part of a creature. pl **bodies.**

bodyguard n a person or persons protecting a king, queen, or other important person.

bog n soft wet ground.

boil 1. v to heat a liquid until it bubbles. 2. to cook something in boiling water. **boiling, boiled.** 3. n a very painful spot under the skin.

boiler *n* 1. a large tank in which steam is made, for driving a steam engine. 2. a small tank over a fire in a house, supplying hot water to the taps.

boisterous *adj* rough and noisy: *He is a boisterous child.*

bold *adj* brave.

bolt 1. *n* a sliding bar to fasten a door or gate. 2. a thick metal pin like a screw without a point. 3. a sudden dash. 4. *v* to fasten with a bolt. **bolting, bolted.**

bomb *n* an explosive shell.

bomber *n* an aeroplane or person attacking with bombs.

bone *n* one of the pieces that make up a skeleton.

bonfire *n* a fire lit out of doors.

bonnet *n* the part of a car covering the engine.

bony *adj* 1. made of bone. 2. full of bones.

book 1. *n* a number of printed pages bound together for reading. 2. a number of blank pages bound together for writing on. 3. *v* to reserve. **booking, booked.**

boom *n* a deep rumbling sound.

boomerang *n* a curved stick that can turn in the air and come back to the thrower.

boot *n* 1. a leather, rubber, or plastic cover for the foot and ankle. 2. a covered space for luggage in a car.

border *n* 1. an outside edge. 2. the line, or frontier, where two countries meet.

bore 1. *n* a hole or well made by drilling. 2. a dull person who talks too much. 3. *v* to drill a hole. 4. to make someone weary by dull talk. **boring, bored.** 5. see **bear**².

born *v* brought into life.

borne see **bear**².

borrow *v* to take something for a while, promising to give it back later: *Jane borrowed my pen.* **borrowing, borrowed.**

boss *n* a person in charge.

both *adj* the two: *Both boys went out.*

bother *v* 1. to annoy. 2. to take great care when you are doing something. **bothering, bothered.**

bottle *n* a container for liquids, usually of glass, with a narrow neck.

bottom *n* 1. the lowest part. 2. the part of your body that you sit on.

bough *n* a large branch of a tree.

bought see **buy.**

boulder *n* a very large rock or stone.

bounce *v* to jump up and down or come back from a wall, like a rubber ball. **bouncing, bounced.**

bound 1. *n* a leap. 2. *v* to leap. **bounding, bounded.** 3. see **bind.**

out of bounds outside the area where you are allowed to walk and play.

boundary *n* a line marking a limit. *pl* **boundaries.**

bouquet *n* a bunch of flowers.

bout *n* a fit of illness.

bow¹ (rhymes with **so**) *n* 1. a ribbon tied in loops. 2. a weapon for shooting arrows. 3. a stick with horsehair tied to it for playing a violin.

bow² (rhymes with **cow**) 1. *n* the front part of a ship. 2. a bending forward of the body from the waist, to show respect. 3. *v* to bend forward to show respect. **bowing, bowed.**

bowl 1. *n* a deep round dish. 2. a wooden ball used in the game of bowls. 3. *v* to toss the ball to the batsman in cricket. **bowling, bowled.**

box 1. *n* a container that you can open and shut. 2. *v* to fight with thick gloves on, for sport. **boxing, boxed.**

boy *n* a male child or teenager.

brace *n* 1. a piece of metal or wood used to support or straighten something. 2. a pair: *a brace of pheasants.* 3. *pl* a pair of straps worn to keep up trousers.

bracelet *n* a ring worn on the wrist or arm.

brackets *n pl* 1. supports for a shelf. 2. a pair of marks, ( ) or [ ], to put round words in printing or writing.

brag *v* to boast. **bragging, bragged.**

brain *n* the grey matter in the skull of humans and animals with which they think and remember.

brainy *adj* intelligent. **brainier, brainiest.**

brake *n* the part of a bicycle, car, or train that makes it go slower or stop moving.

bramble *n* the wild blackberry bush.

bran *n* the outer covering of wheat and other grains.

branch *n* 1. an arm of a tree growing out from the trunk. 2. one of a number of shops and offices of the same kind, but not the chief one.

brand *n* 1. a particular kind of goods. 2. a mark to show the owner or maker.

brass *n* a yellow metal, made of copper and zinc.

brave 1. *adj* not afraid of pain or danger. 2. *n* a North American Indian warrior.

bray *v* to make the noise of a donkey. **braying, brayed.**

bread *n* a food made by baking a mixture of flour, yeast, and water.

breadth *n* the measurement or distance across anything.

break 1. *v* to smash, crack, or snap. 2. (with **into** or **in**) to interrupt. **breaking, broke, I have broken.** 3. *n* a short rest from doing something.

breakdown *n* when something will not work: *The car had a breakdown.*

breast *n* the chest.

breath *n* air taken into and sent out of your lungs.
    out of breath puffing and panting after running.

breathe *v* to draw air into your lungs and then send it out. **breathing, breathed.**

breed 1. *n* a particular kind of animal. 2. *v* to rear young animals. **breeding, bred.**

breeze *n* a gentle wind.

bribe *v* to offer money or a gift in return for help in something dishonest. **bribing, bribed.**

brick *n* a block of baked clay used in building.

bride *n* a woman on her wedding-day.

bridegroom *n* a man on his wedding-day.

bridesmaid *n* an unmarried girl or woman who walks behind the bride.

bridge *n* 1. a road or path built across a river, road or railway line. 2. the captain's platform on a ship.

bridle *n* the part of a harness fitting over a horse's head.

brief *adj* short.

brigade *n* a part of an army.

bright *adj* 1. shining strongly. 2. intelligent.

brilliant *adj* very bright.

brim *n* 1. the edge of a cup or bowl. 2. the part of a hat that sticks out all round the edge.

bring *v* to fetch. **bringing, brought.**
    to bring up to feed and look after.

brisk *adj* quick.

bristle *n* a short stiff hair.

brittle *adj* hard but easily broken.

broad *adj* wide.

broadcast *v* to tell something to everyone, especially by radio or television. **broadcasting, broadcasted, I have broadcast.**

broke, broken see **break.**

bronze *n* a metal made of copper and tin.

brooch *n* an ornament fastened to clothing.

brood 1. *n* a group of chicks hatched together. 2. *v* to worry in a quiet way. **brooding, brooded.**

brook *n* a small stream.

broom *n* a long-handled sweeping brush.

broth *n* soup.

brother *n* a man or boy who has the same parents as someone else.

brought see **bring.**

brow *n* 1. the forehead. 2. the top of a hill.

brown *n* the colour of chocolate or the earth.

Brownie *n* a junior Guide.

bruise *n* a dark mark on the skin caused by a hard knock.

brush *n* a cluster of hairs or bristles fastened to a handle, for cleaning or painting.

brutal *adj* savage.

brute *n* a cruel person behaving like an animal.

bubble *n* 1. a thin balloon of liquid filled with air. 2. a little ball of air or gas rising in a liquid.

buck *n* a male deer, rabbit, or hare. *fem* **doe.**

bucket *n* a large container with a curved handle.

buckle *n* a metal clasp on a belt or shoe.

bud *n* a young growth on a plant stem that becomes a leaf or flower.

budge *v* to move slightly. **budging, budged.**

budgerigar, budgie *n* a small, usually brightly coloured cagebird.

buffalo *n* a wild ox of North America, Africa, and India. *pl* **buffaloes** or **buffalo.**

bugle *n* a musical instrument like a short trumpet.

build *v* to construct something of bricks, stones, or other parts. **building, built.**

building *n* anything with walls made of bricks, concrete, stones, or wood.

built see **build.**

bulb *n* 1. the round root, shaped like an onion, of some plants. 2. a round glass electric lamp.

bulge *v* to swell out or curve outwards. **bulging, bulged.**

bull *n* the male of cattle and some other animals. *fem* **cow.**

bulldog *n* a sturdy kind of dog with a flattened face.

bulldozer *n* a powerful tractor with a large blade in front that can push rocks and earth.

bullet *n* a piece of metal made to be fired from a gun.

bully *n* someone who frightens or hurts a weaker person. *pl* **bullies.**

bulrush *n* a tall plant growing in wet ground.

bump 1. *n* a dull thud. 2. a collision. 3. a swelling. 4. *v* to knock into or against. **bumping, bumped.**

bumper *n* a metal bar at the front and back of a car to protect it.

bunch *n* a group of things growing or fastened together.

bundle *n* a loose mass of things, sometimes tied together: *a bundle of rags.*

bungalow *n* a house with no upstairs.

bungle *v* to fail to do something, or to do it very badly. **bungling, bungled.**

bunk *n* a narrow bed, usually in a ship.

bunny *n* a rabbit. *pl* **bunnies.**

buoy *n* an object floating at sea and fastened to the sea bed, to guide ships.

burglar *n* someone who enters a building by force to steal.

burial *n* the burying of a body at a funeral.

buried see **bury.**

burn 1. *v* to be on fire. 2. to hurt or damage something by fire or heat. **burning, burned** or **burnt.** 3. *n* a burnt spot on skin or cloth.

burrow *n* a hole in the ground made by an animal and used as its home.

burst *v* 1. to blow up. 2. to break open: *The water pipe burst.* 3. to rush: *She burst into the room.* **bursting, burst.**

bury *v* 1. to cover up and hide. 2. to place a body in the ground at a funeral. **he buries, burying, buried.**

bus *n* a large vehicle taking passengers to places for payment.

bush *n* a plant or small tree with many branches.

business *n* 1. a company. 2. the work that someone does. 3. something that is to do with you.

busy *adj* 1. hard at work or having plenty to do. 2. with a lot of activity. **busier, busiest.**

but 1. *conj* though: *I will go, but I do not want to.* 2. *prep* except: *All but Simon went.*

butcher *n* a shopkeeper who sells meat.

butter *n* a yellow food made from cream.

buttercup *n* a wild flower with yellow petals.

butterfly *n* an insect with large wings which are often brightly coloured. *pl* **butterflies.**

button *n* 1. a circular piece of plastic stitched to your clothes for fastening them. 2. a small knob: *a starter button.*

buy *v* to give money for something you want. **buying, bought.**

buzz *n* the sound made by some flying insects: *bees buzz.*

by *prep* 1. at the side of. 2. because of someone's action or efforts: *It was painted by me.* 3. earlier than: *Finish it by Tuesday.* 4. past: *He walked by.* 5. on or in: *We went by train.*

Cc

cab *n* 1. a taxi. 2. the part in a train, lorry, or bus where the driver sits.

cabbage *n* a large round green vegetable.

cabin *n* 1. a small wooden house. 2. a room in a ship or aeroplane.

cable *n* 1. a strong rope or wire. 2. a bundle of wires to carry electric power, or telephone messages under the sea.

cactus *n* a prickly plant. *pl* **cacti** or **cactuses.**

cafe *n* a small restaurant where you can get a light meal.

caftan *n* a long loose dress.

cage *n* a box or room with wires or metal bars, to keep a bird or animal in.

cake *n* a mixture of flour, butter, eggs, and sugar cooked in an oven.

calculate *v* to find out by using numbers. **calculating, calculated.**

calculator *n* a small machine that can do sums.

calendar *n* a list of the days, weeks, and months of the year.

calf *n* 1. a young bull, cow, elephant, or whale. 2. the back of your leg between your knee and your ankle. *pl* **calves.**

caliper, calliper *n* a metal rod worn to support a weak leg.

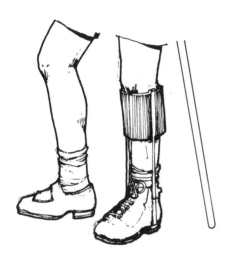

call *v* 1. to shout out. 2. to name. 3. to telephone. **calling, called.**

calm *adj* 1. quiet and still: *a calm day*. 2. not excited.

came see **come.**

camel *n* an animal of the desert with one, or two humps.

camera *n* a box with a lens which takes photographs.

camouflage *v* to hide something by changing its colour or shape. **camouflaging, camouflaged.**

camp *n* a number of tents or huts set up together.

can 1. *v* to be able. *past* **could.** 2. *n* a metal container.

canal *n* a man-made waterway for barges and boats.

canary *n* a yellow singing cagebird. *pl* **canaries.**

cancel *v* to stop something happening which has been arranged. **cancelling, cancelled.**

candle *n* a stick of wax with a wick in it that burns to give light.

cane *n* 1. a long thin stick. 2. the hard stem of a bamboo or sugar plant.

cannibal *n* someone who eats human flesh.

cannon *n* 1. a gun that fires shells. 2. a large gun used in olden times to fire iron balls.

cannot *v* am not able to, is not able to, are not able to. *past* **could not.**

canoe *n* a very light narrow boat moved by using a paddle.

can't *v* short for cannot.

canter *v* for a horse to move in a gentle gallop. **cantering, cantered.**

canvas *n* a strong cloth used for tents and sails.

cap *n* 1. a soft hat with a peak at the front. 2. a metal lid for a bottle. 3. a small round paper with explosive for a toy pistol.

capacity *n* the largest amount of something that a container can hold.

capital 1. *n* a chief city. 2. *adj* or *n* a large letter: *capital B*.

capsize *v* to overturn: *The canoe capsized*. **capsizing, capsized.**

capsule *n* 1. a hollow pill with liquid or solid medicine inside. 2. the part of a spaceship that astronauts travel in.

captain *n* 1. a sailor in command of a ship. 2. a soldier in command of a company. 3. someone who leads a sports team.

captivity *n* being held in prison.

capture *v* to seize and hold: *to capture a fort*. **capturing, captured.**

car *n* a three- or four-wheeled vehicle usually driven by a petrol engine.

caravan *n* a small house on wheels.

card *n* 1. a piece of stiff paper, often with a printed message. 2. one of a set of small pieces of card used in games.

cardboard *n* thick card, used for making boxes.

cardigan *n* a knitted jacket with several buttons at the front.

care *v* to feel concern about. **caring, cared. to take care of** to look after.

careful *adj* being sure to do things in a safe and proper way.

caretaker *n* someone who looks after a building.

cargo *n* goods carried by ship or aeroplane. *pl* **cargoes.**

carnival *n* a procession often in fancy dress with music and dancing.

carol *n* a Christmas hymn.

carpenter *n* someone who makes things out of pieces of wood.

carpet *n* a thick soft covering for floors and stairs.

carriage *n* a vehicle carrying passengers, pulled by an engine or a horse.

carrot *n* a vegetable with a long orange root.

carry *v* to take something from one place to another. **she carries, carrying, carried.**

cart *n* a two-wheeled vehicle often pulled by a horse.

cartoon *n* 1. a film made with drawings. 2. a funny drawing.

carve *v* 1. to cut wood or stone into a shape. 2. to cut meat into slices. **carving, carved.**

case *n* a box for keeping things in.
in case if it should happen.

cash *n* money in the form of coins or notes.

cassette *n* a closed plastic container with a tape-recording or a film inside.

cast *n* a list of the characters and actors in a film or play.

castaway *n* someone shipwrecked in a lonely place.

castle *n* a large building with thick stone walls and towers.

catapult *n* a piece of elastic fastened to a forked stick for shooting stones.

catch *v* 1. to seize something that is moving and hold it. 2. to be in time for. 3. to be made ill by a disease. **catching, caught.**

caterpillar *n* a long grub that will turn into a butterfly or moth.

cathedral *n* the chief church of a large district.

catkin *n* a soft fluffy flower, without petals, that grows on some trees.

cattle *n pl* bulls, cows, oxen, and their young.

caught see **catch.**

cauliflower *n* a vegetable with a large white flower-head.

cause *v* to make something happen. **causing, caused.**

cavalry *n* soldiers on horses.

cave, cavern *n* a large hole in a cliff or hillside, or underground.

ceiling *n* the flat roof of a room.

celebrate *v* to do something special because you are very happy about something. **celebrating, celebrated.**

celery *n* a vegetable with long white stalks.

cell *n* 1. a small room in a prison. 2. a very tiny part of every living thing. 3. part of an electric battery.

cellar *n* an underground storeroom.

cello *n* a musical instrument like a violin, but much larger. *pl* **cellos.**

cement *n* a grey powder used in making concrete, and in sticking bricks together.

cemetery *n* a burial-ground for the dead. *pl* **cemeteries.**

centigrade *n* a way of measuring temperature on a scale that gives 0 degrees for freezing water and 100 degrees for boiling water.

centimetre *n* one hundredth part of a metre.

centipede *n* an insect with many pairs of feet.

central *adj* at the centre.
central heating heating a building by a central boiler.

centre *n* the middle part or the middle point.

century *n* a hundred years. *pl* **centuries.**

cereal *n* corn, rice, or other grain used for food.

ceremony *n* a solemn and dignified service or celebration. *pl* **ceremonies.**

certain *adj* 1. sure. *opp* **uncertain.** 2. one, or some, in particular: *a certain person, certain things.*

certificate *n* a signed statement, written or printed, proving that something is true.

chain *n* a number of rings joined together in a line.

chair *n* a seat with a back, for one person.

chalk *n* 1. a soft white rock. 2. a stick of this for writing on blackboards.

challenge *v* to dare someone to try to beat you in a competition or game. **challenging, challenged.**

champion *n* someone who is better than anyone else at some sport or game.

chance *n* 1. luck. 2. a risk. 3. an opportunity to do something that you cannot do at other times: *You can have one more chance.*

change 1. *v* to make or become different. **changing, changed.** 2. *n* something which has been made different: *a change of address.* 3. money you get back when you pay too much.

channel *n* 1. a long narrow stretch of water, joining two larger stretches. 2. a groove in the ground for water to flow down.

chapati, chapatti *n* a type of flat Indian bread.

chapel *n* 1. a small church. 2. part of a large church.

chapter *n* a part of a book or story, often numbered 1, 2, 3, and so on.

character *n* 1. the nature of a person. 2. a person in a film or play.

charge *n* 1. money paid for something: *a charge for parking.* 2. an attack by soldiers. 3. a case brought against someone by the police.
in charge of taking care of.

chariot *n* a Roman two-wheeled cart pulled by horses.

charm *n* 1. a magic spell. 2. a brooch or other thing that is supposed to bring good luck. 3. a pleasant manner that makes people like you.

charred *adj* blackened with fire.

chart *n* 1. a sheet of paper with a display of information. 2. a map used by sailors.

chase *v* to run after. **chasing, chased.**

chat *v* to talk in an easy friendly way. **chatting, chatted.**

chatter *v* 1. to talk quickly and without stopping. 2. to make a rattling noise: *chattering teeth.* **chattering, chattered.**

chauffeur *n* a man in uniform paid to drive a car.

cheap *adj* not costing much.

cheat *v* 1. to break the rules in order to do well. 2. to deceive someone. **cheating, cheated.**

check 1. *v* to examine carefully to make sure everything is all right. **checking, checked.** 2. *n* a pattern of squares.

cheek *n* 1. one of the sides of your face, between your nose and one of your ears. 2. being rude.

cheer *v* to shout encouragement or because you are pleased. **cheering, cheered.**
to cheer up 1. to feel happier. 2. to make someone happier.

cheerful *adj* bright and smiling: *She is always cheerful at school.*

cheese *n* food made from curdled milk.

chemist *n* 1. someone who sells medicines in a shop. 2. someone who makes new substances, such as dyes and medicines.

cherry *n* 1. a small round red or black fruit with a hard seed inside. 2. the tree on which the fruit grows. *pl* **cherries.**

chess *n* a board game played by two people.

chest *n* 1. the part of your body around your ribs. 2. a large strong box.

chestnut *n* 1. the brown nut of the chestnut tree. 2. a reddish-brown colour.

chew *v* to turn food over in your mouth while biting it with your teeth. **chewing, chewed.**

chewing gum *n* a sweet that you chew.

chick, chicken *n* a young bird of any kind, especially a young farmyard hen.

chicken-pox *n* an illness that covers you in red spots that itch.

chief 1. *n* the head man or leader of a tribe. 2. *adj* most important.

chilblain *n* a painful swelling on a finger or toe, caused by cold.

child *n* a young boy or girl. *pl* **children.**

chill *n* a cold, with shivering.

chilly *adj* cold. **chillier, chilliest.**

chime *v* 1. (of bells) to ring out. 2. (of a clock) to strike the hour. **chiming, chimed.**

chimney *n* a long pipe or passage, letting smoke escape from a fire. *pl* **chimneys.**

chimpanzee *n* an African animal like a large monkey with no tail.

chin *n* the part of the face below the mouth.

china *n* very thin cups, saucers, and plates made from special clay.

chink *n* a thin slit.

chip 1. *n* a long thin slice of fried potato. 2. a piece broken off. 3. *v* to break off a small piece. **chipping, chipped.**

chisel *n* a tool for cutting wood or stone.

chocolate *n* a type of sweet or drink.

choice *n* 1. choosing something. 2. the thing chosen.

choir *n* a group of trained singers, especially in a church.

choke *v* 1. not to be able to breathe properly. 2. to block up: *The pipe is choked with waste food.* **choking, choked.**

choose *v* 1. to pick. 2. to decide: *I chose to go out.* **choosing, chose, I have chosen.**

chop 1. *v* to cut by hitting hard with a sharp tool. **chopping, chopped.** 2. *n* a small piece of meat on a bone.

chop-sticks n pl two small sticks used by the Chinese for eating with.

chorus n 1. a group of people singing together. 2. the parts of a song in which everyone joins in.

chose, chosen see **choose.**

christen v to give a baby its Christian name or names in church. **christening, christened.**

christening n the ceremony of naming a baby.

Christian n a follower of the teachings of Jesus Christ.

Christmas n the festival held on December 25th, to honour the birth of Jesus Christ.

chrysalis n a covering made by a caterpillar before it becomes a butterfly or moth.

chuckle v to laugh quietly to yourself. **chuckling, chuckled.**

chum n a close friend.

chunk n a thick piece: a chunk of meat.

church n a building in which people worship God.

cigar n tobacco leaves tightly rolled for smoking.

cigarette n a thin paper tube containing pieces of tobacco for smoking.

cinders n pl half-burned pieces of coal or wood.

cinema n a building for people to watch films on a screen.

circle n the shape of a perfectly round coin.

circus n a travelling show with clowns, acrobats, and animals.

city n a large important town. pl **cities.**

civilised adj educated and well-behaved. opp **uncivilised.**

claim v to say that something belongs to you. **claiming, claimed.**

clan n a Scottish group of families under one chief.

clang n a deep ringing sound.

clank n a harsh sound of pieces of metal rattling.

clap v to slap your hands together. **clapping, clapped.**

clash n a loud noise made by things banging together.

class n 1. a group of pupils who are taught together. 2. a group of people or things that are very similar.

clatter n sharp rattling sounds.

claw n the sharp hooked nail of a bird and some animals.

clay n a smooth sticky kind of earth used for making bricks and pottery.

clean adj not dirty.

clear adj 1. easy to understand, see, or hear: The teacher made it clear to me. 2. easy to see through: clear glass.

clenched adj tightly closed: a clenched fist.

clergyman n a man in charge of a church. pl **clergy** or **clergymen.**

clerk n a person who works in an office, writing letters or adding money.

clever adj 1. quick at learning. 2. able to do things well. **cleverer, cleverest.**

click n a sharp little sound: the click of a camera.

cliff n high steep rock usually close to the sea.

climate n the kind of weather that a place usually has: Antartica has a very cold climate.

climb v to get up (or down) a steep place. **climbing, climbed.**

cling v to hold tightly to. **clinging, clung.**

clinic n a building usually outside a hospital, where doctors and nurses make people better.

clip 1. n a fastener. 2. v to trim with scissors or shears. **clipping, clipped.**

cloak n a coat without sleeves.

cloakroom n a small room where hats and coats are hung up.

clock n a machine that shows us the time.

clockwork n a motor used to drive clocks or toys, which works when a spring is wound up.

clog 1. n a wooden or leather shoe with a wooden sole. 2. v to choke up: Grease clogged the waste pipe. **clogging, clogged.**

close¹ (rhymes with **nose**) v 1. to shut. 2. to come to an end. **closing, closed.**

close² (rhymes with **dose**) 1. adv near. 2. adj careful: a close look. 3. warm and stuffy: The weather was very close.

cloth n woven material for making things like clothes.

clothes, clothing n pl the things that we wear.

cloud n 1. a white or grey mass of tiny drops of water floating in the sky. 2. anything like a cloud: a cloud of insects.

clover n a meadow plant with leaves in three parts, and white or pink flowers.

clown n someone in a circus with a painted face and funny clothes, who makes people laugh.

club n 1. a thick stick used as a weapon. 2. a stick used for playing golf. 3. a group of people who meet to enjoy some game or hobby. 4. one of the four kinds of playing cards.

clue *n* some small thing that helps in solving a mystery.

clumsy *adj* awkward in moving about and in doing things. **clumsier, clumsiest.**

clung see **cling.**

cluster *n* a bunch: *a cluster of nuts.*

clutch *v* 1. to hang on to. 2. (with **at**) to grab at. **clutching, clutched.**

coach *n* 1. a bus hired to carry people somewhere. 2. a railway carriage. 3. a large four-wheeled carriage drawn by horses in olden days. 4. someone who trains a sports team.

coal *n* a kind of black rock burnt for heating.

coarse *adj* rough: *coarse cloth.*

coast *n* the edge of land where it meets the sea.

coat *n* 1. an outer garment with buttons down the front and sleeves. 2. the hairy covering of some animals.

coax *v* to persuade gently, using kind words. **coaxing, coaxed.**

cobbler *n* someone who mends boots and shoes.

cobweb *n* a spider's net to catch flies.

cock *n* a male bird, especially a male farmyard fowl. *fem* **hen.**

cockerel *n* a male farmyard fowl. *fem* **hen.**

cockle *n* a shellfish found on the seashore.

cockroach *n* a kind of beetle found in buildings.

cocoa *n* a powder made from cocoa beans, used to make a drink and to make chocolate.

coconut *n* the fruit of the palm tree.

cod *n* a sea fish that we eat. *pl* **cod.**

code *n* 1. signs or words used to make a secret message. 2. a set of rules: *the Highway Code.*

coffee *n* a drink made from the roasted seeds of the coffee bush.

coffin *n* the wooden box in which a dead person is put.

cog *n* one of the teeth on the edge of some wheels.

coil *n* a wire or rope wound round in a spiral.

coin *n* a piece of metal money.

coke *n* coal from which the gas has been taken out, that can be used as fuel.

Coke *n* the trade name of a fizzy brown drink.

cold 1. *adj* being without warmth. 2. *n* an illness causing you to sneeze and blow your nose.

collage *n* a picture made from different sorts of paper and material.

collapse *v* to fall down suddenly. **collapsing, collapsed.**

collar *n* 1. the part of some clothes that goes round your neck. 2. a band worn round the neck: *a dog-collar.*

collect *v* to gather together: *John collects stamps.* **collecting, collected.**

collection *n* 1. a number of things collected. 2. money collected in church or for some good cause.

college *n* a place where you can go on studying after you have left school.

collide *v* to bump into something. **colliding, collided.**

colliery *n* a coal-mine. *pl* **collieries.**

collision *n* a big crash between two or more moving things.

colon *n* a punctuation mark (:).

colonel *n* an army officer who commands a regiment.

colour *n* red, blue, yellow, and others, are all colours.

colt *n* a young male horse. *fem* **filly.**

column *n* 1. a pillar. 2. a list of numbers or short lines of words, one below another.

comb *n* 1. a piece of plastic or metal with a row of teeth, to smooth your hair. 2. the red crest on a cock's head.

combine-harvester *n* a machine that cuts corn and takes out the seeds.

come *v* 1. to move here. 2. to arrive. **coming, came, I have come.**

comedian *n* someone on the stage, radio or television who makes you laugh.

comfort 1. *n* being without aches or pain. *opp* **discomfort.** 2. *v* to give freedom from worry. **comforting, comforted.**

comfortable *adj* pleasant to wear, to sit on, or to be in. *opp* **uncomfortable.**

comic *n* 1. a funny person. 2. a paper with stories told in pictures.

comical *adj* funny.

comma *n* a punctuation mark (,), used in writing and printing.

command *v* to tell someone to do something. 2. to be in charge of. **commanding, commanded.**

commence *v* to begin. **commencing, commenced.**

committee *n* a small group of people elected to decide things.

common 1. *adj* happening or found everywhere. *opp* **uncommon.** 2. *n* an area of grassland open to anyone.

commotion *n* a lot of noise.

companion *n* a friend who is with you when you are doing something.

company *n* 1. a business firm. *pl* **companies.** 2. being together with someone else: *I like your company.*

compartment *n* a separate section of a box or a railway carriage.

compass *n* an instrument with a needle that always points to the north.

compasses *n pl* a two-legged instrument for drawing circles.

compel *v* to force someone to do something. **compelling, compelled.**

competition *n* a contest between a number of people, with each trying to win.

competitor *n* someone who takes part in a contest or competition.

complain *v* to tell someone that you are not happy about something. **complaining, complained.**

complaint *n* 1. something that you are not happy about. 2. an illness.

complete 1. *adj* whole. *opp* **incomplete.** 2. *v* to finish. **completing, completed.**

complicated *adj* 1. difficult. 2. having a lot of different parts: *complicated machinery. opp* **uncomplicated.**

compliment *n* words praising a person you are speaking to or writing to.

composer *n* someone who writes music.

composition *n* a piece of writing or music.

computer *n* a machine that can work out complicated things very quickly.

comrade *n* a close friend.

conceal *v* to hide. **concealing, concealed.**

conceited *adj* having too high an opinion of yourself.

concentrate *v* to give careful attention to one thing only. **concentrating, concentrated.**

concern *n* business: *Do not interfere, this is my concern!*

concert *n* a musical entertainment.

conclusion *n* 1. an ending. 2. an opinion: *My conclusion is that the watch was stolen.*

concrete *n* a kind of stone used in building, made from cement, gravel, sand, and water.

condition *n* the state something is in.

conduct 1. (<u>kon</u> dukt) *n* behaviour. 2. (kon <u>dukt</u>) *v* to lead. 3. to direct a choir or an orchestra. **conducting, conducted.**

conductor *n* 1. someone who sells tickets on a bus. 2. someone who keeps an orchestra playing in time. *fem* **conductress.**

cone *n* 1. anything shaped like a clown's hat, circular at one end and with a point at the other: *an ice-cream cone.* 2. the fruit of the fir or pine tree.

confess *v* to admit to something you have done wrong. **confessing, confessed.**

confetti *n* tiny bits of coloured paper thrown at weddings.

confident *adj* sure of yourself: *a confident driver.*

confuse *v* 1. to mix up. 2. to become mixed up. **confusing, confused.**

congratulate *v* to tell someone that you are glad about something special that has happened to him or her. **congratulating, congratulated.**

congregation *n* a gathering of people in church.

conjunction *n* a word connecting two phrases or short sentences. In 'I came and I talked to her' the word 'and' is a conjunction, joining 'I came' to 'I talked to her'.

conjuror or **conjurer** *n* someone who can do clever tricks as if by magic.

conker *n* the shiny brown nut of the horse-chestnut tree.

connect *v* to join one thing to another. **connecting, connected.** *opp* **disconnect.**

conquer *v* to beat in a battle. **conquering, conquered.**

conscious *adj* awake and aware of everything around you. *opp* **unconscious.**

consent *v* to agree to something. **consenting, consented.**

consider *v* to think about carefully. **considering, considered.**

consist *v* (with **of**) to be made up of: *Custard consists of powder and milk.* **consisting, consisted.**

consonant *n* any letter of the alphabet which is not one of the five vowels a, e, i, o, u.

constable *n* an ordinary policeman or policewoman.

construct *v* to build. **constructing, constructed.**

contain *v* to have inside: *This box contains nails.* **containing, contained.**

contented *adj* satisfied. *opp* **discontented.**

contents *n pl* what is inside something like a box or book.

contest *n* a competition.

continent *n* a very large mass of land: *Europe, Asia, Africa, America, and Australia are continents.*

continual *adj* often happening.

continue *v* to keep on doing something: *It continued raining all day.* **continuing, continued.**

continuous *adj* happening without stopping.

contradict *v* to tell someone that what he or she says is untrue. **contradicting, contradicted.**

contrary *adj* opposite: *My opinion is contrary to yours.*

contribute *v* (with **towards**) to give something for a special purpose. **contributing, contributed.**

control *v* 1. to have power over. 2. to hold back: *Control your dog!* **controlling, controlled.**

convenient *adj* 1. helpful: *a convenient route.* 2. suitable: *It will be convenient for you to come today.* *opp* **inconvenient.**

convent *n* a building in which nuns live.

conversation *n* a friendly talk between two or more people.

convict *n* someone who has been sent to prison.

cook *v* to prepare food by heating it. **cooking, cooked.**

cookery *n* the study of how food should be cooked.

cool *adj* slightly cold.

copper *n* a reddish-brown metal.

copy 1. *n* an imitation. 2. one of a number of papers or books printed exactly alike. *pl* **copies.** 3. *v* to make something exactly like something else. 4. to do the same as someone else. **he copies, copying, copied.**

cord *n* thin rope.

core *n* the part in the centre of a thing: *the core of an apple.*

cork *n* something used to close the top of a bottle. It is often made from the bark of a cork tree.

corn *n* 1. a plant, such as wheat or oats, whose grain is used for food. 2. a hard lump on your foot.

corner *n* a place where two walls of a room or two streets meet.

cornflakes *n pl* a cereal eaten with milk at breakfast.

coronation *n* the crowning of a king or queen.

corpse *n* the body of a dead person.

correct 1. *adj* having no mistakes. *opp* **incorrect.** 2. *v* to put right. **correcting, corrected.**

corridor *n* a long passage in a building, or along a railway carriage.

cost *n* the price of anything.

costume *n* 1. the clothes worn by someone in a play. 2. a style of dress: *Dutch national costume.*

cosy *adj* warm and comfortable. **cosier, cosiest.**

cot *n* a baby's bed.

cottage *n* a small house, especially one in the country.

cotton *n* white thread made from the cotton plant. It can be woven into cotton cloth or used for sewing.
    cotton-wool a very soft fluffy pad made from cotton.

couch *n* a long seat for three or four people.

cough *v* to make a loud noise to clear your throat. **coughing, coughed.**

could see **can.**

council *n* a group of people elected to govern a town, city, or county.

count 1. *v* to find out how many things there are by using numbers. 2. to say numbers in order. **counting, counted.** 3. *n* a nobleman in some countries. *fem* **countess.**

counter *n* 1. the long table in a shop across which things are sold. 2. a small plastic disc used in some games.

countess see **count** and **earl.**

country n 1. land away from towns. 2. the land belonging to one nation: *the country of France*. pl **countries.**

county n a part of Great Britain or Ireland. pl **counties.**

couple n a pair.

coupon n a printed ticket which you can exchange for something of value.

courage n bravery.

course n 1. the direction which something takes. 2. a part of a meal. 3. an area of ground where some sport takes place: *a golf course*. **of course** certainly.

court n 1. a place where some game is played. 2. a place where criminals are tried. 3. a royal palace and the people who help or serve a monarch.

courteous adj polite.

cousin n the son or daughter of an uncle and aunt.

cove n a small bay.

cover v to spread one thing over another. **covering, covered.**

cow n the name given to some female animals. *masc* **bull.**

coward n someone who is afraid and runs away from trouble or danger.

cowboy n a man who looks after cattle on an American ranch.

crab n a shellfish with a round body and ten legs including two claws.

crack v 1. to split: *to crack a vase*. 2. to break open: *to crack a nut*. 3. to make a sharp sound: *to crack a whip*. **cracking, cracked.**

cracker n 1. a small firework that you pull at a party. 2. a kind of crisp biscuit.

crackle v to make a cracking noise. **crackling, crackled.**

cradle n a baby's cot which can be rocked.

crafty adj sly. **craftier, craftiest.**

crag n a rugged steep rock or point.

cram v to stuff: *He crammed the food into his mouth*. **cramming, crammed.**

crane n 1. a big machine with a long arm for lifting very heavy weights. 2. a wading bird with a long beak and long legs.

crash n 1. the noise of something being smashed. 2. a collision.

crawl 1. v to move on hands and knees. 2. to move slowly. **crawling, crawled.** 3. n a way of swimming.

crayon n a coloured stick of wax for drawing pictures.

craze n a popular fashion which lasts for a short time.

crazy adj 1. mad. 2. silly. **crazier, craziest.**

creak n a rough squeaking noise.

cream n the thicker liquid on the top of milk.

crease n a mark made when cloth or paper is folded and pressed.

create v to make something new. **creating, created.**

creature n any living animal.

credit n honour: *She passed her test with credit*.

creep v to move slowly and quietly. **creeping, crept.**

crêpe paper n a kind of coloured paper.

crescent n 1. the shape of the new moon. 2. a curved row of houses.

cress n a plant with small round leaves, used in salads.

crest n the highest point.

crew n the people who work on a ship or in an aeroplane or train.

cricket n 1. a summer game played with bats, ball, and two sets of wickets. 2. a long-legged insect like a grasshopper.

cried see **cry.**

crime n a bad deed that is against the law.

criminal n someone guilty of a crime.

crimson n a deep red colour.

crinkled adj wrinkled by constant use.

cripple n someone who has seriously damaged an arm or leg and cannot use it properly.

crisp 1. n a thin dry slice of fried potato. 2. adj dry and easily broken. 3. firm and fresh: *a crisp lettuce*.

croak v to make a deep rough noise in the throat that a frog makes. **croaking, croaked.**

crockery n cups, saucers, plates, and dishes.

crocodile n a large reptile with a long snout living in water in hot lands.

crocus n a small spring flower growing from a bulb.

crook n 1. someone who robs or cheats people. 2. a long hooked stick used by shepherds.

crooked adj 1. full of bends. 2. not honest.

crop n plants grown for food in one season.

cross 1. n a mark shaped like + or ×. 2. a medal shaped like a cross. 3. the sign of Christianity. 4. v to go from one side to another. **crossing, crossed.** 5. adj angry.

crossroads *n* a place where one road crosses another.

crouch *v* to bend your body and your knees. **crouching, crouched.**

crow *n* a big black bird.

crowd *n* a great number of people.

crown *n* 1. the large ring of gold and jewels worn on the head by a king or queen. 2. the top: *the crown of a hill.*

cruel *adj* very unkind and sometimes causing pain.

cruise *n* a voyage in a ship for pleasure.

crumb *n* a tiny bit of bread or cake.

crumble *v* to break into small pieces. **crumbling, crumbled.**

crumple *v* to make something very creased. **crumpling, crumpled.**

crunch *v* to grind noisily with your teeth, or with your feet. **crunching, crunched.**

crush *v* to break or damage by squeezing. **crushing, crushed.**

crust *n* a hard outer covering: *pie-crust.*

cry *v* 1. to shout out loudly. 2. to shed tears. **he cries, crying, cried.**

crystal *n* 1. a hard glass-like material found in the earth. 2. a tiny glass-like piece of sugar or salt.

cub *n* the young of some animals such as foxes, wolves, and tigers.

Cub *n* a junior scout.

cube *n* a solid object with six square faces all alike.

cuckoo *n* a grey bird of which the male calls 'cuck-oo'.

cucumber *n* a long green vegetable.

cuddle *v* to hug gently. **cuddling, cuddled.**

cuff *n* the end of a sleeve near the wrist.

culprit *n* someone who is to blame for doing something wrong.

cultivate *v* to prepare the ground ready to grow crops. **cultivating, cultivated.**

cunning *adj* crafty.

cupboard *n* shelves with doors in front for holding crockery, clothes, books, or other things.

cupful *n* as much as a cup will hold. *pl* **cupfuls.**

curate *n* a clergyman who helps a vicar.

curdle *v* for milk to go sour. **curdling, curdled.**

cure *v* to drive away an illness. **curing, cured.**

curious *adj* 1. wanting to know. 2. unusual: *a curious fact.*

curl *n* a twisted piece of hair.

curly *adj* in curls. **curlier, curliest.**

currant *n* 1. a small dried grape. 2. a small berry growing on a bush: *a redcurrant.* Note: do not spell this word 'current'.

current *n* a flow of water, air, or electricity. Note: do not spell this word 'currant'.

curry *n* food cooked with special spices that give a strong hot flavour.

curse *v* 1. to use bad language. 2. to wish evil on someone. **cursing, cursed.**

curtain *n* a hanging cloth covering a window or a stage.

curve *n* a smooth bend.

cushion *n* a soft pillow to lean against or sit on.

custard *n* a yellow sauce that is poured over puddings.

custom *n* a habit.

customer *n* someone who buys something in a shop.

cut *v* to divide something with a knife or scissors. **cutting, cut.**

cutlery *n* knives, forks, and spoons.

cycle *v* to ride a bicycle. **cycling, cycled.**

cyclist *n* someone riding a bicycle.

cygnet *n* a young swan.

cylinder *n* something shaped like a soup tin.

cymbals *n* a musical instrument made of two round pieces of metal that you bang together.

Dd

dab *v* to pat gently. **dabbing, dabbed.**

dad, daddy *n* father. *pl* **dads, daddies.**

daffodil *n* a yellow flower growing from a bulb.

dagger *n* a short pointed knife with sharp edges.

daily *adv* every day.

dainty *adj* pretty, graceful, and delicate. **daintier, daintiest.**

dairy *n* a place where butter and cheese are made from milk. *pl* **dairies.**

daisy *n* a small common flower with white petals and a yellow centre. *pl* **daisies.**

dale *n* a valley.

dam *n* a wall built across a river to hold back water.

damage *n* harm.

dame n a lady's title, equal to that of a knight.

damp adj slightly wet.

dance v to move about in time to music. **dancing, danced.**

dandelion n a common yellow flower.

danger n something that may cause injury or death.

dangerous adj likely to cause injury or death.

dangle v to hang loosely. **dangling, dangled.**

dare v 1. to be brave enough to do something. 2. to challenge someone: I dare you to jump the fence. **daring, dared.**

dark adj 1. without light. 2. not light in colour: a dark coat.

darling n someone greatly loved.

darn v to sew over a hole in cloth to mend it. **darning, darned.**

dart 1. v to move quickly and suddenly. **darting, darted.** 2. n a small arrow, often thrown at a board.

dash 1. v to rush. **dashing, dashed.** 2. n a mark (—) used in writing or printing.

date n 1. the day, month, and year of some event. 2. the brown sticky fruit of the date-palm.
out-of-date old fashioned.
up-to-date very new.

daughter n a girl or woman who is someone's child.

dawdle v to walk so slowly that you waste time. **dawdling, dawdled.**

dawn n the first light of day.

day n 1. a period of 24 hours, from one midnight to the next. 2. the part of the day when it is light.

daydream n a dream while you are awake.

dazed adj stunned.

dazzle v to blind for a time with a bright light. **dazzling, dazzled.**

dead adj not alive: a dead body.
dead-heat a race with two or more runners coming equal first.

deadly adj able to cause death: a deadly poison.

deaf adj unable or unwilling to hear.

deafen v to make deaf. **deafening, deafened.**

deal 1. n an amount. 2. v (often with **with**) to do business with someone. 3. to share out cards to play a game. **dealing, dealt** (delt).

dear adj 1. loved. 2. expensive.

death n the end of life.

debt n something you owe to someone.

decay v to go bad. **decaying, decayed.**

deceive v to make someone believe something that is not true. **deceiving, deceived.**

December n the twelfth month of the year.

decent adj suitable: decent behaviour. opp **indecent.**

decide v to make up your mind. **deciding, decided.**

decimal adj numbered in tens and tenths: The number 2·3 is a decimal number and is equal to $2\frac{3}{10}$.

decision n something that is decided.

deck n a floor on a ship or bus.

declare v to say something in a firm way. **declaring, declared.**

decorate v to make something look nicer. **decorating, decorated.**

decorator n someone who is paid to decorate houses.

decrease v 1. to make smaller. 2. to become smaller. **decreasing, decreased.**

deed n something special that someone has done.

deep adj measuring a long way from top to bottom.

deer n a fast-running wild animal. pl **deer.**

defeat v to beat someone in a game or battle. **defeating, defeated.**

defend v to protect. **defending, defended.**

definite adj certain. opp **indefinite.**

defy v to refuse to obey. **he defies, defying, defied.**

degree n 1. a measurement for temperature. 2. a mark on a scale for measuring angles. 3. a university honour.

delay v 1. to put off doing something until later. 2. to make somebody or something late. **delaying, delayed.**

deliberate adj done on purpose. opp **undeliberate.**

delicate adj likely to become ill or damaged.

delicious adj very enjoyable to eat or smell.

delight n great pleasure.

delivery n taking or bringing something to someone's house. pl **deliveries.**

deluge n a very heavy fall of rain.

demand v to ask firmly for something that you think you should have. **demanding, demanded.**

demon n an evil spirit in fairy tales.

demonstrate v to show how something should be done or how something works. **demonstrating, demonstrated.**

demonstration *n* a lot of people walking together through the streets to protest about something.

den *n* a cave or shelter where a wild animal lives.

denim *n* strong blue cotton cloth.

dense *adj* very thick.

dent *n* a small hollow made by a knock: *The hammer made a dent in the wood.*

dental *adj* concerning teeth: *a dental clinic.*

dentist *n* someone who takes care of your teeth.

deny *v* to say that something is not true. **he denies, denying, denied.**

depart *v* to leave. **departing, departed.**

department *n* a part of a big shop or office: *the furniture department.*

depend *v* (with **on**) 1. to rely on: *I depend on you to help me.* 2. to follow from: *That depends on what you want.* **depending, depended.**

deposit *v* to put something down. **depositing, deposited.**

depot *n* a warehouse.

depressed *adj* feeling sad.

depth *n* how deep something is.

descend *v.* to go down. **descending, descended.**

describe *v* to tell all about something or someone. **describing, described.**

description *n* words that tell you about someone or something: *a description of the thief.*

desert[1] (<u>dez</u> ert) *n* a very dry sandy or stony land where little grows.

desert[2] (di <u>zert</u>) *v* to abandon. **deserting, deserted.**

deserve *v* to have earned a reward or a punishment. **deserving, deserved.**

design *n* a drawing or a pattern for something.

desire *v* to want very much. **desiring, desired.**

desk *n* a small writing-table, as used in classrooms.

despair *n* being without hope.

desperate *adj* made reckless by despair: *a desperate murderer.*

despise *v* to regard someone or something with scorn: *He despises meanness.* **despising, despised.**

dessert *n* sweet food that you eat after the main part of a meal.

destination *n* the place you are travelling to.

destroy *v* 1. to ruin completely. 2. to kill an animal that is too sick or too badly hurt to get better. **destroying, destroyed.**

destroyer *n* a small fast warship.

destruction *n* when something is destroyed.

detail *n* a tiny part.

detect *v* to discover. **detecting, detected.**

detective *n* someone who tries to find out who has committed a crime.

determined *adj* with your mind firmly made up: *He was determined to win.*

detest *v* to hate. **detesting, detested.**

develop *v* to grow bigger or better: *a child develops into a man or a woman.* **developing, developed.**

devoted *adj* very fond of.

devour *v* to eat greedily. **devouring, devoured.**

dew *n* drops of water that appear at night on things outside as the air cools down.

diagonal *n* a straight line joining opposite corners of a square or rectangle.

diagram *n* a drawing or plan that shows how something works or is made up.

dial *n* the face of a clock, meter, telephone, or something similar.

diamond *n* 1. a very hard precious stone like sparkling glass. 2. one of the four kinds of playing cards. 3. the shape ◇.

diary *n* a small notebook in which you write down what has happened each day. *pl* **diaries.**

dice *n pl* small cubes with six sides marked with one to six dots.

dictionary *n* a book that gives words in alphabetical order, telling you what each word means. *pl* **dictionaries.**

did see **do.**

die *v* to stop living. **dying, died.**

diesel *n* an engine that uses oil as fuel.

difference *n* the way in which one thing is not like another.

different *adj* not the same.

difficult *adj* not easy.

dig v to turn over the earth with a spade or trowel. **digging, dug.**

digestion n absorbing food into the body from the stomach.

dignified adj serious and proud: a dignified way of walking.

dim adj not bright: a dim light. **dimmer, dimmest.**

dimple n a little hollow in your flesh, especially in your cheek or chin.

din n a loud continuous noise.

dine v to eat your dinner. **dining, dined.**

dinghy (ding gee) n a small boat. pl **dinghies.**

dingy (din jee) adj dark and dirty looking.

dining-room n the room that you eat in.

dinner n the main meal of the day.

dinosaur n one of a number of different animals that lived millions of years ago on land.

dip v 1. to put one thing into another for a short time: to dip your hand into water. 2. to slope down: The road dipped into the valley. **dipping, dipped.**

direct 1. v to tell someone what to do. 2. to tell or show the way. **directing, directed.** 3. adj straight: the direct route to London.

direction n the point towards which something moves: The ship sailed in a westerly direction.

dirt n earth or mud.

dirty adj marked with dirt or stains. **dirtier, dirtiest.**

dis- a prefix meaning 'not': A disadvantage (not an advantage).

disabled adj crippled.

disagree v not to agree with someone. **disagreeing, disagreed.**

disagreeable adj not nice.

disappear v to pass out of sight. **disappearing, disappeared.**

disappointed adj unhappy at not finding what you hoped for.

disaster n a great misfortune, accident, or tragedy.

disc n a thin round plate.

discipline n training in obedience.

disco, discotheque n a place where you go to dance to music on records.

discontented adj not satisfied.

discover v to see or learn something new. **discovering, discovered.**

discovery n the finding of something new. pl **discoveries.**

discuss v to talk about something with other people. **discussing, discussed.**

disease n any form of illness.

disgrace n shame: She was in disgrace for telling lies.

disguise n a change of clothing and appearance so that people will not recognise you.

disgust n strong dislike.

dish n 1. a shallow bowl. 2. a kind of food: a tasty dish.

dishonest adj not honest.

dislike v not to like. **disliking, disliked.**

dismal adj gloomy.

dismiss v to send away. **dismissing, dismissed.**

disobedient adj not doing what you are told.

disobey v not to obey. **disobeying, disobeyed.**

display n a show: a firework display.

dissatisfied adj not content.

dissolve v to mix something with water, or other liquid, until it disappears. **dissolving, dissolved.**

distance n 1. the amount of space between two places. 2. a place far off: away in the distance.

distant adj a long way off.

distinct adj heard or seen clearly.

distinguished adj important and respected: a distinguished writer.

distress n great worry, unhappiness, or trouble.

district n a part of a city or country.

disturb v 1. to upset someone's peace. 2. to move something out of place. **disturbing, disturbed.**

disturbance n something that upsets someone's peace.

ditch n a long trench cut in the ground to drain water away.

dive v to go head-first, usually into water. **diving, dived.**

diver n someone who works under water, usually in a diving-suit.

divide v 1. to share out. 2. to split something into smaller pieces. 3. in arithmetic, to see how many times one number goes into another. **dividing, divided.**

division n 1. seeing how many times one number goes into another. 2. dividing. 3. one of the four groups of top football teams: the first division.

dizzy adj feeling that everything is spinning round you. **dizzier, dizziest.**

do v to carry out something. **I do, he does, doing, did, I have done.**

dock *n* I. a place where a ship can load, unload, or be repaired. 2. a weed with large leaves.

doctor *n* someone who helps sick and injured people to get better.

dodge *v* to move to one side quickly to avoid getting hurt by something. **dodging, dodged.**

doe *n* a female rabbit, deer, or hare. *masc* **buck.**

does see **do.**

doll, dolly *n* a toy baby or child. *pl* **dolls, dollies.**

dollar *n* a silver coin, or a note, used in the United States and some other countries.

dolphin *n* a sea animal like a porpoise.

domino *n* an oblong piece of wood or bone, with dots on one side, used in the game of dominoes. *pl* **dominoes.**

done see **do.**

donkey *n* a long-eared animal like a small horse. *pl* **donkeys.**

don't short for do not.

door *n* a wooden barrier closing the way into a house or room.

doorway *n* a way into a building.

dormitory *n* a large bedroom, with many beds. *pl* **dormitories.**

dose *n* the amount of medicine to be taken at one time.

dot *n* a small round mark.

double *adj* twice as much or many.

doubt *v* not to be sure. **doubting, doubted.**

doubtful *adj* not sure.

dough *n* a mixture of flour and water, used to make bread and cakes.

dove *n* a kind of pigeon.

down I. *prep* or *adv* to a lower position. 2. *n* very soft feathers.

doze *v* to have a light sleep. **dozing, dozed.**

dozen *n* twelve.

drab *adj* dull.

drag *v* I. to pull something heavy along the ground. 2. for time to pass by slowly. **dragging, dragged.**

dragon *n* an imaginary monster with wings, that breathes out fire.

dragonfly *n* a large winged insect with long legs. *pl* **dragonflies.**

drain *n* a ditch or large pipe carrying away unwanted water.

drake see **duck.**

drama *n* I. a play. 2. an exciting happening.

dramatic *adj* exciting: *a dramatic rescue.*

drank see **drink.**

draught *n* a cold current of air blowing into a warmer room.

draughts *n* a game played with round counters on a squared board.

draw *v* I. to make a likeness on paper with pen, pencil, or crayon. 2. to finish a game with neither side winning: *We drew one goal each.* 3. to pull. **drawing, drew, I have drawn.**

drawbridge *n* the bridge to a castle, that can be raised when the castle is attacked.

drawer *n* a sliding container in a piece of furniture.

drawing *n* a picture made with pen, pencil, or crayon.

drawn see **draw.**

dread *v* to be very afraid. **dreading, dreaded.**

dreadful *adj* very bad.

dream *v* to imagine things are happening, while you are asleep. **dreaming, dreamt.**

dreary *adj* dull. **drearier, dreariest.**

drenched *adj* very wet all over.

dress *n* I. a garment worn by women and girls that consists of a skirt and top in one piece. 2. clothing: *informal dress.*

dressing *n* I. a bandage on a cut or wound. 2. a sauce: *salad dressing.*

dressing-table *n* a piece of bedroom furniture with drawers and a mirror.

drew see **draw.**

dribble *v* I. for a baby to drip water from its mouth. 2. (in football) to push the ball forward with little taps of your foot. **dribbling, dribbled.**

dried see **dry.**

drier *n* a machine for drying clothes.

drift *v* to be carried along by a current of wind or air. **drifting, drifted.**

drill *n* I. a tool for boring holes. 2. exercises carried out by soldiers.

drink *v* to swallow liquid. **drinking, drank, I have drunk.**

drip *v* to fall in drops, like water from a leaking tap. **dripping, dripped.**

drive *v* to steer and control a vehicle or an animal. **driving, drove, I have driven.**

drizzle *n* very light rain.

droop *v* to hang down with no strength: *The flowers drooped.* **drooping, drooped.**

drop I. *n* a spot of liquid. 2. *v* to fall down from a height. 3. to let something fall. **dropping, dropped.**

drought *n* a long period of very dry weather.

drove see **drive.**

drown v to die in water when there is no air to breathe. **drowning, drowned.**

drowsy adj feeling very sleepy.

drum n 1. a musical instrument with a stretched skin which is tapped with sticks. 2. a large metal container for liquids: an oil drum.

drunk see **drink.**

dry 1. adj not wet or damp. **drier, driest.** 2. v to make dry. 3. to become dry. **he dries, drying, dried.**

duchess n the wife of a duke.

duck 1. n a female water bird. masc **drake.** 2. v to bend down quickly to avoid something. **ducking, ducked.**

due adj 1. expected: The train is due. 2. owing: Some money is due to me.
due to caused by: late due to fog.

duel n a fight between two people using the same sort of weapon.

duffle coat n a thick overcoat with a hood and narrow buttons which go through loops.

dug see **dig.**

duke n a nobleman of the highest rank. fem **duchess.**

dull adj 1. not bright. 2. not interesting. 3. not sharp: a dull explosion.

dumb adj not able to speak.

dummy n a model of a person in a tailor's shop. pl **dummies.**

dump 1. n a place where rubbish is thrown away. 2. v to put something down carelessly. **dumping, dumped.**

dungarees n pl a kind of overall.

dungeon n an underground prison in a castle.

during prep in the time of: during the morning.

dusk n just before it gets dark in the evening.

dust n dry powdered dirt.

dustbin n a container with a lid, for rubbish.

duster n a cloth to wipe dust from furniture.

duty n something you have to do. pl **duties.**

dwarf n 1. a little man. 2. any living thing that is much smaller than usual. pl **dwarfs.**

dwell v to live in some place. **dwelling, dwelt** or **dwelled.**

dwindle v to become smaller, to shrink. **dwindling, dwindled.**

dye n a special liquid used to colour cloth.

dying see **die.**

dynamite n a powerful explosive used for blowing things up.

Ee

each pron or adj every single one.

eager adj anxious to have or to do something.

eagle n a large bird of prey.

ear n 1. one of the two parts of the head through which we hear. 2. the top of a stalk of corn where the seeds are found.

earring n an ornament worn in the ear.

earl n a nobleman of high rank. fem **countess.**

early adj or adv 1. before the fixed time. 2. near the beginning: early on Friday. **earlier, earliest.**

earn v to get something, usually payment, by working. **earning, earned.**

earnest adj serious.

earth n 1. the world. 2. soil.

earthquake n a violent shaking of the earth.

earwig n a brown crawling insect.

ease n rest. opp **unease.**

easel n a stand to rest a blackboard or picture on.

easily adv without trouble.

east n the direction of the rising sun.

Easter n a Christian festival in memory of the rising of Jesus after his death.

eastern adj in or of the east.

easy adj 1. not hard to do or understand. 2. comfortable. **easier, easiest.**

eat v to chew and swallow food. **eating, ate, I have eaten.**

echo *n* a sound that bounces back from a wall when you shout at it. *pl* **echoes.**

eclipse *n* a time when for example the moon stops light from the sun reaching the earth.

edge *n* 1. a rim or border. 2. the sharp side of a blade.

editor *n* a person in charge of a newspaper or magazine.

educate *v* to teach people. **educating, educated.**

eel *n* a long thin fish like a snake.

effect *n* the result of something. Note: do not get mixed up with 'affect'.

effort *n* the strength or energy needed to do something.

egg *n* an object with a thin shell, laid by a bird or a reptile, from which a young one hatches.

eiderdown *n* a bed-covering filled with soft feathers.

eight *n* and *adj* one more than seven, 8. *adj* **eighth.**

eighteen *n* and *adj* ten more than eight, 18. *adj* **eighteenth.**

eighty *n* and *adj* ten times eight, 80. *adj* **eightieth.**

either *adj* or *pron* one or the other: *either Stephen or Fred.*

elastic *n* a rubber band that stretches when pulled and then goes back to its normal size.

elbow *n* the joint between your lower arm and your upper arm.

elder *adj* older: *Jill's elder sister.*

elderly *adj* old: *an elderly woman.*

eldest *adj* the oldest.

election *n* choosing people by voting.

electric, electrical *adj* having to do with electricity: *an electric lamp, an electrical engineer.*

electrician *n* a person who deals with anything electrical.

electricity *n* a powerful force that gives light, heat, or makes machines work.

elephant *n* the largest living land animal.

eleven *n* and *adj* one more than ten, 11. *adj* **eleventh.**

elf *n* a mischievous fairy. *pl* **elves.**

elm *n* a large kind of tree.

else *adj* or *adv* other in addition: *somebody else. What else can I do?*

elsewhere *adv* in some other place.

elves see **elf.**

emblem *n* a badge.

embroidery *n* designs sewn on cloth.

emerald *n* 1. a bright green jewel. 2. the colour of this.

emergency *n* a sudden happening that must be dealt with at once. *pl* **emergencies.**

emigrate *v* to make your home in another country. **emigrating, emigrated.**

emperor *n* the ruler over an empire. *fem* **empress.**

empire *n* a group of countries under the same ruler.

employ *v* to pay someone for working for you. **employing, employed.**

empress see **emperor.**

empty *adj* with nothing inside or on top: *an empty table.* **emptier, emptiest.**

enamel *n* 1. a hard glossy paint. 2. the hard surface of your teeth.

enchanted *adj* under a magic spell.

enclosed *adj* 1. put in a wrapping or envelope. 2. surrounded by a fence or wall.

encourage *v* to give someone hope and courage to do something difficult. **encouraging, encouraged.** *opp* **discourage.**

encyclopedia *n* a book or sets of books that tell you a lot of different things.

end, ending *n* the last part.

enemy *n* someone fighting against you or your country. *pl* **enemies.**

energetic *adj* full of the power to do a lot of things.

energy *n* the power to do things.

engaged *adj* 1. hired to work for someone. 2. having promised to marry someone. 3. occupied by someone else.

engine *n* a machine that makes its own power and can make things move: *The diesel engine pulled the train up the hill.*

engineer *n* someone who plans the building of machinery, roads, or bridges.

engraved *adj* carved in stone or metal.

enjoy *v* to like doing something. **enjoying, enjoyed.**

enjoyable *adj* giving pleasure: *a most enjoyable day.*

enormous *adj* very big.

enough *n* or *adj* as much or as many as are wanted: *enough to eat.*

enquire, enquiry see **inquire, inquiry.**

enter *v* 1. to go in or come in. 2. to take part in: *Sam entered the competition.* **entering, entered.**

entertain *v* I. to amuse. 2. to hold a party and have guests. **entertaining, entertained.**

enthusiasm *n* a great interest in something.

enthusiastic *adj* full of enthusiasm: *an enthusiastic welcome.* opp **unenthusiastic.**

entire *adj* all of anything.

entirely *adv* completely.

entrance *n* a way in: *the entrance to a cinema.*

entry *n* I. coming or going in. 2. a way in. *pl* **entries.**

envelope *n* a paper cover for a letter.

envious *adj* full of envy.

envy *n* a wish for something that someone else has.

equal *adj* of the same number, value, or size as something else. opp **unequal.**

equator *n* an imaginary line around the world, half-way between the North and South Poles.

equipment *n* the special things needed to do something.

erect *v* to build. **erecting, erected.**

errand *n* a small journey to collect or deliver something for someone.

error *n* a mistake.

escalator *n* a moving staircase.

escape *v* to get away from. **escaping, escaped.**

Eskimo *n* one of the people living in north Canada and other regions round the North Pole. *pl* **Eskimoes.**

especially *adv* most of all.

estimate *v* to guess the value or amount of something. **estimating, estimated.**

eternal *adj* lasting for ever.

eve *n* the day before a special event: *New Year's Eve.*

even I. *adj* level: *even ground.* 2. equal: *The score was even.* opp **uneven.** 3. (of numbers) able to be divided by 2. 4. *adv* still: *Even now it is not too late.*

evening *n* the end of the day before it changes to night.

event *n* I. some special happening. 2. one of the items in a sports programme.

ever *adv* at any time: *Will you ever go?*
for ever always.

evergreen *adj* (of a tree) always having green leaves.

every *adj* each: *I pass the house every day.*

everybody, everyone *n* each person.

everything *n* all the things.

everywhere *adv* in every place.

evident *adj* plain to see.

evil *adj* wicked.

ewe *n* a female sheep. *masc* **ram.**

ex- a prefix meaning 'at one time': *Joe Louis, ex-champion boxer.*

exact *adj* correct: *the exact time.* opp **inexact.**

exaggerate *v* to say something is bigger, better, or worse than it really is. **exaggerating, exaggerated.**

examination *n* I. a close look at. 2. an important test of what you know.

example *n* I. anything that shows what something is like or how it works. 2. a person or thing to be copied.

excellent *adj* very good indeed.

except *prep* apart from: *everyone except Gareth.*

exchange *v* to give one thing in return for another. **exchanging, exchanged.**

excite *v* to make someone have strong feelings, usually of pleasure because of something that is going to happen. **exciting, excited.**

excitement *n* being excited.

exclaim *v* to shout out with excitement or surprise. **exclaiming, exclaimed.**

exclamation *n* an excited shout.
exclamation mark a mark (!) used in writing and printing to show excitement: *'Hurray, we have won!'*

excursion *n* a journey for pleasure.

excuse I. *n* a reason why you did not do something that you should have done. 2. *v* to forgive: *Excuse me.* **excusing, excused.**

exercise *n* I. practice in doing something like sums. 2. the using of your body to make it strong and healthy: *Take plenty of exercise and be healthy.*

exhaust I. *v* to tire out. **exhausting, exhausted.** 2. *n* the pipe on a motor-vehicle leading away the burnt gases from the engine.

exhibition *n* a display: *an art exhibition.*

exist *v* I. to be. 2. (with **on**) to live on: *They existed on berries for a week.* **existing, existed.**

exit *n* a way out.

expand *v* to grow larger: *the town is expanding.* **expanding, expanded.**

expect *v* to think something will happen: *I expect him to come.* **expecting, expected.**

expedition *n* a journey for some special purpose such as exploring.

expense *n* the cost of anything.

expensive *adj* costing a lot. *opp* **inexpensive.**

experience *n* I. having practised something for a long time. *opp* **inexperience.** 2. anything that has happened to you: *a terrifying experience.*

experiment *n* a test to find out what will happen.

expert *n* someone who knows a lot about something.

explain *v* to make the meaning of something clear. **explaining, explained.**

explanation *n* something said or written to explain.

explode *v* to burst into pieces or blow up with a loud noise. **exploding, exploded.**

explore *v* I. to look round for the first time. 2. to travel to discover new lands. **exploring, explored.**

explosion *n* a bursting into pieces or a blowing up with a loud noise.

export *v* to send goods to be sold in another country. **exporting, exported.**

express I. *n* a fast train that stops at only a few stations. 2. *v* to put something into words. **expressing, expressed.**

expression *n* a look on your face: *a sad expression.*

exterior *n* the outside of anything. *opp* **interior.**

extinguish *v* to put out a flame or fire. **extinguishing, extinguished.**

extra *adj* more than usual.

extraordinary *adj* very unusual.

extreme *adj* I. the greatest: *Take extreme care.* 2. the furthest: *the extreme south of the island.*

eye *n* one of the two parts of your head through which you see.

eyebrow *n* the small ridge of hair over each eye.

eyelash *n* one of the short hairs that grow around the edge of each eye.

eyesight *n* the power to see.

Ff

fable *n* a short story from which people can learn a lesson.

face I. *n* the front of your head. 2. the front of a clock, building, or playing card. 3. *v* to have the front towards: *Our house faces a church.* **facing, faced.**

fact *n* something that is true.

factory *n* a building in which things are made with the help of machines. *pl* **factories.**

fade *v* I. to lose colour in sunshine or by washing. 2. (of light or sound) to grow weak. **fading, faded.**

fail *v* I. not to do something you try to do. 2. not to do something you ought to do: *Tony failed to turn up in time.* **failing, failed.**

failure *n* something that has failed.

faint I. *adj* weak: *a faint noise.* 2. *v* to lose your senses and fall down. **fainting, fainted.**

fair I. *adj* light in colour. 2. honest: *a fair trial. opp* **unfair.** 3. bright and dry: *fair weather.* 4. *n* a place for fun with stalls and roundabouts.

fairy *n* an imaginary little creature with magical powers. *pl* **fairies.**

faith *n* I. religious belief. 2. trust.

faithful *adj* loyal. *opp* **unfaithful.**

fake *adj* made to look like something better: *fake jewels.*

fall *v* I. to drop from a high place. 2. to die away: *The wind fell.* **falling, fell, I have fallen.**

false *adj* I. untrue. 2. artificial: *false teeth.*

falter *v* I. to stumble. 2. to hesitate when speaking. **faltering, faltered.**

fame *n* being well known.

familiar *adj* well known. *opp* **unfamiliar.**

family *n* a father, mother, and their children. *pl* **families.**

famine *n* a great shortage of food in a district or in a country.

famous *adj* well known and honoured.

fan *n* I. something to make a cooling breeze. 2. someone who likes a sports team or a popular person very much.

fancy I. *v* to want. **he fancies, fancying, fancied.** 2. *adj* worn to imitate someone else: *fancy dress.*

fang *n* I. a long sharp tooth of a dog or wolf. 2. a snake's poison-tooth.

fantastic *adj* amazing.

far *adj* or *adv* a long way off: *He sailed to far countries*. **farther, farthest** or **further, furthest.**

fare *n* the price of a journey from one place to another.

farewell *n* a goodbye.

farm *n* land for growing crops and rearing animals.

farmer *n* a man who manages a farm.

farther, farthest see **far.**

fashion *n* an up-to-date style of dress.

fast I. *adj* quick. 2. (of a clock) showing a time after the correct time. 3. *adv* quickly. 4. not able to move: *a ship stuck fast on rocks*. 5. *v* to go without food. **fasting, fasted.**

fasten *v* to make tight: *to fasten a rope*. **fastening, fastened.** *opp* **unfasten.**

fat I. *adj* plump. **fatter, fattest.** 2. *n* the white greasy part of meat. 3. any type of grease used in cooking.

father *n* I. a man who is a parent. 2. a Roman Catholic priest.

fault *n* I. a mistake. 2. something wrong that spoils someone or something.

favour *n* a kindness: *Please do me a favour*.

favourite *n* the one most liked.

fawn *n* I. a young deer. 2. a pale yellowish-brown colour.

fear *v* to feel afraid of. **fearing, feared.**

feast *n* a splendid meal for a lot of people.

feat *n* a deed of great courage or strength.

feather *n* the covering on a bird's wing or body.

February *n* the second month of the year.

fed see **feed.**

feeble *adj* weak.

feed *v* to give food to. **feeding, fed.**

feel *v* I. to touch. 2. to be in a mood: *Ruth felt happy*. 3. to have an opinion: *I feel that this is wrong*. **feeling, felt.**

feeler *n* one of the two thin rods on the head of some insects.

feeling *n* I. the sense of touch. 2. a mood you are in.

feet see **foot.**

fell *v* I. to cut down. **felling, felled.** 2. see **fall.**

fellow *n* a man or boy.

felt I. *n* a thick kind of cloth. 2. *v* see **feel.**

female *n* a girl, woman, or animal that can have babies. *opp* **male.**

feminine *adj* having to do with women or girls. *opp* **masculine.**

fence I. *n* a kind of wall made of wood. 2. *v* to fight with swords. **fencing, fenced.**

fern *n* a plant with long leaves like feathers.

ferret *n* an animal kept to drive rabbits out of their burrows.

ferry *n* a boat that carries people and vehicles across water. *pl* **ferries.**

fertile *adj* good for growing crops: *fertile land*. *opp* **infertile.**

festival *n* a time of celebration.

fetch *v* to go and get. **fetching, fetched.**

fête *n* a kind of outdoor party with stalls and competitions.

fever *n* an illness that makes you very hot.

few *n* and *adj* not many.

fibre *n* a thread of any kind.

fiction *n* a made-up story that did not really happen.

fiddle I. *n* a violin. 2. *v* to play around with something. **fiddling, fiddled.**

fidget *v* to move your body about because you cannot keep still. **fidgeting, fidgeted.**

field *n* a piece of land with a hedge or fence round.

fierce *adj* cruel and angry.

fifteen *n* and *adj* one more than fourteen, 15. *adj* **fifteenth.**

fifth *adj* one more than fourth, 5th.

fifty *n* and *adj* five times ten, 50. *adj* **fiftieth.**

fig *n* a soft round fruit full of seeds.

fight *v* to struggle or battle against someone or something. **fighting, fought.**

figure *n* I. a number. 2. the shape of someone's body: *the figure of a giant*.

file *n* I. a tool with a rough side to make things smooth. 2. a box or folder for keeping important papers in order.
in single file one behind another.

fill *v* to put into a container as much as it will hold. **filling, filled.**

filly *n* a young female horse. *pl* **fillies.** *masc* **colt.**

film *n* I. moving photographs, usually with sound. 2. a roll of material on which you take photographs.
film-star a chief actor or actress in a cinema film.

filthy *adj* very dirty. **filthier, filthiest.**

fin *n* one of the short flat parts of a fish that help it to balance and swim.

final *adj* the last: *the final part of a play*.

finch *n* one of various kinds of small bird.

find *v* 1. to come across something either by accident or when you are looking for it. 2. (with **out**) to discover. **finding, found.**

fine *adj* 1. sunny and dry. 2. very good. 3. thin: *fine cloth.*

finger *n* one of the four long tips of your hand.

fingerprint *n* a mark made by the tip of a finger, showing a pattern.

finish *n* the end: *the finish of a race.*

fir *n* a tall evergreen tree with cones and needle-like leaves.

fire 1. *n* the heat and light from something burning. 2. *v* to shoot with a gun or rifle. **firing, fired.**

fire-engine *n* a big motor-vehicle with men ready to go to a fire.

fire-escape *n* a ladder or stairs helping people to escape from a fire.

fireplace *n* a place under the chimney in a house, where a fire burns.

fireworks *n pl* small cardboard tubes filled with gunpowder that will send out coloured sparks, lit at special celebrations.

firm 1. *adj* steady. 2. *n* a business.

first 1. *adj* chief: *the first prize.* 2. *adv* before all others.
   first aid help given to a hurt or sick person before a doctor comes.
   first-class of the best kind.

fish *n* an animal with scales and fins, that breathes through gills and lives only in water. *pl* **fish** or **fishes.**

fisherman *n* a man who catches fish.

fist *n* a tightly-closed hand.

fit 1. *v* to be of the right size and shape. **fitting, fitted.** 2. *adj* to be suitable. 3. to be well. *opp* **unfit.**

five *n* and *adj* one more than four, 5. See **fifth.**

fix 1. *v* to make something firm. 2. to put something right. **fixing, fixed.** 3. *n* a difficulty.

fizzy *adj* having a lot of tiny bubbles that burst.

flag *n* an oblong piece of cloth with the emblem of a country, or a society.

flake *n* a small thin piece.

flame *n* a tongue of fire.

flannel *n* a piece of soft cloth for washing yourself.

flap 1. *v* to move up and down, or sideways: *A bird flaps its wings.* **flapping, flapped.** 2. *n* a part that hangs down loosely: *the flap of an envelope.*

flare *v* to blaze up suddenly. **flaring, flared.**

flash *v* to shine suddenly. **flashing, flashed.**

flask *n* a bottle with a narrow neck, for holding liquids.

flat 1. *adj* smooth and level. **flatter, flattest.** 2. *n* a home that is a set of rooms in a house, all on one floor.

flatten *v* to make flat. **flattening, flattened.**

flavour *n* the taste of something.

flaw *n* a small fault: *a flaw in pottery.*

flea *n* a small hopping insect that sucks blood.

flee *v* to run away. **fleeing, fled.**

fleece *n* a sheep's woollen coat.

fleet *n* a number of ships or cars grouped together.

flesh *n* 1. meat. 2. the soft part of your body under your skin.

flew see **fly.**

flick *v* to hit quickly with a finger. **flicking, flicked.**

flight *n* 1. the movement of birds, insects, or aeroplanes through the air. 2. a journey by aeroplane. 3. a running away from danger. 4. a series of steps.

flimsy *adj* easily torn or broken. **flimsier, flimsiest.**

flinch *v* to move back slightly from something threatening. **flinching, flinched.**

fling *v* to throw hard. **flinging, flung.**

flint *n* a very hard kind of stone.

flipper *n* the flat leg of a seal, walrus, or turtle.

float *v* to rest on water like a ship, or on air like a balloon. **floating, floated.**

flock *n* a group of birds, or some animals.

flog *v* to beat hard with a whip or a stick. **flogging, flogged.**

flood *n* 1. a great overflow of water. 2. anything like this: *a flood of letters.*

floor *n* the bottom of a room, on which we walk.

flop *v* to drop down heavily: *She flopped down.* **flopping, flopped.**

florist *n* someone who sells flowers.

flour *n* a white powder got by grinding grain, used for baking.

flow *v* to move along smoothly, as water does. **flowing, flowed.**

flower *n* the blossom of a plant.

flown see **fly.**

flu *n* an illness when you have a cold, a fever, and aches all over your body.

fluffy *adj* covered with soft hair or fur.

flung see **fling.**

flush *v* I. to go red with excitement. 2. to wash out with water. **flushing, flushed.**

flute *n* a musical instrument that you blow.

flutter *v* to wave backwards and forwards quickly and lightly. **fluttering, fluttered.**

fly I. *n* any of various kinds of small insect that fly. *pl* **flies.** 2. *v* to move along through the air. 3. to make something keep up in the air: *to fly a kite.* **it flies, flying, flew, it has flown.**

flyover *n* a bridge carrying one road over another one.

foal *n* a young horse or donkey.

foam *n* white froth, as on a wave.

fog *n* a thick cloud of mist.

fold I. *v* to double something over. **folding, folded.** 2. *n* a crease caused by folding.

-fold an ending meaning 'times': *Threefold* (three times).

folder *n* a cover for keeping papers in.

foliage *n* the leaves on trees and plants.

folk *n* people.

folk music *n* the old music and songs of a country.

follow *v* I. to come or go after. 2. to understand: *I don't follow you.* **following, followed.**

fond *adj* (with **of**) liking very much.

food *n* what we eat to keep us alive.

fool *n* a silly person.

foolish *adj* silly.

foot *n* I. the part of each leg on which you stand. 2. a length of twelve inches. *pl* **feet.** 3. the bottom part: *the foot of the cliff.*

football *n* a large leather ball, used to play football.

footprint *n* the mark of a foot.

footsteps *n pl* the sound of someone walking.

forbid *v* to say that someone is not to do something. **forbidding, forbade, I have forbidden.**

force I. *n* power. 2. *v* to make some person or animal do something. 3. to do something, using force. **forcing, forced.**

ford *n* a place where you can cross a river on foot or in a car.

fore- a prefix meaning 'in front'.

forecast *v* to say what is likely to happen. **forecasting, forecast.**

forehead *n* the part of your face above your eyebrows.

foreign *adj* belonging to another country.

forest *n* a large area of country thickly covered with trees.

forgave see **forgive.**

forge I. *n* a blacksmith's workshop. 2. *v* to copy someone's signature, or print notes of money, for a dishonest reason. **forging, forged.**

forget *v* not to remember. **forgetting, forgot, I have forgotten.**

forgive *v* to stop being angry with someone: *I forgave him for telling a lie.* **forgiving, forgave, I have forgiven.**

forgot, forgotten see **forget.**

fork *n* I. a small tool with prongs, for eating with. 2. a big garden tool with prongs, for lifting earth or roots. 3. a place where a road or river branches in two.

form I. *n* a shape: *the form of a square.* 2. a class in school. 3. a bench. 4. a printed paper asking questions, with spaces for the answers. 5. *v* to make into a shape. **forming, formed.**

forsake *v* to leave for ever. **forsaking, forsook, I have forsaken.**

fort, fortress *n* a strong castle.

fortnight *n* two weeks.

fortunate *adj* lucky. *opp* **unfortunate.**

fortune *n* I. a lot of money. 2. luck: *good fortune.*

forty *n* and *adj* ten times four, 40. *adj* **fortieth.**

forward *adv* ahead: *Forward march!*

fossil *n* the remains of an ancient plant or animal that has turned to stone, found in rock.

foster-mother *n* a woman who looks after a child in place of the real mother.

fought see **fight.**

foul *adj* I. filthy. 2. unfair: *foul play.* 3. stormy: *foul weather.*

found see **find.**

fountain *n* a jet of water shooting upwards.

four *n* and *adj* one more than three, 4. *adj* **fourth. on all fours** on hands and knees.

fourteen n and adj one more than thirteen, 14. adj **fourteenth.**

fowl n a bird, especially a cock or a hen.

fox n a reddish-brown wild animal, with a dog-like head. fem **vixen.**

fraction n a part of a whole amount: A quarter ($\frac{1}{4}$) is a fraction.

fragile adj delicate, easily broken.

fragment n a small piece of something.

frame n a border of wood or metal around something: a picture frame.

framework n the parts that support something.

frank adj saying openly what you think.

fraud n 1. a trick. 2. a person who cheats.

fray v (of cloth) to wear away. **fraying, frayed.**

freak adj very unusual: a freak wave.

freckles n pl light brown spots on the skin caused by the sun.

free adj 1. able to do as you like. 2. costing nothing. 3. generous: free with his money.

freedom n being free.

freeze v 1. to become very cold. 2. to turn into ice. **freezing, froze, it has frozen.**

freezer n a machine that freezes food put inside it, to keep it fresh.

frequent adj often happening or appearing. opp **infrequent.**

fresh adj 1. not old or used: fresh milk, fresh air. 2. not tinned: fresh fruit.

fret v to worry a lot about something. **fretting, fretted.**

Friday n the sixth day of the week.
Good Friday the Friday before Easter, the day when Jesus died.

fridge short for **refrigerator.**

fried see **fry.**

friend n someone you know well and like.

fright n a scare.

frighten v to make someone afraid. **frightening, frightened.**

frill n an edge of lace or cloth on a dress.

fringe n 1. a border of loose threads on a dress or curtain. 2. hair cut low across the forehead.

frock n a dress.

frog n a small jumping animal that lives in and out of water.

from prep 1. out of. 2. between: from four to five o'clock. 3. beginning at: Read from the first line. 4. because of: The plant died from the frost.

front n the forward part.

frost n powdered ice you see on the ground on a cold day.

froth n masses of tiny bubbles on the top of a liquid.

frown v 1. to wrinkle your forehead when you are puzzled or angry. 2. (with **at**) to glare at someone. **frowning, frowned.**

froze, frozen see **freeze.**

fruit n the fleshy food, containing the seed, that follows the blossom on a fruit tree.

fry v to cook in oil or fat. **he fries, frying, fried.**

frying-pan n a pan for frying things in.

fudge n a kind of soft, sweet toffee.

fuel n anything that is burned to give heat or energy.

fulfil v to carry out something you have started or promised to do. **fulfilling, fulfilled.**

full adj filled completely: The hall is full of people.
full stop a punctuation mark (.).

fumble v 1. to handle something awkwardly. 2. to feel about: to fumble for a key. **fumbling, fumbled.**

fumes n pl unpleasant gases or smoke from something burning.

fun n enjoyment.

fund n money put by for a special purpose: a church fund.

funeral n a service when a dead person's body is buried or burnt.

funnel n 1. a chimney on a ship or steam locomotive. 2. a tube with a wide mouth to help you pour things into bottles.

funny adj 1. amusing. 2. strange. **funnier, funniest.**

fur n the soft hairy coat of some animals.

furious adj very angry.

furnace n a very hot fire in a closed fireplace.

furnish v to supply a house with furniture. **furnishing, furnished.**

furniture n the chairs, tables, wardrobes, and other movable things in a house.

furrow n a shallow trench made by a plough.

furry adj covered with fur.

further 1. adv to a greater distance: Ted moved further away. See **far.** 2. adj in addition.

fury n great anger.

fuse n 1. a piece of paper or cord that you burn to start an explosion. 2. a piece of wire that will melt to stop too much electricity flowing into something.

fuselage n the body of an aeroplane.

fuss *n* a commotion, especially about things that are not very important.

future *n* the time that lies ahead.

Gg

gag *v* to tie something over someone's mouth so that the person can't call out. **gagging, gagged.** *opp* **ungag.**

gaily *adj* merrily.

gain *v* 1. to win. 2. to increase: *Judy has gained in weight.* **gaining, gained.**

gala *n* a friendly festival or competition.

galaxy *n* a very large group of stars. *pl* **galaxies.**

gale *n* a very strong wind.

gallant *adj* brave and honourable: *a gallant soldier.*

galleon *n* a large Spanish sailing ship of olden times.

gallery *n* 1. a long room where pictures are shown. 2. a high balcony in a theatre. *pl* **galleries.**

galley *n* 1. a ship of olden times moved by sails and oars. 2. a ship's kitchen. *pl* **galleys.**

gallop *v* (of a horse) to run at full speed. **galloping, galloped.**

gamble *v* 1. to play a game of luck and try to win money. 2. to take unnecessary risk. **gambling, gambled.**
to take a gamble to take a risk.

game *n* 1. a competition between two people or two sides. 2. wild birds or animals hunted by people for sport or food.

gamekeeper *n* a man who looks after wild birds and animals.

gander see **goose.**

gang *n* 1. a group of criminals working together. 2. a group of men working together.

gangway *n* 1. a narrow passage between rows of seats in a hall or cinema. 2. a movable bridge for getting on or off a ship.

gaol, jail *n* a prison.

gap *n* an opening between two objects.

garage *n* a building where vehicles are kept or repaired.

garden *n* a place where plants, vegetables, and fruit are grown.

garment *n* any piece of clothing.

gas *n* 1. anything, such as air, that is neither liquid nor solid. *pl* **gases.** 2. a special kind of gas that burns and is used for heating and cooking.

gash *n* a long deep cut.

gasp *v* to open your mouth and breathe in deeply. **gasping, gasped.**

gate *n* a hinged door in a fence or wall round a piece of land.

gather *v* 1. to collect. 2. to come together: *A crowd gathered round.* **gathering, gathered.**

gave see **give.**

gay *adj* 1. merry. 2. having bright colours.

gaze *v* to stare at. **gazing, gazed.**

gazelle *n* a small deer of Africa and Asia.

geese see **goose.**

gem *n* a precious stone.

general 1. *adj* common to most people or things. 2. *n* an army commander.

generous *adj* ready to give or share what you have.

genius *n* someone who is very clever.

gentle *adj* 1. quiet. 2. soft. 3. gradual.

gentleman *n* a polite name for a man.

genuine *adj* real.

geography *n* the study of the world and the people who live in different countries.

gerbil *n* a small brown animal like a large mouse.

germ *n* a very small living thing that can cause illness.

get *v* 1. to obtain or fetch. 2. to become: *to get cold.* 3. to ask: *I got him to come.* **getting, got.**

ghastly *adj* horrible, terrible: *He made a ghastly mistake.*

ghost *n* the spirit of a dead person, which some people think walks about at night.

giant *n* 1. a man of enormous size. 2. anything much larger than usual.

giddy *adj* dizzy. **giddier, giddiest.**

gift *n* a present.

gigantic *adj* enormous in size.

giggle *v* to laugh in a silly way. **giggling, giggled.**

gills *n pl* two openings for breathing, in the head of a fish.

ginger *n* a reddish-brown colour.

gingerbread *n* a cake that tastes of ginger.

gipsy, gypsy *n* one of the wandering people who often live in caravans. *pl* **gipsies, gypsies.**

giraffe *n* a tall African animal with a long neck.

girl *n* 1. a female child. 2. a young woman.

give *v* to hand over something to someone. **giving, gave, I have given.**
to give in, to give up to surrender.
to give way to collapse.

glacier *n* a huge river of ice that moves very slowly down a mountain side.

glad *adj* pleased.

glade *n* a small open space in a wood or forest.

glance *v* to take a quick look. **glancing, glanced.**

glare *v* to look angrily at someone. **glaring, glared.**

glaring *adj* 1. shining brightly. 2. fierce and angry: *a glaring look.*

glass *n* 1. a hard brittle substance you can see through. 2. a cup made of glass that has no handle.

glasses *n pl* spectacles.

gleam *n* a soft light.

glen *n* a narrow Scottish valley.

glide *v* to move along smoothly. **gliding, glided.**

glider *n* a light aeroplane with no engine that can glide through the air.

glimmer *n* a faint shine.

glimpse *n* a quick sight of something.

glisten *v* to shine like something that has drops of water on it. **glistening, glistened.**

glitter *v* to flash brightly. **glittering, glittered.**

globe *n* a ball with a map of the world on it.

gloomy *adj* 1. dim. 2. miserable. **gloomier, gloomiest.**

glorious *adj* splendid.

glory *n* 1. great beauty. 2. great fame.

glossy *adj* smooth and shining. **glossier, glossiest.**

glove *n* a covering for your hand with separate parts for your thumb and each finger.

glow *v* to give out a warm light. **glowing, glowed.**

glue *n* a substance used to stick things together.

glum *adj* sad and gloomy.

gnat *n* a small fly that sucks blood.

gnaw *v* to keep biting something: *to gnaw a bone.* **gnawing, gnawed.**

gnome *n* in fairy-tales, a dwarf.

go *v* 1. to move away. 2. (of a machine) to be working. **he goes, going, went, he has gone** (gon).

goal *n* 1. the two posts between which the ball must go to score a point in some games. 2. an aim: *Sandra's goal was to win.*

goalkeeper, goalie *n* the person who defends the goal in a ball-game.

goat *n* an animal with horns and a beard. *masc* **billy-goat.** *fem* **nanny-goat.** *young* **kid.**

gobble *v* to eat something quickly and noisily. **gobbling, gobbled.**

goblin *n* in fairy-tales, a mischievous ugly fairy.

god *n* a powerful spirit that people once worshipped. *fem* **goddess.**

God *n* the Creator of everything.

goddess see **god.**

goggles *n pl* large spectacles worn to keep dust out of one's eyes.

go-kart *n* a small simple racing car.

gold *n* a very valuable yellow metal.

golden *adj* 1. made of gold. 2. coloured like gold.

goldfish *n* a small orange fish kept as a pet.

golf *n* a game played with clubs and small white balls.

gone see **go.**

good *adj* 1. pleasing. 2. kind. 3. well-behaved. **better, best.**
good natured kind.

goodbye *n* the word said when you leave.

goods *n pl* things that can be bought and sold.

goose *n* a large female web-footed bird. *pl* **geese.** *masc* **gander.** *young* **gosling.**

gooseberry *n* a yellowish-green fruit that grows on bushes. *pl* **gooseberries.**

gorge *n* a narrow valley between high cliffs.

gorgeous *adj* magnificent.

gorilla *n* the largest kind of ape.

gorse *n* a prickly shrub covered with small yellow flowers.

gospel *n* any one of the first four books of the New Testament.

gossip *v* to chatter for a long time, especially about people. **gossiping, gossiped.**

got see **get.**

govern *v* to be in charge of a country or place. **governing, governed.**

government *n* the people who govern a country.

gown *n* a long loose dress.

grab *v* to take hold of suddenly. **grabbing, grabbed.**

grace *n* 1. a beautiful way of moving or standing. 2. a short prayer said before a meal.

gradual *adj* happening a bit at a time.

grain *n* 1. the seeds of wheat, rice, etc. 2. a speck. 3. the lines in wood.

gram *n* a very small weight, equal to one-thousandth of a kilogram.

grammar *n* the study of how to speak and write correctly.
grammar school in England and Wales, a secondary school for boys and girls over 11 years of age.

grand *adj* 1. magnificent. 2. great: *a grand piano.*

grandchild *n* a child of a son or daughter.

grand-dad, grandfather, grandpa *n* the father of a mother or father.

grandma, grandmother, grannie, granny *n* the mother of a father or mother.

granite *n* a very hard rock.

grape *n* a green or purple fruit growing in clusters on vines.

grapefruit *n* a yellow fruit like a large orange.

graph *n* a diagram giving you information about sets of figures.

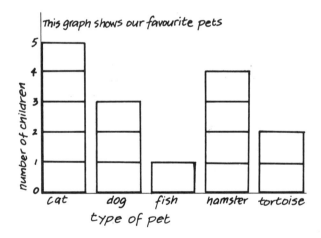

This graph shows our favourite pets

grasp *v* to hold something tightly. **grasping, grasped.**

grass *n* the green plant making up a lawn or meadow.

grasshopper *n* a jumping insect with long legs.

grate 1. *n* the part of a fireplace that holds burning fuel. 2. *v* to make an unpleasant noise by scraping one thing against another. 3. to rub something into little pieces. **grating, grated.**

grateful *adj* full of thanks. *opp* **ungrateful.**

grating *n* a frame of iron bars, often placed over the opening of a drain.

grave 1. *n* a hole in the earth in which a dead person is buried. 2. *adj* serious.

gravel *n* a lot of small smooth stones together.

gravity *n* the force pulling things towards the earth.

gravy *n* the juice of cooked meat or a brown liquid sauce made to look like this.

gray see **grey.**

graze *v* 1. to hurt your skin by rubbing it hard against something. 2. to eat grass while it is growing: *Cows graze in the fields.* **grazing, grazed.**

grease *n* fat or thick oil.

great *adj* 1. large. 2. important: *a great artist.* 3. very good.

greedy *adj* wanting more than your share. **greedier, greediest.**

green *n* 1. the colour of grass. 2. a large area of grass.

greengrocer *n* someone who sells fruit and vegetables in a shop.

greenhouse *n* a glass building where plants are grown.

greet *v* to welcome or say hello to someone. **greeting, greeted.**

grew see **grow.**

grey, gray *n* a colour between black and white.

grief *n* great sadness.

grim *adj* not looking pleased or friendly.

grimy *adj* dirty and difficult to clean. **grimier, grimiest.**

grin *n* a wide smile.

grind *v* 1. to crush to powder. 2. to rub together: *to grind your teeth.* **grinding, ground.**

grip *v* to hold tightly. **gripping, gripped.**

grit *n* small bits of stone or sand.

groan *n* a sigh of disappointment or pain.

grocer *n* a shopkeeper who sells dry or tinned foods such as tea, sugar, and soup.

groceries *n pl* things sold by a grocer.

groom *n* 1. someone who looks after horses. 2. a bridegroom.

groove *n* a long narrow hollow cut into something.

grope *v* to feel around for something when you cannot see. **groping, groped.**

gross *n* twelve dozen, or 144.

ground 1. *n* the earth we walk on. 2. *v* see **grind.**

group *n* a number of people, animals, or things together.

grouse 1. *v* to grumble. **grousing, groused.** 2. *n* a wild bird shot for food. *pl* **grouse.**

grove *n* a small wood.

grow *v* 1. to get bigger. 2. to plant for food. **growing, grew, I have grown.**

growl *v* to make a deep angry sound. **growling, growled.**

grown see **grow.**

grown-up *n* a man or a woman.

grub *n* a soft crawling creature that will later turn into an insect.

grudge *n* a bad feeling against someone.

gruff *adj* deep and rough: *a gruff voice.*

grumble *v* to complain. **grumbling, grumbled.**

grunt *v* to make a noise like a pig. **grunting, grunted.**

guard *n* 1. a man in charge of a train. 2. someone who keeps watch and protects: *a guard at the castle.*

guardian *n* someone who looks after a child whose parents cannot take care of him or her.

guess *v* to say or believe what you think is true, without being sure. **guessing, guessed.**

guest *n* someone who is invited.

guide *v* to show the way. **guiding, guided.**

guilty *adj* having done wrong or taken part in a crime: *guilty of stealing.*

guinea pig *n* a small animal that has no tail and is kept as a pet.

guitar *n* a musical instrument with strings that are plucked.

gull see **seagull.**

gulp *v* to swallow quickly and in a noisy way. **gulping, gulped.**

gum *n* 1. pink flesh round your teeth. 2. a sweet that you keep chewing. 3. a stickly liquid for fastening things together.

gun *n* a cannon, rifle, or revolver.
   gunpowder black explosive powder used in fireworks and once used in guns.

gurgle *v* to make a noise like that of water going out of the bath. **gurgling gurgled.**

gush *v* (of a liquid) to burst out. **gushing, gushed.**

gusty *adj* (of the wind) blowing in sudden rushes.

gutter *n* a long narrow hollow at the side of a road or along the edge of a roof, to take away rain water.

guy *n* a model of Guy Fawkes made to be put on a bonfire on 5th November.

gym, gymnasium *n* a special room for exercising in.

gymkhana *n* a meeting for horse riding competitions.

gypsy see **gipsy.**

Hh

habit *n* something you do very often, sometimes without even realising it.

had see **have.**

hadn't short for had not.

haggard *adj* looking tired and distressed.

hail *n* frozen rain.

hair *n* one of the fibres that grow on your skin.

hairdresser *n* someone who cuts and arranges hair.

half *n* one of two equal parts which make up a whole, $\frac{1}{2}$. *pl* **halves.**

hall *n* 1. the entrance space behind the door of a building. 2. a large room for concerts, meetings, and dances. 3. a large old country house.

Hallowe'en *n* October 31st, when all the witches are said to come out.

halt *v* to stop for a time. **halting, halted.**

halve *v* to divide into two equal parts. **halving, halved.**

halves see **half.**

ham *n* cooked meat from a pig's thigh.

hamburger *n* a round flat cake of chopped meat that is fried and often eaten in a bread roll.

hammer *n* a tool for knocking in nails.

hammock *n* a bed made of netting or canvas, hung up by cords tied to each end.

hamster *n* a small furry animal kept as a pet.

hand *n* 1. the part at the end of your arm. 2. a pointer on a clock. 3. a deal of cards. 4. a member of a ship's crew.

handbag *n* a lady's bag, carried by hand.

handcuffs *n pl* steel bracelets to lock a prisoner's hands together.

handful *n* as much as a hand will hold. *pl* **handfuls.**

handicap *n* anything that makes it more difficult for you to do something.

handkerchief, hankie, hanky *n* a cloth for wiping your nose. *pl* **handkerchiefs, hankies.**

handle *n* the part of a cup, pan, or tool by which you hold it.

handlebar *n* the part of a bicycle you steer with.

handsome *adj* good-looking.

handy *adj* 1. clever with your hands. 2. useful to have near by. **handier, handiest.**

hang *v* to fasten something so that it swings but does not fall. **hanging, hung.**

hangar *n* a large shed for aircraft.

hanger *n* a frame to hang clothes on.

hankie, hanky short for **handkerchief.**

haphazard *adj* done anyhow, not carefully carried out: *Terry works in a haphazard way.*

happen *v* 1. to take place. 2. to do something by chance: *I happened to see a fox.* **happening, happened.**

happily *adv* in a happy way.

happiness *n* being happy.

happy *adj* pleased or cheerful. **happier, happiest.**

harbour *n* a sheltered place for ships, on a coast.

hard *adj* 1. not soft: *hard rock.* 2. tiring. 3. difficult.

hard-hearted *adj* cruel.

hardly *adv* only just: *I can hardly reach it.*

hardship *n* hard conditions.

hardy *adj* able to stand hard conditions: *hardy plants.* **hardier, hardiest.**

hare *n* an animal like a large rabbit.

harm *v* to hurt. **harming, harmed.**

harmful *adj* causing harm: *These berries are harmful to eat.* opp **harmless** or **unharmful.**

harness *n* the leather straps worn by a horse when ridden or pulling a cart or plough.

harp *n* a large musical instrument played by plucking its strings.

harpoon *n* a spear, with a rope fastened to it, fired at whales by a gun.

harsh *adj* severe: *a harsh frost.*

harvest *n* the gathering of corn, fruit, and vegetables at the end of the growing season: *the apple harvest.*

haste *n* a great hurry: *He ran off in haste.*

hat *n* a covering for the head.

hatch 1. *v* to be born by breaking out of an egg. **hatching, hatched.** 2. *n* a door in a ship's deck.

hate *v* to dislike very much. **hating, hated.**

hatred *n* strong dislike.

haul *v* to pull with difficulty. **hauling, hauled.**

haunted *adj* supposed to be visited by ghosts.

have *v* 1. to own. 2. to contain: *The pond has three frogs in it.* 3. (before another verb, to show something has been finished): *I have eaten, you have slept.* **he has, having, had. to have to** must: *I have to go.*

hawk *n* a bird of prey.

hawthorn *n* a prickly tree that blossoms in May.

hay *n* grass cut and dried as food for animals.

haystack *n* a large pile of dried hay.

haze *n* slight mist or smoke.

head 1. *n* the top part of your body. 2. the top or front of anything. 3. *adj* the chief: *head cook.*

headache *n* a pain in the head.

headmaster *n* the head teacher in a school. *fem* **headmistress.**

heal *v* 1. to make well again. 2. to become well again: *The wound has healed.* **healing, healed.**

health *n* the condition of your mind and body, whether you are well or ill.

healthy *adj* in good health. **healthier, healthiest.** opp **unhealthy.**

heap *n* a pile: *a heap of rubbish.*

hear *v* 1. to listen to. 2. to have news. **hearing, heard.**

heart *n* 1. the pump in your chest that you can feel beating, and which sends blood round your body. 2. the centre of something: *the heart of the problem.* 3. one of the four kinds of playing cards.

hearth *n* the floor of a fireplace.

heat *n* 1. warmth. 2. (in sports) one of several races to pick out the best runners for the final race.

heath *n* a stretch of moorland.

heather *n* a low-growing moorland plant with small white or purple flowers.

heave *v* to lift up or pull with a great effort. **heaving, heaved.**

heaven *n* the place believed to be the home of God.

heavy *adj* 1. having much weight. 2. in great quantities: *heavy rain.* **heavier, heaviest.**

hedge *n* a line of bushes forming a fence.

hedgehog *n* a small animal covered with prickles.

heel *n* the back of your foot, or the back of a sock, stocking, or shoe.

height *n* how high or tall anything is.

heir *n* someone who will become the owner of another person's title, money, or property when that person dies. *fem* **heiress.**

held see **hold.**

helicopter *n* an aircraft without wings that can rise straight up from the ground, pulled by a propeller on its roof.

helm *n* the wheel or handle used to steer a ship.

helmet *n* a hard hat worn as protection.

help *v* to share someone's work or troubles by doing something for them. **helping, helped.**

helpful *adj* giving help. *opp* **unhelpful.**

helping *n* a share: *helping of pudding.*

hem *n* the edge of a piece of cloth turned over and stitched.

hen *n* a female bird, which lays eggs.

her, hers *adj* and *pron* referring to a girl, woman, or female animal.

herb *n* a plant used in cooking to give flavour.

herd *n* a group of cattle or other large animals.

here *adv* I. in this place. 2. to this place: *Come here!*

hermit *n* a person who lives alone, usually in a lonely place.

hero *n* I. someone who has done something very brave. 2. the chief man or boy in a book or play. *pl* **heroes.** *fem* **heroine.**

heron *n* a large wading bird with a long beak and long legs.

herring *n* a sea fish used for food.

hers see **her.**

herself see **himself.**

hesitate *v* to pause because you are not sure whether to do something. **hesitating, hesitated.**

hibernate *v* (of some animals) to sleep through the winter. **hibernating, hibernated.**

hiccup *n* a sudden noise in your throat, made after you have eaten or drunk something too quickly.

hid see **hide.**

hide I. *v* to keep out of sight. 2. to put out of sight. **hiding, hid, I have hidden.** 3. *n* the skin of an animal.
hide-and-seek a game in which you hide and someone tries to find you.

hideous *adj* very ugly.

high *adj* I. a long way up from the ground. 2. very great: *a high price.* 3. at the top of a musical scale: *a high note.*
high school a secondary school for older boys and girls.

highway *n* a road that everyone can use.

highwayman *n* in olden days, a man who robbed travellers on the roads. *pl* **highwaymen.**

hijack *v* to threaten a pilot or a driver, and tell him or her to go where you want to go. **hijacking, hijacked.**

hike *v* to go for a long walk in the country. **hiking, hiked.**

hill *n* high land lower than a mountain.

hilt *n* the handle of a sword or dagger.

him *pron* referring to a boy, man, or male animal.

himself *pron* he alone. *fem* **herself.**

hind I. *adj* at the back: *hind legs.* 2. *n* a female deer. *masc* **stag.**

hinder *v* to get in someone's way so that it is difficult for something to be done. **hindering, hindered.**

hinge *n* a movable metal joint letting a door or lid swing.

hint *n* I. a helpful piece of advice. 2. some information given to someone to make him or her guess exactly what you mean.

hip *n* the joint at the top of your thigh.

hippopotamus *n* a large thick-skinned African animal that lives near water. *pl* **hippopotamuses.**

hire *v* to use something for a while in return for payment. **hiring, hired.**

his *pron* and *adj* belonging to him.

hiss *v* to make a sharp 's' sound with your mouth. **hissing, hissed.**

history *n* what happened in past times.

hit *v* to strike. **hitting, hit.**

hitch-hike *v* to travel by obtaining lifts on the way. **hitch-hiking, hitch-hiked.**

hive *n* a house for bees.

hoard *v* to store in a secret place: *Squirrels hoard nuts in the ground.* **hoarding, hoarded.**

hoarse *adj* with a rough voice.

hobble *v* to walk slowly with short steps as if lame. **hobbling, hobbled.**

hobby *n* a favourite pastime. *pl* **hobbies.**

hockey *n* a game played on a pitch with two goals as in football, but with each player having a curved stick to hit a small ball.

hoe *n* a long-handled tool for loosening the soil.

Hogmanay *n* the celebration of New Year's Eve in Scotland.

hoist *v* to lift up something by using a rope. **hoisting, hoisted.**

hold 1. *v* to keep in your hand. 2. to contain. 3. to defend. 4. to have: *to hold a meeting.* **holding, held.** 5. *n* the space below deck for a ship's cargo.
to hold up 1. to lift. 2. to cause delay. 3. to rob.

hole *n* 1. an opening. 2. a pit.

holiday *n* a time free from work or school.

hollow 1. *adj* with a space inside. 2. *n* a shallow hole.

holly *n* an evergreen shrub with prickly leaves, and with red berries in winter.

holster *n* a container for carrying a gun, often worn on a belt round the waist.

holy *adj* having to do with God or a god. *opp* **unholy.**

home *n* the place where you live.

homesick *adj* longing for home when you are away.

homework *n* schoolwork done at home.

honest *adj* never cheating, stealing, or telling lies. *opp* **dishonest.**

honesty *n* acting in an honest way.

honey *n* a sweet food made by bees.

honour *n* respect. *opp* **dishonour.**

hood *n* a covering for the head and neck, sometimes fastened to a coat or anorak.

hoof *n* the hard part of the foot of some animals such as a horse or a cow. *pl* **hoofs** or **hooves.**

hook *n* a bent piece of metal, sometimes with a point, made to catch or hold something: *a fish-hook, a meat-hook.*

hoop *n* a wooden or metal ring round a barrel.

hoot *n* 1. the sound of a motor horn. 2. the cry of an owl.

hooves see **hoof.**

hop 1. *v* to jump on one leg, or (of some birds and some animals) with both feet at the same time. **hopping, hopped.** 2. *n* a plant of which the fruit is used to flavour beer.

hope *v* to wish that something will happen. **hoping, hoped.**

hopeless *adj* 1. giving no hope of success or rescue: *a hopeless position.* 2. not able to do something well.

hopscotch *n* a game where you skip along squares.

horizon *n* the line where sea and sky, or land and sky, seem to meet.

horn *n* 1. a pointed bone that grows out of the heads of some animals. 2. a musical instrument that you blow. 3. a warning sound: *a motor horn.*

horrible *adj* very unpleasant.

horrid *adj* nasty: *a horrid smell.*

horrified *adj* 1. filled with horror. 2. having had a nasty surprise.

horror *n* great fear.

horse *n* an animal with hooves, used for riding and pulling carts. *masc* **stallion.** *fem* **mare.** *young* **foal.**

horse-chestnut *n* the tree that conkers grow on.

horseshoe *n* a curved piece of iron nailed under a horse's hoof.

hose *n* a long tube taking water from a tap.

hospital *n* a building where people who are ill or hurt are looked after by doctors and nurses.

host *n* 1. anyone who entertains visitors. *fem* **hostess.** 2. a large number: *a host of sparrows.*

hostile *adj* very unfriendly.

hot *adj* 1. very, very warm. 2. having a very strong taste. **hotter, hottest.**
hot dog a hot sausage eaten in a bread roll.

hotel *n* a large building with many rooms where people can pay to sleep and eat.

hound *n* a hunting-dog.

hour *n* a length of time equal to 60 minutes.

house *n* a building in which people live.

hover *v* to fly in the air staying over one spot. **hovering, hovered.**

hovercraft *n* a vehicle without wings or wheels that can glide over land or water.

how *adv* in what way: *How did you do it?*

however I. *adv* in what way. 2. *conj* and yet: *I put the clock right; however it stopped again.*

howl *n* a long cry.

hub *n* the centre of a wheel.

huddle *v* to press close: *The animals huddled together.* **huddling, huddled.**

hug *v* to clasp in your arms. **hugging, hugged.**

huge *adj* very big: *a huge elephant.*

hull *n* the frame of a ship or boat.

hum *v* I. to make a noise like a bee. 2. to make a tune with your lips closed. **humming, hummed.**

human *adj* having to do with people, not animals.

humble *adj* not proud, wealthy, or grand.

humorous *adj* funny.

humour *n* fun.

hump *n* a large lump, usually on the back.

hundred *n* and *adj* ten times ten, 100. *adj* **hundredth.**

hung see **hang.**

hunger *n* a great wish for food.

hungry *adj* having a great wish for food. **hungrier, hungriest.**

hunt *v* I. to chase after something in order to catch or kill it. 2. (with **for**) to search for. **hunting, hunted.**

hurdle *n* a movable fence for runners or horses to jump over in a race.

hurl *v* to throw something with all your strength. **hurling, hurled.**

hurricane *n* a storm with a wind violent enough to blow down buildings.

hurry *v* I. to move quickly. 2. to do something quickly because there is not much time. **he hurries, hurrying, hurried.**

hurt *v* to make a person or an animal feel pain. **hurting, hurt.**

husband *n* a married man. *fem* **wife.**

husk *n* the outside shell of a seed.

husky *adj* having a hoarse voice.

hustle *v* I. to hurry. 2. to make others hurry by pushing them along. **hustling, hustled.**

hut *n* a small house, often made of wood.

hutch *n* a box for rabbits to live in.

hyacinth *n* a spring plant with sweet-smelling flowers growing from a bulb.

hymn *n* a song of praise to God.

hyphen *n* a short dash (-) used to join two words. *Bumble-bee has a hyphen.*

Ii

ice I. *n* frozen water. 2. *v* to become covered with ice. 3. to cover with icing: *to ice a cake.* **icing, iced.**

ice cream a frozen food that tastes of cream.

iceberg *n* a mountain of ice floating in the sea.

icicle *n* a spike of hanging ice.

icing *n* a sweet covering on cakes.

icy *adj* as cold as ice: *an icy wind.*

idea *n* I. something you have thought of. 2. a plan.

ideal *adj* perfect: *an ideal spot.*

idiot *n* a stupid person.

idle *adj* I. not wanting to work. 2. not working: *machinery standing idle.*

idol *n* a statue worshipped as a god.

if *conj* I. on condition that: *I will go if you wish.* 2. whether: *Let me know if it rains.*

igloo *n* an Eskimo's hut made of blocks of snow.

ignorant *adj* knowing nothing or very little.

ignore *v* to pretend not to see. **ignoring, ignored.**

ill *adj* not well: *I felt ill and went to bed.*

illness *n* something that makes people ill.

ill-treat *v* to treat badly. **ill-treating, ill-treated.**

illuminate *v* I. to light up. 2. to decorate with lights. **illuminating, illuminated.**

illuminations *n pl* a lot of coloured lights used to decorate streets or buildings.

illustrate *v* to add pictures to: *to illustrate a story in a book.* **illustrating, illustrated.**

im- a prefix meaning 'not': *Impatient* (not patient).

image *n* I. a likeness: *an image in a mirror.* 2. a picture or statue.

imaginary *adj* not real.

imagination *n* being able to picture things in your mind.

imagine *v* I. to picture a thing in your mind. 2. to pretend: *Imagine you are a princess.* **imagining, imagined.**

imitate *v* to copy a person or animal: *A parrot can often imitate voices.* **imitating, imitated.**

immediately *adv* at once.

immense *adj* very large.

immigrant *n* a person who leaves his or her country to live and work in your country.

imp *n* 1. a little goblin. 2. a mischievous child.

impatient *adj* not patient.

imperfect *adj* not perfect.

impertinent *adj* rude.

implore *v* to beg strongly. **imploring, implored.**

import *v* to bring goods into a country from another country. **importing, imported.**

important *adj* worth taking notice of. *opp* **unimportant.**

impossible *adj* not possible.

impressed *adj* having a high opinion of. *opp* **unimpressed.**

imprison *v* to put in prison. **imprisoning, imprisoned.**

improve *v* 1. to make better. 2. to become better. **improving, improved.**

improvement *n* a better result.

in- a prefix meaning 'not'.

incapable *adj* not capable.

inch *n* a measure of length. One inch is about $2\frac{1}{2}$ centimetres.

include *v* to count in: *everyone including Parveen.* **including, included.**

incorrect *adj* not correct.

increase *v* 1. to make bigger. 2. to become bigger. **increasing, increased.**

indeed *adv* certainly: *Yes indeed, I believe you.*

independent *adj* able to do things on your own.

index *n* a list, usually at the end of a book, telling you the things in the book, and the pages on which you can find them.

indigestion *n* a feeling when digestion is painful.

indignant *adj* angry at something unfair that someone has said or done.

individual *n* single thing or person: *Each individual must show his ticket.*

indoor *adj* inside a building: *an indoor game.*

indoors *adv* inside: *Douglas stayed indoors.*

industry *n* making things of a certain type, or using certain materials, in works and factories: *the car industry, the steel industry.* pl **industries.**

infant *n* a baby or a very young child.

infectious *adj* of a disease, likely to pass from one person to another: *Influenza is infectious.*

influenza see **flu.**

inform *v* to tell. **informing, informed.**

information *n* facts.

inhabit *v* to live in a land or country. **inhabiting, inhabited.**

inherit *v* to receive money, property, or a title from someone who has died: *John inherited some money from his uncle.* **inheriting, inherited.**

initial *n* the first letter of a name.

injection *n* a prick in the skin using a hollow needle so that a medicine will go into your body to cure or prevent illness.

injure *v* to hurt. **injuring, injured.**

injury *n* harm to part of your body. pl **injuries.**

ink *n* coloured liquid used with a pen for writing.

inland *adj* and *adv* right in the country and away from the sea.

inn *n* a small hotel or public house for travellers to stay in.

inner *adj* inside: *the inner walls of a castle.*

innings *n* a turn at batting in rounders or cricket.

innocent *adj* not guilty.

inquire, enquire *v* to ask about something. **inquiring, inquired,** or **enquiring, enquired.**

inquiry, enquiry *n* 1. a question. 2. the asking of a lot of questions. pl **inquiries, enquiries.**

inquisitive *adj* 1. wanting to know. 2. being nosey. *opp* **uninquisitive.**

insect *n* a small creature such as an ant, bee, or fly, with six legs and three parts to its body, very often with wings.

inside 1. *adv* within. 2. *n* the inner side or part.

insist *v* to say firmly and strongly. **insisting, insisted.**

inspect *v* to examine very closely. **inspecting, inspected.**

inspector *n* 1. someone who makes sure that everything is in order. 2. a policeman of high rank.

instalment *n* 1. one of the parts of a serial story. 2. one of the payments you make when you pay for something a bit at a time.

instance *n* an example.
for instance for example.

instant *n* a moment.

instead *adv* (sometimes with **of**) in place of.

instinct *n* something that makes people or animals do things without having learnt to do them.

instructions *n pl* words that tell people what to do.

instructor *n* a kind of teacher: *a swimming instructor.*

instrument *n* I. a tool that helps you to do something carefully or to find out something: *Pens, compasses, and thermometers are all instruments*. 2. anything that makes musical sounds.

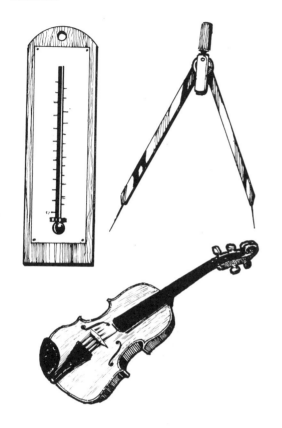

insult *v* to speak to someone with contempt. **insulting, insulted.**

intelligent *adj* quick at learning and understanding. *opp* **unintelligent.**

intend *v* to mean to do something. **intending, intended.**

interest *v* to make someone want to look, listen, or learn more. **interesting, interested.**

interfere *v* I. (sometimes with **with**) to take part in something that is not your business. 2. (with **with**) to hinder. **interfering, interfered.**

interior *n* the inside. *opp* **exterior.**

international *adj* having to do with more than one country: *an international agreement*.

interrupt *v* to break into what someone is saying or doing. **interrupting, interrupted.**

interval *n* a break.

interview *n* a meeting arranged between people, for questions to be asked and answered.

into *prep* I. to the inside of. 2. to the form of: *The snow turned into rain*.

introduce *v* to tell people each other's names when they meet, so that they begin to know each other. **introducing, introduced.**

invade *v* I. to enter another country with an army, in order to conquer it. 2. to do anything in this way: *Ants invaded the garden*. **invading, invaded.**

invalid *n* someone who is weak because of illness or injury.

invent *v* to plan or make something that is completely new. **inventing, invented.**

invention *n* a new thing that has been invented.

inventor *n* someone who makes or thinks of something for the first time.

inverted commas *n pl* marks ('…' or "…") to show the words that someone speaks.

investigate *v* to inquire and search into carefully. **investigating, investigated.**

invisible *adj* not able to be seen.

invitation *n* asking someone to your house, or to join you in doing something: *an invitation to the party*.

invite *v* to ask someone to join you at home or to do something. **inviting, invited.**

inward(s) *adj* or *adv* towards the inside.

iris *n* I. the coloured part of your eye. 2. a tall garden plant.

iron I. *n* a strong hard metal. 2. *v* to press clothes with a hot piece of smooth iron, usually heated electrically. **ironing, ironed.**

ironmonger *n* a shopkeeper who sells metal things such as nails and tools.

irritable *adj* easily annoyed.

irritate *v* I. to make angry. 2. to make sore. **irritating, irritated.**

Islam *n* the Muslim religion.

island *n* a piece of land with water round it.

isle *n* an island.

isn't short for is not.

itch *v* to make you feel that you want to scratch somewhere on your skin. **itching, itched.**

item *n* a single thing in a list or group of things.

its *adj* belonging to it: *The cat drank its milk*.

it's short for 'it is'. Note: do not mix up **its** with **it's.**

itself *pron* it alone: *The dog stretched itself*.

ivory *n* a hard white material like bone, of which elephant's tusks are made.

ivy *n* an evergreen climbing plant.

Jj

jab *v* to push suddenly at something with the end of your finger, or with something pointed. **jabbing, jabbed.**

jack *n* 1. a tool that can raise heavy things. 2. one of the picture playing-cards.

jackal *n* a wild animal that looks like a dog.

jackdaw *n* a black bird like a small crow.

jacket *n* a short coat.

jagged *adj* with a rough uneven edge.

jaguar *n* a wild animal like a leopard.

jail *n* a prison.

jam *n* 1. fruit boiled with sugar until it becomes thick. 2. a tight mass of traffic.

January *n* the first month of the year.

jar *n* a pot or glass container with a wide mouth.

javelin *n* a light spear thrown by hand.

jaw *n* one of the two bones in which teeth are fixed.

jealous *adj* feeling annoyed because someone is luckier than you or in a better position than you.

jeans *n pl* strong cotton trousers, usually blue.

jeep *n* a small powerful motor-vehicle.

jeer *v* (with **at**) to make fun of. **jeering, jeered.**

jelly *n* a cold sweet slippery food flavoured with a fruit juice. *pl* **jellies.**

jellyfish *n* a sea animal with a soft body, like jelly.

jerk *v* to pull or move something quickly. **jerking, jerked.**

jersey *n* a pullover with long sleeves. *pl* **jerseys.**

jet *n* 1. a stream of liquid, air, or gas from a narrow opening. 2. a type of aeroplane pushed forwards by jets of hot gases from its engines.

jetty *n* a small pier. *pl* **jetties.**

Jew *n* a person descended from the old Hebrews. *fem* **Jewess.**

jewel *n* a valuable stone such as a diamond.

jewellery *n* ornaments that people wear, such as rings, and often containing jewels.

jig *n* a lively dance.

jigsaw, jigsaw-puzzle *n* a puzzle in which you put together pieces to make a picture.

jingle *n* the sound that very small bells make.

job *n* 1. a piece of work. 2. regular work: *a job in a factory.*

jockey *n* someone who rides horses in races. *pl* **jockeys.**

jodhpurs *n pl* special trousers for riding.

jog *v* to run along at a slow pace. **jogging, jogged.**

join *v* 1. to fasten together. 2. to become a member of a group. **joining, joined.**

joint *n* 1. a place where two parts meet: *a finger joint.* 2. a large piece of meat for roasting.

joke *n* something said that makes you laugh.

jolly *adj* merry. **jollier, jolliest.**

jolt *v* to give a sudden knock or jerk. **jolting, jolted.**

jot (with **down**) *v* to make a quick note in writing. **jotting, jotted.**

journalist *n* someone who writes for a newspaper or magazine.

journey *n* travel from one place to another. *pl* **journeys.**

joy *n* happiness.

judge *n* 1. a person in charge of a prisoner's trial in a court of law. 2. someone who decides the result of a competition such as a flower show.

jug *n* a container with a handle, for pouring liquids.

juggler *n* someone who entertains by throwing, catching, and balancing things cleverly.

juice *n* the liquid in fruits and meat.

July *n* the seventh month of the year.

jumble-sale *n* a sale of second-hand things to raise money for a good purpose.

jump *v* to move into the air with both feet off the ground. **jumping, jumped.**

jumper *n* a pullover.

junction *n* a place where railway lines or roads meet.

June *n* the sixth month of the year.

jungle *n* land in hot countries thickly covered with trees and bushes.

junior *n* someone who is younger.

junk *n* 1. things that are almost useless. 2. a Chinese sailing-ship.

jury *n* a group of 12 people who sit in a court of law to decide whether someone is guilty of a crime or not. *pl* **juries.**

just 1. *adj* fair. *opp* **unjust.** 2. *adv* almost not succeeding: *Connie could just do it.*

justice *n* a fair way of doing things.

jut *v* to stick out. **jutting, jutted.**

Kk

kaftan see **caftan.**

kangaroo *n* an Australian animal with long back legs on which it jumps.

kayak *n* a canoe used by Eskimoes.

kebab *n* small pieces of meat cooked on a stick.

keel *n* a long piece of wood or metal along the bottom of a ship or boat.

keen *adj* 1. enthusiastic. 2. sharp.

keep *v* 1. to look after: *Keep it until later.* 2. to have something as your own and not throw it away. 3. (often with **on**) to continue. 4. not to go bad. **keeping, kept.**

kennel *n* a small hut for keeping a dog in.

kerb *n* the edge of a pavement.

kernel *n* the inside part of a nut.

kettle *n* a metal container with a handle and a spout, in which you boil water.

key *n* 1. a piece of metal shaped so that it will open or close a lock, or wind a clock. 2. one of the parts on a piano or typewriter that you press down. *pl* **keys.**

kick *v* to hit with your foot. **kicking, kicked. kick-off** the start of a football match.

kid *n* a young goat.

kidnap *v* to take someone away by force: *the pirates kidnapped the children.* **kidnapping, kidnapped.**

kidney *n* one of two small parts inside your body. *pl* **kidneys.**

kill *v* to make someone or something die. **killing, killed.**

kilogram *n* a measure of weight equal to 1,000 grams.

kilometre *n* a measure of distance equal to 1,000 metres.

kilt *n* a pleated tartan skirt worn by Scottish Highlanders.

kind 1. *adj* helpful and friendly. *opp* **unkind.** 2. *n* a sort: *A tiger is a kind of wild cat.*

king *n* 1. the ruler of a country. *fem* **queen.** 2. a playing-card with the picture of a king.

kingdom *n* a country ruled by a king or queen.

kingfisher *n* a brightly coloured river bird.

kiosk *n* a small stall where newspapers and tobacco are sold.

kipper *n* a herring that has been salted and dried in smoke.

kiss *v* to touch someone with your lips. **kissing, kissed.**

kitchen *n* a room in a house for cooking.

kite *n* a light framework with paper or cloth over it, flown at the end of a string.

kitten *n* a young cat.

knee *n* the joint in the middle of your leg. **knee-cap** the flat bone over your knee.

kneel *v* to go down on your knees. **kneeling, knelt.**

knew see **know.**

knickers *n pl* short underpants worn by girls and women.

knife *n* a sharp blade fastened to a handle. *pl* **knives.**

knight *n* a man with the title of 'Sir', who in olden times dressed in armour and fought on horseback for his king.

knit *v* to weave woollen or cotton threads, using long needles. **knitting, knitted.**

knives see **knife.**

knob *n* the round handle of a door or drawer.

knock *v* to hit, sometimes with the knuckles. **knocking, knocked.**

knocker *n* a hinged piece of metal on a door, to tap the door with.

knot *v* to tie together two pieces of string or rope. **knotting, knotted.** *opp* **unknot.**

know *v* I. to understand. 2. to have some information. 3. to recognise someone. **knowing, knew, I have known.**

knowledge *n* things that you know.

knuckle *n* one of the joints in a finger.

koala *n* an Australian animal that looks like a small bear.

Koran *n* the holy scriptures of Islam.

Ll

label *n* a piece of card or sticky paper fastened to something to show whose it is, where it is going, or what is inside.

laboratory *n* a place where scientific work is done. *pl* **laboratories.**

labour *n* hard work.

lace *n* I. a cord for tying. 2. material made of thin threads with a pattern of holes.

lack *n* a shortage: *a lack of food.*

lad *n* a boy.

ladder *n* a set of steps between two poles.

ladle *n* a deep spoon with a long handle, used for serving.

lady *n* I. a polite name for a woman. 2. a title given to a woman or the wife of a nobleman. *pl* **ladies.** *masc* **gentleman.**

ladybird *n* a small flying beetle, usually red with black spots.

lag *v* to walk slowly behind other people. **lagging, lagged.**

laid see **lay.**

lain see **lie.**

lake *n* a large area of water with land all round.

lamb *n* a young sheep.

lame *adj* not able to walk properly.

lamp *n* a light, usually in a glass cover.

lance *n* a spear carried by a knight on a horse.

land I. *n* all the earth above the sea or any part of it. 2. a country. 3. *v* (of an aeroplane) to arrive. **landing, landed.**

landing *n* I. a flat space at the top of a stairway. 2. the arrival of an aeroplane.

landlord *n* the owner of a rented house, an inn, or a stretch of land. *fem* **landlady.**

landscape *n* the appearance of country scenery.

lane *n* a narrow road.

language *n* the words used by a person or by people in different countries.

lantern *n* a glass case with a light inside.

lap I. *n* the top of your thighs when you are sitting down. 2. once round a race-track. 3. *v* (of an animal) to drink with the tongue. **lapping, lapped.**

lard *n* pig's fat used in cooking.

larder *n* a small room for keeping food in.

large *adj* big.

lark *n* I. a skylark. 2. a bit of fun.

lash *v* I. to hit hard, usually with a whip. 2. to tie firmly to something. **lashing, lashed.**

lasso *n* a rope with a loop at the end, for catching cattle. *pl* **lassos.**

last I. *adj* after all the others. 2. *v* to go on for some time. **lasting, lasted.**
at last finally, after waiting.

latch *n* a metal bar that fastens a door or gate.

late *adj* and *adv* I. behind the expected time. 2. at or near the end of a day, month, or year.

lather *n* a foam made with soap and water.

laugh *v* to make sounds to show that you are happy or that something is funny. **laughing, laughed.**

laughter *n* the sound of laughing.

launch 1. *v* to push a boat into the water. 2. to send a rocket into space. **launching, launched.** 3. *n* an open motor-boat.
launching-pad the place from which a rocket can be launched.

launderette *n* a laundry where you pay to wash clothes in a machine.

laundry *n* a place where clothes can be left to be washed. *pl* **laundries.**

lava *n* molten rock from a volcano.

lavatory *n* a place where waste from the body can be flushed away. *pl* **lavatories.**

law *n* a rule made by a government.

lawn *n* a level area of grass that is mown.

lawyer *n* someone who knows the law and advises people about it.

lay *v* 1. to put something down. 2. (of a bird) to drop an egg into a nest. **laying, laid.** 3. see **lie. to lay the table** to put things like knives and forks in place on the table.

layer *n* something that lies over or under another surface: *a layer of paint.*

lazy *adj* not willing to work. **lazier, laziest.**

lead[1] (leed) 1. *v* to be or go in front. **leading, led.** 2. *n* a strap to hold a dog.

lead[2] (led) *n* a heavy grey metal.

leader (lee der) *n* a person or animal that goes in front.

leaf *n* one of the small flat green parts that grow on trees and other plants. *pl* **leaves.**

league *n* a group of sports teams that play against one another: *the football league.*

leak *n* a small hole or crack through which gas or liquid escapes.

lean 1. *v* (with **against**) to rest against. 2. to slant. **leaning, leaned** or **leant.** 3. *adj* thin. 4. having little fat.

leap *v* to jump. **leaping, leaped** or **leapt** (lept). **leap-year** every fourth year, in which February has an extra day making 366 days for that year.

learn *v* 1. to get to know new facts about something. 2. to find out how to do something. **learning, learned** or **learnt.**

least *adj* smallest.

leather *n* a material made from an animal's skin.

leave *v* 1. to go away from. 2. to let something stay where it is. **leaving, left.**

leaves see **leaf.**

lecture *n* a talk that teaches you something.

led see **lead**[1].

ledge *n* a narrow shelf.

leek *n* a vegetable with a long white stem, tasting like an onion.

left 1. *n* the side or direction opposite to right. Most people use a fork in their left hand. 2. *v* see **leave.**
left-handed using the left hand to write and to do most other things.

leg *n* 1. one of the limbs on which a person or animal stands or walks. 2. anything like a leg: *a table leg.*

legend *n* a story of ancient times that is probably not true: *the legend of King Arthur and his knights.*

leisure *n* time when you are free to do what you like.

lemon *n* yellow fruit with a sour taste.

lemonade *n* a drink made from lemons, sugar, and water.

lend *v* to let someone use something of yours for a time. **lending, lent.**

length *n* 1. how long a thing is. 2. a piece of rope or cloth.

lengthen *v* 1. to make longer. 2. to become longer. **lengthening, lengthened.**

lens *n* a curved piece of glass used in spectacles, cameras, and telescopes to bend light.

lent see **lend.**

Lent *n* the six weeks before Easter.

leopard *n* a wild animal with dark spots, found in Africa and Asia.

leotard *n* a piece of clothing worn by dancers and acrobats.

less *adj* not as much or as many.

-less an ending meaning 'without': *painless* (without pain).

lesson *n* 1. something you have to learn. 2. a period of time when someone teaches you: *a music lesson.*

let *v* 1. to allow. 2. to allow someone to live in a house in return for paying rent. **letting, let.**

-let an ending meaning 'small': *A booklet is a small book.*

letter *n* 1. a written message put in an envelope and sent to someone. 2. one of the parts of an alphabet.

lettuce *n* a green vegetable eaten raw in salads.

level *adj* 1. smooth and flat. 2. equal or side by side.
level-crossing a place where railway lines cross the surface of a road.

lever *n* a bar that is pulled down to raise or move something heavy, or to make a machine work.

liable *adj* (with **to**) likely to: *The dog is liable to bite if teased*.

liar *n* someone who does not tell the truth.

librarian *n* someone in charge of a library.

library *n* a room or building where books are kept on shelves. *pl* **libraries.**

licence *n* a printed paper allowing you to own or use something.

lick *v* to move your tongue over something. **licking, licked.**

lid *n* the movable top of a container.

lie *v* 1. to rest with your body flat. **lying, lay, I have lain.** 2. to say something that is not true. **lying, lied.**

life *n* 1. being alive. 2. all the time you are alive. *pl* **lives** (rhymes with dives).

lifeboat *n* a boat built to save people from drowning at sea.

lift 1. *v* to raise. **lifting, lifted.** 2. *n* a kind of cage that can take people up and down inside a building. 3. a ride given to help someone.
lift-off the moment when a rocket leaves the launching-pad.

light 1. *n* energy from the sun, a lamp, or something burning, which lets you see things. 2. anything which gives off light. 3. *v* to set fire to. **lighting, lit.** 4. *adj* not heavy. 5. pale: *light green*.

lighthouse *n* a tower by the sea with a powerful light to warn ships of dangerous rocks.

lightning *n* a flash of electricity in a thunderstorm.

like 1. *v* to think that something or someone is pleasant. **liking, liked.** *opp* **dislike.** 2. *prep* similar to. *opp* **unlike.**

likely *adj* probable. *opp* **unlikely.**

lilac *n* 1. a garden shrub with white or purple flowers. 2. a pale purple colour.

lily *n* a tall garden flower growing from a bulb. *pl* **lilies.**

limb *n* an arm, a leg, or a wing.

lime *n* a green fruit like a small lemon.

limestone *n* a soft greyish-white rock.

limit *n* a point that you cannot or should not pass: *a speed limit*.

limp 1. *v* to walk as if lame. **limping, limped.** 2. *adj* drooping.

line *n* 1. a long thin mark. 2. a row: *a line of soldiers*. 3. a cord or rope. 4. a railway track. 5. a company providing a service of aeroplanes or ships.

linen *n* 1. a strong type of cloth. 2. things like table-cloths made of linen.

liner *n* a large passenger ship or aeroplane.

linger *v* to be slow to leave a place. **lingering, lingered.**

lining *n* a thin inside layer to clothes.

link 1. *v* to join things together. **linking, linked.** 2. *n* one of the rings in a chain.

lino, linoleum *n* a canvas covering for floors that is shiny.

lion *n* a wild animal of Africa and South Asia. *fem* **lioness.** *young* **cub.**

lip *n* one of the two soft edges of your mouth.

lipstick *n* a stick of grease-paint to make the lips a different colour.

liquid *n* something that can be poured.

liquorice *n* a kind of black sweet.

list *n* a number of things written one under the other.

listen *v* to pay attention so that you hear something. **listening, listened.**

lit see **light.**

litre *n* a measure of liquid, containing 1,000 cubic centimetres.

litter *n* 1. rubbish left lying around. 2. a number of animals all born together: *a litter of pigs*.

little *adj* 1. small. 2. not much. **less, least.**

live[1] (liv) *v* 1. to be alive. 2. to have your home in a place. **living, lived.**

live[2] (lyve) *adj* living.

lively (lyve li) *adj* full of life and energy: *a lively pup*. **livelier, liveliest.**

liver *n* an inside part of your body which helps in the digestion of food.

lives see **life.**

lizard *n* an animal like a snake with four short legs.

load 1. *v* to put goods in or on a ship, wagon, or other vehicle. 2. to put a bullet into a gun. **loading, loaded.** *opp* **unload.** 3. *n* a cargo or pile of goods to be carried.

loaf *n* a large lump of bread. *pl* **loaves.**

loan *n* anything that is lent to someone.

loaves see **loaf.**

lobster *n* a shellfish with eight legs and two large claws.

local *adj* belonging to a certain place or district: *our local grocer*.

loch *n* a Scottish lake. *pl* **lochs.**

lock *n* 1. a fastening for a door or lid worked by a key. 2. a section of a canal where the water level can be raised or lowered. 3. a piece of hair cut off.

locker *n* a small cupboard.

locomotive *n* a railway engine.

locust *n* a grasshopper of Africa or Asia which feeds on crops.

lodge *v* to live in someone else's house. **lodging, lodged.**

loft *n* the space beneath a sloping roof of a building.

lofty *adj* very tall. **loftier, loftiest.**

log *n* a sawn-off part of a tree.

loiter *v* to dawdle. **loitering, loitered.**

loll *v* to sit, stand, or lean in a lazy way. **lolling, lolled.**

lollipop, lolly *n* a sweet at the end of a stick.

lone *adj* on your own.

lonely *adj* 1. feeling sad because you are alone. 2. a long way from others: *a lonely tree.* **lonelier, loneliest.**

long 1. *adj* measuring a lot from end to end. 2. taking a lot of time. 3. *v* (with **for**) to want very much. **longing, longed.**

longing *n* a great wish.

look 1. *v* to turn your eyes to see something. 2. to seem. 3. to face: *The house looks east.* **looking, looked.** 4. *n* a glance.
to look after to take care of.
to look for to try to find something.
to look forward to to wait for something with pleasure.

looking-glass *n* a mirror.

look-out *n* a careful watch.

loom 1. *v* to appear with an unclear shape in darkness or fog. **looming, loomed.** 2. *n* a machine for weaving cloth.

loop *n* a ring made in something like rope.

loose *adj* 1. not tight. 2. not fastened to anything.

loosen *v* 1. to make loose. 2. to become loose. **loosening, loosened.**

lop-sided *adj* with one side lower than the other.

lord *n* 1. a nobleman. 2. a title. *fem* **lady.**

lorry *n* a heavy wagon for carrying goods by road. *pl* **lorries.**

lose *v* 1. to be without something that you cannot find. 2. to be without something you once had. 3. to be beaten in a game. **losing, lost.**

loss *n* something lost.

lost see **lose.**

lot *n* 1. a large number. 2. the whole number: *He bought the lot.*

loud *adj* 1. noisy. 2. easy to hear.

loudspeaker *n* the part of a radio, television, or record-player from which the sound comes.

lounge *n* a room with comfortable chairs in it.

lovable *adj* worth loving.

love *n* to like very much. **loving, loved.**

lovely *adj* beautiful. **lovelier, loveliest.**

low *adj* not high.

lower *v* to let down: *to lower a flag.* **lowering, lowered.**

lowland *n* flat low-lying country.

lowly *adj* humble. **lowlier, lowliest.**

loyal *adj* true to your friends or country. *opp* **disloyal.**

luck *n* chance.

lucky *adj* having good luck. **luckier, luckiest.**

ludo *n* a board game that you play with counters and a dice.

luggage *n* a traveller's bags and cases.

lukewarm *adj* slightly warm.

lullaby *n* a song to send a baby to sleep. *pl* **lullabies.**

lump *n* 1. a piece of anything. 2. a swelling.

lunar *adj* having to do with the moon.

lunatic *n* a mad person.

lunch *n* the midday meal.

lung *n* one of the two parts inside your chest which you fill with air when you breathe in.

lurch *v* to lean suddenly to one side. **lurching, lurched.**

lurk *v* to lie in wait. **lurking, lurked.**

luxury *n* something very nice that you do not really need. *pl* **luxuries.**

lying see **lie.**

lynx *n* a kind of wild cat.

Mm

mac see **mackintosh.**

macaroni *n* tubes of flour paste used as food.

machine *n* a set of working parts that does something to help the person using it: *a washing machine, a machine-gun.*

machinery *n* 1. machines in a factory. 2. the moving parts of a machine.

mackerel *n* a silver and black sea fish. *pl* **mackerel.**

mackintosh *n* a raincoat. (**mac** for short.)

mad *adj* 1. crazy. 2. very angry. 3. very silly. **madder, maddest.**

madam *n* a polite way of speaking or writing to a woman.

made see **make.**

magazine *n* a thin book with pictures and stories, that appears weekly or monthly.

maggot *n* a grub that will turn into a fly.

magic *n* 1. the clever tricks of a conjuror. 2. the power to make things that seem impossible come true.

magician *n* a person who can do things by magic.

magistrate *n* a man or woman who judges small crimes in a court of law.

magnet *n* a bar of iron or steel that can draw pieces of iron or steel towards it and make them stick to it.

magnificent *adj* splendid.

magnify *v* to make something look larger. **it magnifies, magnifying, magnified.**

magpie *n* a black and white bird.

maid *n* a woman servant.

maiden *n* in olden times, a young girl.

mail *n* 1. anything sent by post. 2. chain armour worn by soldiers in olden days.

main *adj* the most important: *a main road.*

maize *n* a kind of corn.

majesty *n* a title for a king or queen: *Your Majesty. pl* (their) **majesties.**

major *n* an army officer, next in rank above a captain.

make 1. *v* to build. 2. to force someone to do something. 3. to create: *They made Pamela captain.* **making, made.** 4. *n* a brand: *a make of bicycle.*

male *n* a person or animal that can become a father. *fem* **female.**

mammal *n* an animal that feeds its young with its own milk and has warm blood: *A cow, a goat, and a whale are all mammals.*

mammoth *n* a prehistoric elephant.

man *n* a grown-up male human being. *pl* **men.** *fem* **woman.**

manage *v* 1. to be able to do something that is difficult for you. 2. to be in charge of a business or part of it. **managing, managed.**

manager *n* someone in charge of a business or a hotel. *fem* **manageress.**

mane *n* the long hair on the neck of some animals such as horses or lions.

manger *n* a container in a stable holding hay for horses or cattle.

mankind *n* the human race.

manner *n* the way something happens or is done.

manners *n pl* behaviour towards other people.

mansion *n* a large important house.

mantelpiece *n* a shelf above a fireplace.

manufacture *v* to make things in large quantity in a factory. **manufacturing, manufactured.**

manure *n* animal droppings and straw put in the ground to make plants grow better.

many *adj* a great number of people or things. **more, most.**

map *n* a drawing of some part of the earth's surface showing towns, roads, and rivers.

marble *n* 1. a hard stone used to make statues and fine buildings. 2. a small glass ball used in the game of marbles.

March *n* the third month of the year.

march 1. *v* (of soldiers) to walk together with steps of the same length. **marching, marched.** 2. *n* a piece of music to march to.

mare *n* a female horse. *masc.* **stallion.** *young* **foal.**

margarine *n* a food made of vegetable oils and fats.

margin *n* a space between the edge of a page and writing or a picture.

mark *n* 1. a scratch, stain, or cut. 2. a score in a test.

market *n* a place with several stalls, where food and other things are sold.

marmalade *n* jam made from oranges or lemons.

maroon 1. *n* a brown-red colour. 2. *v* to leave someone alone on an island, as a punishment. **marooning, marooned.**

marriage *n* a wedding.

marrow *n* I. a vegetable like a large cucumber. 2. the fatty matter in the hollow of bones.

marry *v* to become husband and wife. **marrying, married.**

marsh *n* a bog.

marvellous *adj* wonderful.

marzipan *n* a paste made from almonds and sugar.

mascot *n* an animal, doll, or charm that is supposed to bring luck: *Our mascot for the football match is a bear.*

masculine *adj* having to do with men or boys. *opp* **feminine.**

mash *v* to crush into a soft wet mass. **mashing, mashed.**

mask *n* a covering over the face, worn as a disguise or a protection.

mass *n* I. a great lump or quantity. 2. the ceremony of Holy Communion in the Roman Catholic church.

massive *adj* huge and heavy: *a massive rock.*

mast *n* a pole holding up sails, a flag or an aerial.

master *n* I. a man in charge of people. 2. an expert. *fem* **mistress.** 3. a title given to a young boy.

mat *n* I. a small rug to wipe your feet on. 2. a small piece of thick material for putting hot plates on.

match I. *n* a small thin piece of wood with a tip that lights when rubbed. 2. a game between two sides. 3. *v* to be like something in colour, shape, or some other way. **matching, matched.**

mate *n* a companion.

material *n* I. the stuff that anything is made of. 2. any woven cloth.

mathematics, maths *n pl* the study of numbers, measurement, and shapes.

matter I. *n* something that is your concern. 2. *v* to be important. *past* **mattered.**

mattress *n* the thick soft part of a bed.

May *n* the fifth month of the year.

may *v* (usually before another verb) I. to be allowed: *She may go if she wants to.* 2. to be possible: *She may get there in time.*

mayor *n* the head of a council. *fem* **mayoress.**

maypole *n* a pole for dancing round on May Day (May Ist).

maze *n* a confusing series of paths or lines in which it is easy to lose your way.

meadow *n* a field of grass.

meal *n* I. food eaten each day at a certain time. 2. grain ground into a powder: *oatmeal.*

mean I. *adj* not generous. 2. nasty. 3. *v* to have a meaning. 4. to plan in your mind: *I mean to go later.* **meaning, meant.**

meaning *n* what someone has in mind when he or she says something.

measles *n* an illness when your body is covered with red spots.

measure I. *v* to find the size or amount of something. **measuring, measured.** 2. *n* a unit used for measuring.

measurement *n* a size or amount.

meat *n* animal flesh used as food.

mechanic *n* someone who makes or uses machinery.

medal *n* a piece of metal in a special shape, often with a ribbon, given for winning some competition or for bravery.

meddle *v* to interfere. **meddling, meddled.**

medical *adj* having to do with doctors and medicine: *a medical school.*

medicine *n* a liquid or powder which you swallow to make you better when you are ill.

medium *adj* not too big and not too small.

meek *adj* gentle and obedient.

meet *v* I. to come face to face with someone else. 2. to come together. **meeting, met.**

melody *n* a tune. *pl* **melodies.**

melon *n* a large juicy fruit.

melt *v* to become liquid with heat. **melting, melted.**

member *n* a person or thing belonging to a group.

memory *n* I. the power to remember things. 2. something you remember. *pl* **memories.**

men see **man.**

menacing *adj* threatening: *a menacing snarl.*

mend *v* to put right something that is broken or torn. **mending, mended.**

mental *adj* done in your head: *mental maths.*

mention *v* to make a remark about. **mentioning, mentioned.**

menu *n* a list of what there is to eat.

merchant *n* a person who buys and sells things: *a timber merchant.*

mercy *n* kindness and pity shown to someone weak.

merely *adv* only: *I merely asked the time.*

meringue *n* a light, white pudding made from egg whites.

merit *n* a quality worth praising.

mermaid *n* an imaginary woman whose body is like a fish from the waist downwards.

merry *adj* happy and laughing. **merrier, merriest.**

mess *n* things that are untidy or dirty.

message *n* information sent from one person to another.

messenger *n* someone who takes a message.

met see **meet.**

metal *n* a hard material like iron or lead.

meteor *n* a piece of rock or metal that moves through space and burns up in the earth's atmosphere.

meteorite *n* a meteor that has hit the ground.

meter *n* a machine that measures how much of something has been used.

method *n* a way of doing something.

metre *n* a measure of length equal to 100 centimetres.

miaow *v* to make the cry that a cat makes. **miaowing, miaowed.**

mice see **mouse.**

microbe *n* a germ that can cause disease.

microphone *n* an instrument that turns your voice into electrical energy which travels along wires to a loudspeaker or telephone.

microscope *n* an instrument with a tube holding lenses, which makes tiny things look large.

mid- a prefix meaning 'middle'.

middle *n* the part of something that is half the distance between all its sides or edges, or from both of its ends.

might 1. *v* (usually before another verb) will perhaps or would perhaps: *He might come later.* 2. *n* strength.

mighty *adj* very strong. **mightier, mightiest.**

migrate *v* to move to another place or country. **migrating, migrated.**

mild *adj* 1. gentle: *a mild breeze.* 2. not strong: *a mild taste.* 3. neither hot nor cold: *a mild day.*

mile *n* a measure of distance equal to 1,760 yards.

military *adj* having to do with soldiers: *a military camp.*

milk *n* the white liquid with which cows and some other animals feed their young.

mill *n* 1. a factory with machinery where cloth or other goods are made. 2. a place where corn is ground into flour.

millimetre *n* a very small measure, a thousandth part of a metre.

million *n* and *adj* a thousand thousands, 1,000,000. **millionth.**

millionaire *n* a rich man with at least one million pounds. *fem* **millionairess.**

mime *v* to act something without words. **miming, mimed.**

mimic *v* to imitate someone's way of speaking or moving, for fun. **mimicking, mimicked.**

mince 1. *v* to chop into very small pieces. **mincing, minced.** 2. *n* meat chopped into very small pieces.

mincemeat *n* a mixture of chopped fruit and spice.

mind 1. *n* the power to think. 2. *v* to be careful: *Mind the step!* 3. to feel concerned or upset: *Do you mind if we don't go?* **minding, minded.**

mine 1. *adj* and *pron* belonging to me. 2. *n* a hole in the earth where men dig out coal or other things. 3. a bomb in the ground or the sea that explodes when something comes near it or touches it.

miner *n* someone who works down a mine.

mineral *n* 1. anything dug out from a mine. 2. a cold fizzy drink.

mingle *v* to join in with. **mingling, mingled.**

minister *n* 1. a clergyman. 2. the head of a government department.

mink *n* an animal like a weasel whose fur is very valuable.

minor *adj* not very important.

mint *n* 1. a plant with a strong scent. 2. a sweet that tastes of mint. 3. a place where coins are made.

minus *n* the subtraction sign (−) placed before a number to show that number has to be taken away.

minute[1] (<u>min</u> it) *n* sixty seconds of time.

minute[2] (my <u>newt</u>) *adj* very tiny.

miracle *n* something marvellous that has happened although it seems impossible.

mirror *n* a piece of glass in which you can see yourself.

mis- a prefix meaning 'bad' or 'badly'.

misbehave *v* to behave badly. **misbehaving, misbehaved.**

mischief *n* bad or silly behaviour that annoys someone.

miser *n* a person who hoards money and spends as little as possible.

miserable *adj* very unhappy.

misfortune *n* bad luck.

miss *v* 1. to fail to catch, find, hit, or hear something. 2. to be unhappy that someone is no longer with you. **missing, missed.**

missile *n* something that is fired or thrown.

missionary *n* someone who goes to a foreign land to teach the gospel. *pl* **missionaries.**

mist *n* tiny drops of water in the air that make it difficult to see a long way.

mistake 1. *n* something that is wrong. 2. *v* to make a mistake. **mistaking, mistook, I am mistaken.**

mistletoe *n* a climbing plant with white berries that grows up trees.

mistook see **mistake** *v.*

mistress *n* a woman in charge of a class of children.

mittens *n pl* gloves with one part to cover the thumb and the other to cover the palm and fingers.

mix *v* 1. to stir together. 2. (with **up**) to mistake one thing for another: *The wizard mixed up his spells.* **mixing, mixed.**

mixture *n* two or more things mixed together.

moan *v* 1. to make a low noise of pain or sorrow. 2. to complain. **moaning, moaned.**

moat *n* a wide ditch round a castle, often filled with water.

mob *n* a crowd of people out of control.

mock *v* to make fun of. **mocking, mocked.**

model *n* 1. a small copy: *a model ship.* 2. a good example. 3. someone who wears new clothes to show what they look like to other people.

moderate *adj* not very much and not very little.

modern *adj* 1. up-to-date. *opp* **old-fashioned.** 2. having to do with present times: *modern history. opp* **ancient.**

moist *adj* slightly wet.

mole *n* 1. a small furry animal that makes tunnels under the ground. 2. a small dark lump or spot on your skin.

molten *adj* melted: *molten iron.*

moment *n* a very small amount of time.

monarch *n* a royal ruler such as a king, queen, or emperor.

monastery *n* a building where monks live. *pl* **monasteries.**

Monday *n* the second day of the week.

money *n* coins and paper notes.

mongrel *n* a dog that is of mixed breeds.

monitor *n* a boy or girl who has special jobs to do for the teacher.

monk *n* a man who lives a religious life with other monks in a monastery.

monkey *n* an animal with a long tail, living in trees in a hot country. *pl* **monkeys.**

monster *n* a huge frightening creature.

month *n* one of the twelve parts of the year.

monument *n* a statue or building put up in memory of someone or some happening.

moo *v* to make the long deep sound of a cow. **mooing, mooed.**

mood *n* the way you feel.

moon *n* the planet that we often see shining in the sky at night.

moor 1. *n* a large area of land often covered with grass and heather. 2. *v* to fasten a boat so that it will not float away. **mooring, moored.**

moose *n* a North American kind of deer. *pl* **moose.**

mop *n* a sponge or pieces of cloth fastened at the end of a long handle, used for cleaning.

moral *n* a lesson to be learned from a story or fable.

more *adj* and *n* a bigger amount or number of something.

morning *n* the part of the day before midday.

morsel *n* a tiny piece.

mortar *n* a mixture of sand, cement, and water, used to stick bricks together.

mosque *n* an Islamic church.

mosquito *n* a small flying insect that sucks blood. *pl* **mosquitoes.**

moss *n* a small smooth green plant that grows on damp trees and stones.

most 1. *adj* the greatest number or part. 2. *adv* the greatest: *Which sport do you like most?*

moth *n* an insect like a butterfly that flies at night.

mother *n* a woman who is a parent.

motion *n* movement.

motor *n* an engine: *an electric motor*.

motorbike *n* a kind of bicycle with an engine.

motorway *n* a wide road for fast traffic.

mould *n* 1. a hollow shape into which a hot liquid can be poured so that it can cool and set in that shape. 2. a blue-green covering that grows on stale food.

mound *n* a large heap: *a mound of stones*.

mount 1. *v* to get on to a horse or bicycle. **mounting, mounted.** *opp* **dismount.** 2. *n* a mountain: *Mount Everest*. 3. a horse for riding.

mountain *n* a very high hill.

mountaineer *n* someone who climbs mountains.

mourn *v* to feel very sorry because someone or something has died or gone far away. **mourning, mourned.**

mouse *n* a small grey furry animal with a long tail. *pl* **mice.**

moustache *n* hair that grows on a man's top lip.

mouth *n* 1. the opening in your face for speaking, eating, and drinking. 2. any opening shaped like a mouth: *the mouth of a cave*. **mouth-organ** a small musical instrument played with the mouth.

movable *adj* able to be moved.

move *v* 1. to put something in another place. 2. to go to another place. 3. to go to live in another place. **moving, moved.**

movement *n* an act of moving.

movie *n* a cinema film.

mow *v* to cut grass. **mowing, mowed, I have mowed** or **mown.**

much *n* and *adj* a great deal. **more, most.**

mud *n* a thick mixture of soil and water.

muddle *n* confusion.

muddy *adj* covered with mud. **muddier, muddiest.**

mudguard *n* a curved piece of metal over a wheel, to stop mud flying up.

muffin *n* a flat cake, toasted and eaten.

mug *n* a thick cup with a handle, but no saucer.

mule *n* an animal that is half donkey and half horse.

multi- a prefix meaning 'many': *a multistorey carpark*.

multiply *v* to make a number several times larger. **he multiplies, multiplying, multiplied.**

multiplication *n* multiplying one number by another.

mum *n* a word for 'mother'.

mumble *v* to speak with your mouth half-closed so that people cannot hear you clearly. **mumbling, mumbled.**

mummy *n* 1. a word for 'mother'. 2. a dead body that has been prevented from decaying. *pl* **mummies.**

mumps *n* an illness that makes the sides of your face and your neck swell.

munch *v* to chew in a noisy way. **munching, munched.**

murder *v* to kill someone on purpose. **murdering, murdered.**

murmur *v* to say something in a soft voice. **murmuring, murmured.**

muscle *n* one of the parts of your body that make it move.

museum *n* a place where you can go to see old and interesting things.

mushroom *n* a white and brown plant, shaped like a small umbrella, that is cooked and eaten.

music *n* 1. series of pleasant sounds, made by singing or playing on an instrument. 2. signs on paper to show people what notes to play or sing.

musical *adj* having to do with music.

Muslim *n* a follower of the religion of Islam.

muslin *n* a very soft cotton cloth.

mussel *n* a shellfish living in a pair of dark-blue shells.

must *v* to have to: *I must go out.*

mustard *n* a hot-tasting yellow mixture eaten with meat.

musty *adj* smelling stale and dusty. **mustier, mustiest.**

mutiny *n* soldiers or sailors rebelling against their officers. *pl* **mutinies.**

mutter *v* to speak or grumble in a low voice. **muttering, muttered.**

mutton *n* meat from a sheep.

muzzle *n* 1. the mouth and nose of an animal. 2. a cover put over an animal's mouth to stop it biting. 3. the open end of a gun barrel.

my *adj* belonging to me.

myself *pron* I alone: *I cut myself.*
　　by myself on my own.

mysterious *adj* very strange.

mystery *n* something very strange and hard to understand. *pl* **mysteries.**

Nn

nag *v* to keep on scolding and finding fault. **nagging, nagged.**

nail *n* 1. the hard part at the end of a finger or toe. 2. a small piece of metal with a sharp point.

naked *adj* without any clothes on.

name *n* what a person or thing is called.

nanny-goat *n* a female goat. *masc* **billy-goat.**

nap *n* a short sleep.

napkin *n* a square of cloth or paper to protect your clothes while you are eating.

nappy *n* a cloth folded round a baby's bottom and pinned at the waist. *pl* **nappies.**

narrow *adj* not far across. *opp* **wide.**

nasty *adj* not pleasant or kind. **nastier, nastiest.**

nation *n* the people of one country, often with their own government, language, and flag.

national *adj* belonging to a nation: *the national flag.*

native *n* someone who was born in a certain country: *a native of Spain.*

natural *adj* 1. found in nature, not made by man. 2. normal: *It is natural for ducks to swim.* *opp* **unnatural.**

nature *n* 1. the world and everything in it not made by man. 2. the behaviour of a living creature: *Tigers have a cruel nature.*

naught *n* nothing, the figure 0.

naughty *adj* badly behaved. **naughtier, naughtiest.**

naval *adj* having to do with the navy.

navigate *v* to guide a ship, aircraft, or car. **navigating, navigated.**

navy *n* a country's warships and their crews. *pl* **navies.**
　　navy blue the dark-blue colour of a sailor's uniform.

nay *adj* an old-fashioned word for 'no'.

near *prep, adv,* or *adj* not far away from something.

nearly *adv* not quite: *We are nearly home.*

neat *adj* clean and tidy.

necessary *adj* something that we must have, or that must be done. *opp* **unnecessary.**

neck *n* 1. the part of the body that joins the head to the shoulders. 2. something with this shape.

necklace *n* a string of beads or pearls round the neck.

need *v* to find something necessary. **needing, needed.**

needle *n* a thin steel spike, with a hole or 'eye' at one end, to sew with.

neglect *v* not to take care of. **neglecting, neglected.**

Negro *n* a black-skinned man. *pl* **Negroes.** *fem* **Negress.**

neigh *v* to make the noise a horse makes. **neighing, neighed.**

neighbour *n* someone who lives near to you.

neither *adv* not either: *neither Sally nor Connie.*

nephew *n* the son of a brother or sister. *fem* **niece.**

nerve *n* one of the fibres carrying messages between any part of the body and the brain.

nervous *adj* 1. feeling worried and excited about something. 2. easily frightened.

nest *n* a home made by birds for their chicks.

nestle *v* to lie in a warm comfortable place. **nestling, nestled.**

net *n* woven material, usually of string or wire, with large or small spaces between the strings or wires.

netball *n* a game between two teams, in which a ball has to be thrown into a net at the top of a post.

netting n a piece of net: *wire-netting*.

nettle n a plant with leaves that sting.

never adv not at any time.

new adj 1. just made or bought. 2. not seen or known before.

news n information about what has just happened.

newsagent n a newspaper-seller.

newspaper n a daily or weekly paper.

newt n a small animal like a lizard that lives on land and in water.

next adj or adv 1. the nearest. 2. the one after this.

nib n the metal point of a pen for writing with.

nibble v to eat something in small bites. **nibbling, nibbled.**

nice adj pleasant.

nickname n a name that you call someone, often in fun: *Barry's nickname is 'Tubby'.*

niece n the daughter of a brother or sister. *masc* **nephew.**

night n the time when it is dark.

nightdress n a garment worn by girls or women in bed.

nightingale n a brown bird that sings at night.

nightmare n a dream that frightens you.

nil n nothing: *We won the match three-nil.*

nimble adj quick and lively.

nine n and adj one more than eight, 9. adj **ninth.**

nineteen n and adj ten more than nine, 19. adj **nineteenth.**

ninety n and adj ten times nine, 90. adj **ninetieth.**

nip v to pinch or bite someone. **nipping, nipped.**

no 1. adv a word meaning you do not agree with someone or you will not do something. 2. adj not one or not any.
no one no person.

noble 1. adj magnificent. 2. n also **nobleman** a man of high rank.

nobody pron no one.

nod v to bend your head forward quickly, meaning 'yes'. **nodding, nodded.**

noise n a sound that is often loud and unpleasant.

noisy adj making a noise. **noisier, noisiest.**

non- a prefix meaning 'not'.

none pron not one or not any.

nonsense n something meaningless or silly.

noon n twelve o'clock in the daytime.

noose n a loop of rope made so that when the rope is pulled the loop gets smaller.

nor conj and not (after **neither**).

normal adj ordinary.

north 1. n the direction to your right as you face the setting sun. 2. adj from the north: *a north wind.*
north pole the place that is the furthest north in the world.

northern adj in or of the north.

nose n the part of your face through which you breathe, and smell things.

nosey adj always wanting to know what other people are doing.
nosey parker a very inquisitive person.

nostril n one of the two openings in your nose.

not adv a word meaning 'no' or 'the opposite'.

notch n a small cut, shaped like a V.

note n 1. a short letter to someone. 2. a musical sound, or a sign that stands for it in music.

nothing n 1. not anything. 2. (in arithmetic) a nought, the figure 0.

notice 1. v to see something that makes you think. **noticing, noticed.** 2. n something put up for people to read.
to take notice to pay attention.

nought n zero, the figure 0.

noun n a word giving the name of a person or thing. 'Alice', 'honesty', and 'football' are all nouns.

novel 1. n a book with an imaginary story. 2. adj new and interesting.

November n the eleventh month of the year.

now adv at this moment.

nowhere adv in no place.

nozzle n the open end of a pipe or hose.

nudge v to push someone with your elbow to attract his or her attention. **nudging, nudged.**

nugget n a rough lump of ore containing metal: *a gold nugget.*

nuisance n someone or something annoying to other people, or getting in their way.

numb adj without any feeling.

number n 1. a word or sign saying how many. 2. several.

numerous adj very many: *on numerous occasions.*

nun n a woman living a religious life in a convent.

nurse n someone who looks after people who are ill or hurt, or very young children.

nursery n 1. a room or building for very young children. 2. a place where young plants are looked after. pl **nurseries.**

nut *n* 1. a fruit with a wooden shell. 2. a small piece of metal with a hole, which can be twisted on to a bolt.

nutmeg *n* a hard seed that is made into a powder and used for flavouring.

nylon *n* a fibre made from chemicals in a factory, and woven to make stockings and other things.

Oo

oak *n* a tree that bears acorns.

oar *n* a long pole with a flat blade at one end, used for rowing.

oasis *n* a place in a desert where there is water, and trees grow. *pl* **oases.**

oath *n* a solemn promise.

oatmeal *n* ground oats.

oats *n pl* a kind of corn.

obedient *adj* willing to obey. *opp* **disobedient.**

obey *v* to do what you are told. **obeying, obeyed.** *opp* **disobey.**

object¹ (ob jekt) *n* 1. a thing you can see and touch. 2. an aim.

object² (ob jekt) *v* (often with **to**) to say that you are not happy about something. **objecting, objected.**

oblige *v* 1. to compel someone to do something because it is a duty. 2. to do a favour to someone. **obliging, obliged.**

oblong *n* a rectangle.

observant *adj* quick to notice. *opp* **unobservant.**

observe *v* 1. to watch carefully. 2. to mention something that you have noticed. 3. to obey: *to observe the rules.* **observing, observed.**

obstacle *n* something that is in the way.

obstinate *adj* keeping to your opinion and your way of doing things.

obstruct *v* to get in the way. **obstructing, obstructed.**

obtain *v* to get. **obtaining, obtained.**

obvious *adj* easy to see or understand.

occasion *n* the time when something happens.

occasional *adj* happening now and then.

occupation *n* the work that someone does for a living.

occupy *v* 1. to live in something. 2. to take up time. **occupying, occupied.**

occur *v* 1. to take place. 2. to come to mind. **occurring, occurred.**

ocean *n* a large sea.

o'clock short for 'of the clock'.

October *n* the tenth month of the year.

octopus *n* a sea creature with eight arms. *pl* **octopuses.**

odd *adj* 1. strange. 2. (of numbers) not even. 3. not making a perfect pair: *odd socks.* **odds and ends** bits left over.

odour *n* a smell.

of *prep* 1. made from. 2. among: *one of the boys.* 3. holding: *a tin of salt.* 4. about: *I heard of it.*

off *adv* 1. away. 2. away from: *He fell off the ladder.* 3. not on: *The switch is off.*

offence *n* a crime.

offend *v* to hurt someone's feelings. **offending, offended.**

offer *v* 1. to hold out something so that someone can take it if he or she wants it. 2. to say that you are willing to do something. **offering, offered.**

office *n* 1. a room where business is done. 2. an important position: *the office of Mayor.*

officer *n* 1. someone who holds a public position: *a police officer.* 2. someone in command: *an army officer.*

official *n* someone who has a duty to carry out, often to the public: *an airline official.*

often *adv* many times.

ogre *n* in fairy-tales, a man-eating giant.

oil *n* a slippery liquid which will not mix with water.

ointment *n* a grease to be put on a cut or sore to heal it.

old *adj* 1. having existed or lived for a long time. 2. having lived for a certain time: *six years old.* **older** or **elder, oldest** or **eldest. olden days, olden times** years long ago. **old-fashioned** common at some time in the past.

omit *v* to leave out. **omitting, omitted.**

on 1. *prep* placed upon. 2. *adv* further: *Let us go on.*

once *adv* 1. one time. 2. in the past. **at once** now: *Do it at once.* **once upon a time** at some time long ago.

one 1. *adj* single. 2. *n* a single person or thing.

onion *n* a round white vegetable like a bulb, with a strong smell.

only 1. *adv* merely: *I only won one game.* 2. *adj* single: *an only child.* 3. *conj* but: *I wanted to go only I had a cold.*

onward(s) *adv* forward.

open 1. *adj* letting people or things pass through. 2. wide and clear: *the open sky*. 3. *v* to unfasten. 4. to start: *to open a meeting*. **opening, opened.**

opening *n* 1. a space. 2. a beginning: *the opening of the book*.

opera *n* a play set to music, with the words sung.

operate *v* to cut part of the body and do something to make it healthy again. **operating, operated.**

operation *n* the cutting open of the body.

opinion *n* what you think of something.

opponent *n* someone you fight or play against.

oppose *v* to fight or argue against. **opposing, opposed.**

opposite *adj* 1. facing. 2. as different as possible: *opposite ideas*.

optician *n* someone who makes or sells spectacles.

orange *n* 1. a reddish-yellow fruit. 2. a reddish-yellow colour.

orbit *n* the path that something takes in space when it is moving round the earth or sun.

orchard *n* a place where fruit trees are grown.

orchestra *n* a large group of musicians playing together.

ordeal *n* a nervous or painful experience.

order *n* 1. a tidy arrangement: *kept in order*. *opp* **disorder.** 2. a command. 3. a list of things that you want to be brought to you.
alphabetical order arranging things in the order of the first letter of their names, A, B, C, etc.

ordinary *adj* not special.

ore *n* rock containing a valuable substance, usually metal: *iron ore*.

organ *n* a large musical instrument like a piano, with pedals, and pipes.

original *adj* 1. not copied: *an original story*. 2. made before any others.

ornament *n* something used for decoration such as a vase or brooch.

orphan *n* a child whose parents are dead.

ostrich *n* a very large African bird that runs fast but cannot fly.

other *adj* 1. different: *I have other things to do*. 2. opposite: *on the other side*.

otter *n* a furry animal that lives in or near water and feeds on fish.

ought *v* (often with **to**) should: *You ought to go*.

our *adj* belonging to us: *our house*.

ours *pron* belonging to us: *The house is ours*.

ourselves *pron* we alone: *We shall do it ourselves*.
by ourselves on our own.

out *adv* 1. not in. 2. not burning: *The fire is out*.
out of bounds in a place that is forbidden.
out-of-date old-fashioned.

outdoor *adj* in the open air: *outdoor games*.

outdoors *adv* into the open air: *They went outdoors*.

outer *adj* outside: *the outer door*. *opp* **inner.**

outfit *n* a set of clothes.

outing *n* a trip: *an outing to the seaside*.

outlaw *n* in olden times, a bandit who was outside the protection of the law.

outlet *n* a way out.

outline *n* a line drawn to show the shape of an object.

outlook *n* a view: *a wide outlook*.

outside 1. *adv* not inside. 2. *n* the side facing away from the middle of something.

outward *adj* outside: *an outward appearance*.
outward bound of a ship, starting out on a new voyage.

oval *adj* egg-shaped.

oven *n* a heated iron box in which food is cooked.

over 1. *prep* above. 2. more than: *over a pound*. 3. across: *over the bridge*. 4. *adv* finished: *The lesson is over*. 5. too much: *food left over*.

overalls *n pl* a loose garment, with trousers and jacket in one piece, worn over other clothes to keep them clean.

overbalance *v* to fall over. **overbalancing, overbalanced.**

overboard *adv* over a ship's side.

overcoat *n* an outer coat.

overcome *v* to defeat. **overcoming, overcame.**

overdue *adj* behind time: *The train is overdue*.

overflow *v* to flow over the edge of a container. **overflowing, overflowed.**

overgrown *adj* covered with growing plants: *The path is overgrown with weeds*.

overhead *adv* high above: *birds flying overhead*.

overhear *v* to listen to someone speaking, who does not know you are listening. **overhearing, overheard.**

overlap *v* to cover part of something. **overlapping, overlapped.**

overload *v* to put too heavy a load on. **overloading, overloaded.**

overlook *v* 1. to look down on. 2. not to notice. **overlooking, overlooked.**

overseas *adv* in a land across the sea.

overtake *v* to go faster than something else that is moving and go past it. **overtaking, overtook, I have overtaken.**

overthrow *v* to conquer. **overthrowing, overthrew, I have overthrown.**

overturn *v* to turn upside-down or over. **overturning, overturned.**

overwhelm *v* to defeat completely. **overwhelming, overwhelmed.**

owe *v* to have to pay money to someone. **owing, owed.**

owl *n* a bird of prey that hunts at night.

own *v* to have something that belongs to you. **owning, owned.**
  my own belonging only to me.
  on my own by myself.
  to get your own back to get your revenge.
  to own up to confess to something you have done.

ox *n* an animal like a cow kept for its meat or for pulling carts. *pl* **oxen.**

oxygen *n* a gas in the air needed to keep us alive.

oyster *n* a round flat shellfish used for food.

Pp

pace *n* 1. one step when walking. 2. speed: *at a fast pace.*

pack 1. *v* to put things into a case or bag. **packing, packed.** *opp* **unpack.** 2. *n* a bundle carried on the back. 3. a set of cards used in games.

package *n* a parcel.

packet *n* a small parcel: *a packet of seeds.*

pad *n* 1. sheets of paper fastened together: *a writing-pad.* 2. a piece of soft material made into a sort of cushion to protect something.

paddle 1. *v* to walk in shallow water with bare feet. **paddling, paddled.** 2. *n* a short oar used to make a canoe move.

padlock *n* a kind of small metal lock.

page *n* one side of a sheet of paper in a book.

paid see **pay.**

pail *n* a bucket with a handle.

pain *n* a feeling when part of your body is hurt or sick.

painful *adj* giving pain.

paint *n* a coloured liquid that is put on to a surface with a brush.

painting *n* a picture made of paint on paper or canvas.

pair *n* two people, animals, or things that belong together: *a pair of socks.*

palace *n* a very large splendid house for a king, a queen, or a bishop.

pale *adj* 1. almost white: *Vera was very pale.* 2. weak in colour: *pale blue.*

palette *n* a board on which an artist mixes paints.

palm *n* 1. the inside of your hand between your wrist and your fingers. 2. a tree that grows in warm countries and has long leaves.

pamper *v* to be too kind to a person or an animal. **pampering, pampered.**

pan *n* a container with a handle, used in cooking.

pancake *n* a thin round cake of eggs, flour, and milk mixed together and fried.

panda *n* a large black and white animal, like a bear, that lives in China.

pane *n* a sheet of glass in a window frame.

panel *n* a piece of wood sunk into a door or wall.

panic *n* a sudden fear that makes people or animals do things without thinking: *The lion's escape caused a panic in the town.*

pant *v* to gasp in quick breaths. **panting, panted.**

panther *n* 1. a wild cat-like animal of North America. 2. a leopard.

pantomime *n* a musical play about a fairy-tale.

pants *n pl* a piece of clothing like very short trousers, worn next to the skin.

paper *n* 1. material in thin sheets for writing on, printing on, or wrapping. 2. a newspaper.

parable *n* a short story that teaches people something: *the parable about the Good Samaritan.*

parachute *n* an umbrella-shaped sheet of cloth with ropes tied to someone's back so that he or she can jump out of an aeroplane in the air and float safely to the ground.

parade *n* a group of soldiers or other people being inspected or marching while people watch them.

paraffin *n* an oil burnt in fires and lamps for heating and lighting.

paragraph *n* a few sentences grouped together on a page of writing or printing.

parallel *adj* (of two or more straight lines) the same distance apart all the way along.

paralysed *adj* unable to move or feel anything.

parcel *n* something wrapped up in paper.

pardon *v* to forgive. **pardoning, pardoned.**

parent *n* a father or mother.

parish *n* a district with its own church.

park 1. *n* a fenced-off piece of public land for people to play in. 2. *v* to leave a car in a safe place for a time. **parking, parked.**

parliament *n* a council of men and women, chosen at an election, who make a country's laws.

parrot *n* a brightly-coloured bird that lives in hot countries and can learn to repeat words.

parsley *n* a plant whose leaves are chopped and used in cooking.

parsnip *n* a vegetable like a pale yellow carrot.

parson *n* a clergyman or priest in charge of a parish.

part 1. *n* anything that has been taken from, or belongs to, something bigger. 2. a character in a film or play. 3. *v* to separate. **parting, parted.**

particular *adj* having to do with one person or thing: *in this particular case.*

partner *n* 1. someone working with another, or playing a game on the same side: *a tennis partner.* 2. a husband or wife.

partridge *n* a wild bird that is shot for food.

party *n* a group of people enjoying something together: *a birthday party.* pl **parties.**

pass 1. *v* to go past. 2. to hand something to someone. 3. to get through a test. **passing, passed.** 4. *n* a road or path between two mountains.

passage *n* 1. a narrow way in a building. 2. a part taken from a story.

passenger *n* a traveller in a ship, aeroplane or some other vehicle, except the driver and crew.

passer-by *n* someone walking past. *pl* **passers-by.**

passover *n* a Jewish religious feast.

passport *n* special papers that you must have to travel in a foreign country.

past 1. *n* time gone by. 2. *adv* up to and beyond: *Donald ran past us.*

pasta *n* Italian flour paste used to make spaghetti and macaroni.

paste *n* 1. a sticky liquid for fastening papers together. 2. a thick mixture made from meat or fish that is spread on bread and eaten.

pastime *n* an amusement, game, or hobby: *Her favourite pastime is riding.*

pastry *n* a stiff mixture of flour, fat, and water, rolled flat and used for pies.

pasture *n* grassland for cattle to feed on.

pat *v* to tap gently with your hand. **patting, patted.**

patch *n* 1. a small piece of material sewn or stuck over a hole. 2. a small area: *a vegetable patch.*

path *n* a narrow way for walking in the open air.

patience *n* being able to wait for a long time or to work at a difficult job without complaining. *opp* **impatience.**

patient 1. *n* a person who is ill and in a doctor's care. 2. *adj* having patience. *opp* **impatient.**

patrol *n* a small group of soldiers or policemen who are on guard.

patter *v* to make a light tapping sound: *rain pattered on the roof.* **pattering, pattered.**

pattern *n* 1. a model to be copied: *a dress pattern.* 2. a design of lines or shapes drawn on something to decorate it: *a pattern on a curtain.*

pause *v* to stop what you are doing for a short while. **pausing, paused.**

pavement *n* a paved footpath.

pavilion *n* a wooden building on a sports ground where people wait their turn to play.

paw *n* an animal's foot with claws.

pay *v* I. to give money in return for goods, or for work done. 2. to make: *to pay a visit.* **paying, paid.**

payment *n* money that is paid.

pea *n* a small round green seed that grows in a pod.

peace *n* I. a time of quiet. 2. a time when there is no war.

peach *n* a round juicy fruit with a stone inside.

peacock *n* a large bird with beautiful tail feathers that it can open like a fan. *fem* **peahen.**

peak *n* I. a mountain top. 2. the part of a cap that sticks out in front.

peal *n* a loud sound, such as that of bells, thunder, or laughter.

peanut *n* a small nut that grows in a yellow husk.

pear *n* a green or yellow fruit shaped like a cone.

pearl *n* a small shiny whitish ball found in some oyster shells and used as a jewel.

peasant *n* a poor worker on the land in some countries.

peat *n* a type of soil that can be dug up in pieces and burnt instead of coal.

pebble *n* a small round stone.

peck *v* (of a bird) to jab at food and pick it up with its beak. **pecking, pecked.**

peculiar *adj* strange: *a peculiar smell.*

pedal *n* a part of a machine such as a bicycle that you push with your foot to make it work.

pedestrian *n* someone who is walking.

peel *n* the skin or rind of a fruit or vegetable.

peep *v* to take a quick look at. **peeping, peeped.**

peer I. *v* to look hard. **peering, peered.** 2. *n* a nobleman. *fem* **peeress.**

peg *n* I. a small wooden clip. 2. a small metal or wooden pin: *a tent-peg.*

pelican *n* a large bird with a pouch under its beak.

pellet *n* a tiny ball, usually of metal.

pelt I. *n* the fur and skin of an animal. 2. *v* to keep throwing at. **pelting, pelted.**

pen *n* I. a tool for writing with ink. 2. an enclosed space to keep living things in.

penalty *n* (in games) a punishment for breaking the rules. *pl* **penalties.**

pence see **pennies.**

pencil *n* a tool for writing, with a black or coloured centre in a wooden cover.

pendulum *n* a weight at the end of a rod that moves from side to side in some clocks.

penetrate *v* to make or find a way into something. **penetrating, penetrated.**

penguin *n* a black and white sea-bird that cannot fly, found near the South Pole.

penknife *n* a small pocket-knife with blades that fold into the handle. *pl* **penknives.**

penny *n* a small British coin. *pl* **pennies** (concerning number), **pence** (concerning value).

people *n pl* men, women, boys, and girls.

pepper *n* a hot-tasting powder used to flavour food.

perch *n* I. place for a bird to rest on. 2. a kind of river fish.

percussion *n* any musical instrument that has to be hit or shaken to be played.

perfect *adj* so good that it cannot be made better: *a perfect page of sums.* *opp* **imperfect.**

perform *v* to do something in front of an audience. **performing, performed.**

perfume *n* a sweet-smelling liquid.

perhaps *adv* possibly: *Perhaps he will come.*

peril *n* danger.

perimeter *n* the distance round an edge.

period *n* any length of time.

perish *v* I. to die. 2. (of something such as fruit or rubber) to change so that it can no longer be eaten or used. **perishing, perished.**

permission *n* words that allow someone to do something: *permission to go home early.*

permit *v* to allow. **permitting, permitted.**

persevere *v* to keep trying. **persevering, persevered.**

persist *v* to go on doing something: *He persisted in talking.* **persisting, persisted.**

person *n* any human being.

perspire *v* to sweat. **perspiring, perspired.**

persuade *v* to talk to someone and get him or her to agree to something. **persuading, persuaded.**

pest *n* any person or animal that does harm or causes trouble.

pester *v* to keep on being a nuisance. **pestering, pestered.**

pet *n* an animal that you keep and look after.

petal *n* one of the coloured parts of a flower-head.

petrol *n* the liquid used in most car engines.

petticoat *n* a piece of clothing that is worn under a skirt or a dress.

pew *n* a long wooden seat in a church.

pheasant *n* a wild bird with long tail feathers.

phone short for **telephone.**

photo short for photograph. *pl* **photos.**

photograph *n* a picture taken with a camera.

phrase *n* a group of words that is not a full sentence. 'As happy as a lark' is a phrase.

piano *n* a large musical instrument with black and white keys. *pl* **pianos.**

pick 1. *v* to choose. 2. to gather: *to pick fruit.* **picking, picked.** 3. *n* a heavy tool with a point for breaking up hard ground.

pickled *adj* kept in vinegar.

picnic *n* a meal eaten out in the country.

picture *n* a drawing, painting, or photograph.

pie *n* meat or fruit baked in pastry.

piece *n* a part: *a piece of cake.*

pier *n* a long platform built out over water.

pierce *v* to make a hole in. **piercing, pierced.**

piercing *adj* (of sound) high: *a piercing shriek.*

pig *n* an animal that gives pork, bacon, and ham.

pigeon *n* a greyish-white bird, sometimes used for racing.

pigmy see **pygmy.**

pigsty *n* a place where pigs are kept. *pl* **pigsties.**

pigtail *n* a long plait of hair at the back of the head.

pile *n* a number of things on top of one another.

pilgrim *n* a traveller to a holy place.

pill *n* a tablet of medicine to be swallowed.

pillar *n* a large post, usually of stone, to hold up the roof of a big building.

pillow *n* a cushion for resting your head on in bed.

pilot *n* 1. a person who controls an aeroplane. 2. a person who goes on board a ship and guides it into port.

pimple *n* a small swelling on the skin.

pin *n* a thin piece of metal with a head at one end and a point at the other, used to fasten things.

pinafore *n* a large apron worn in front over a dress.

pincers *n pl* 1. a tool for gripping things. 2. the claws of a crab or lobster.

pinch *v* to squeeze between thumb and finger. **pinching, pinched.**

pine 1. *n* a tall tree with cones, and leaves that look like green needles. 2. *v* to miss: *Jane pined for her dog.* **pining, pined.**

pineapple *n* a large sweet fruit that grows in hot countries.

pink *n* a very pale red colour.

pioneer *n* 1. someone who is the first to do something. 2. one of the first people to go to live in a new country.

pip *n* the seed of some fruits: *an orange pip.*

pipe *n* 1. a tube to carry water or gas. 2. a tube ending in a small bowl used for smoking tobacco.

piper *n* a man who plays the bagpipes.

piping *n* a length of pipe.

pirate *n* a robber who steals from ships at sea.

pistol *n* a small gun fired from one hand.

pit *n* 1. any deep hole in the ground. 2. a deep hole leading to a coal-mine.

pitch 1. *n* a piece of ground marked out for a game. 2. *v* to throw. 3. to put up: *to pitch a tent.* **pitching, pitched.**

pitchfork *n* a long fork for lifting hay.

pity 1. *n* a feeling of sorrow for someone in trouble or in pain. 2. *v* to have this feeling. **he pities, pitying, pitied.**

pizza *n* an open pie, usually with cheese or tomatoes on it.

placard *n* a poster.

place 1. *n* a position or space. 2. a town. 3. *v* to put something in a certain spot. **placing, placed.**

plague *n* a deadly disease that spreads very quickly.

plaice *n* a flat sea-fish that can be eaten. *pl* **plaice.**

plain 1. *adj* obvious: *It is plain that you are not well.* 2. not decorated. 3. *n* a large area of level country.

plait *n* three lengths of hair or straw twisted over and under one another.

plan 1. *n* a drawing showing how a building or town is arranged when seen from above. 2. *v* to decide what is going to be done. **planning, planned.**

plane *n* 1. a short word for **aeroplane.** 2. a tool for making wood smooth.

planet *n* a world like ours that moves round the sun, and that is so far away that it looks like a star.

plank *n* a long flat thick piece of wood.

plant *n* a living thing that grows in soil, such as a flower, a vegetable, or a tree.

plaster *n* 1. a strip of cloth with a sticky side and a special part for covering a cut or graze. 2. a soft mixture that is spread smoothly on walls and ceilings, and then goes hard.

plastic *n* a material that is made in factories and then used to make different things such as toys and bowls.

plasticine *n* something like soft clay that you can use for making models.

plate *n* a flat dish for eating from.

platform *n* 1. the part of a railway station beside the track. 2. a raised floor, as in a hall.

play 1. *v* to enjoy oneself, often by being in a game. 2. to make music with a musical instrument. **playing, played.** 3. *n* a story that is acted.

playground *n* a place out of doors for children to play in.

plead *v* to beg for something that you want very much. **pleading, pleaded.**

pleasant *adj* pleasing. *opp* **unpleasant.**

please *v* 1. to make someone happy. **pleasing, pleased.** *opp* **displease.** 2. (a word used when asking politely): *Please may I come in?*

pleasure *n* a feeling of being pleased. *opp* **displeasure.**

pleat *n* a double fold of cloth stitched in position.

plentiful *adj* in great numbers or amounts: *a plentiful supply of food.*

plenty *n* a lot of something: *plenty of people.*

pliers *n pl* pincers that can grip and bend things.

plimsolls *n pl* light canvas shoes with rubber soles.

plod *v* 1. to walk slowly and heavily. 2. to keep on working at something dull. **plodding, plodded.**

plot 1. *n* a small piece of ground. 2. the main points of a story. 3. *v* to make secret plans. **plotting, plotted.**

plough *n* a machine for turning over the soil.

pluck *v* 1. to pull a string or wire and let it go. 2. to pull all the feathers off. **plucking, plucked.**

plug *n* 1. a round piece of material that fits into a hole to stop water from running out. 2. an electrical connection that fits into a special place in a wall where electricity can flow into it.

plum *n* a soft fruit with a stone seed.

plumber *n* someone who connects and mends pipes for water or gas.

plump *adj* fat: *a plump hen.*

plunder *v* to rob a person or place by force and take things. **plundering, plundered.**

plunge *v* to throw yourself into. **plunging, plunged.**

plural *n* more than one: *'Mice' is the plural of 'mouse'.*

plus *prep* added to: *3 plus 2 equals 5.*

plywood *n* several thin layers of wood glued together in sheets.

poach *v* 1. to cook an egg, without the shell, in boiling water. 2. to hunt animals on someone's land without permission. **poaching, poached.**

pocket *n* a small bag sewn into some clothes, for keeping things in.

pod *n* a long part of some plants with seeds inside.

poem *n* lines of words, with a certain number of syllables to the line, and with the lines usually rhyming at the end.

poet *n* someone who writes poems.

poetry *n* poems: *a book of poetry.*

point 1. *n* a sharp end. 2. a mark scored in a game. 3. *v* to direct a finger or a gun towards something. **pointing, pointed.**

poison *n* something that would kill you or make you very ill if you swallowed it.

poisonous *adj* containing poison: *poisonous berries.*

poke *v* 1. to jab with a finger or stick. 2. (with **out**) to stick out: *He poked out his tongue.* **poking, poked.**

poker *n* a metal rod for poking a fire.

polar *adj* having to do with the North or South Pole, or both.

pole *n* 1. a long round piece of wood or metal. 2. one of the two places that are furthest north and south in the world.

police *n* men and women who make sure that the law is obeyed and who catch criminals.

polish *v* to make something shiny by rubbing it. **polishing, polished.**

polite *adj* having good manners. *opp* **impolite.**

pollen *n* a yellow powder at the centre of flowers.

polythene *n* a kind of plastic.

poncho *n* an oblong piece of cloth with a hole to put the head through, that is worn loosely over other clothes.

pond *n* a small lake.

pony *n* a horse of a small breed. *pl* **ponies.**

poodle *n* a pet dog with very curly hair.

pool *n* 1. a small pond, sometimes specially made for swimming in. 2. a small patch of liquid.

poor *adj* 1. having very little money. 2. not good: *This is poor work.* **poorer, poorest.**

pop *v* to make a sudden small noise. **popping, popped.**

pop music *n* popular music that you like to dance to.

Pope *n* the head of the Roman Catholic church.

poplar *n* a tree that grows very tall and straight.

poppadum *n* a kind of Indian biscuit that is fried.

poppy *n* a plant with red flowers. *pl* **poppies.**

popular *adj* liked by a lot of people. *opp* **unpopular.**

population *n* the number of people living in a town or a country.

porch *n* a shelter in front of an outside door of a building.

pore *n* one of many tiny holes in your skin.

pork *n* meat from a pig.

porpoise *n* a sea-animal like a small whale.

porridge *n* a breakfast food made by boiling oatmeal with water.

port *n* 1. a harbour, or town with a harbour. 2. the left side of a ship as you face the front or bow. *opp* to **starboard.**

porter *n* someone who carries luggage or loads.

porthole *n* one of the small round windows in the side of a ship.

portion *n* 1. a part of something. 2. a helping.

portrait *n* a picture of someone.

position *n* a place for something or someone.

positive *adj* certain: *I am positive that I did it.*

possess *v* to own. **possessing, possessed.**

possessions *n pl* all the things that belong to you.

possible *adj* able to happen or to be done: *a possible mistake. opp* **impossible.**

post 1. *n* the carrying of letters and parcels. 2. an upright pole fixed in the ground. 3. *v* to send letters and parcels by post. **posting, posted. post office** a shop selling stamps, postal orders, and dealing with the post.

postage *n* the money you pay for posting a letter or parcel.

postal order *n* special paper money you can send by post.

postcard *n* a card that you can write a message on and post.

poster *n* a large notice stuck up on a board or wall.

postman *n* a man who collects and delivers letters and parcels.

pot *n* a round container: *a flower-pot.*

potato *n* a vegetable that is a swollen part of a root, grown for food. *pl* **potatoes.**

pottery *n* 1. things made of baked clay. 2. a place where these are made.

pouch *n* a small bag to hold things.

poultry *n* birds, such as hens or ducks, kept for their meat and eggs.

pounce *v* to attack by suddenly jumping on something. **pouncing, pounced.**

pound *n* 1. a measure of weight equal to 454 grams. 2. British money equal to 100 pence.

pour *v* 1. to rain heavily. 2. to tip a liquid out of a container. **pouring, poured.**

powder *n* anything like dry dust.

power *n* strength.

practice *n* something you keep doing so that you get better at it. Note: the noun 'practice' is spelt with a 'c' at the end.

practise *v* to keep doing something so that you get better at it. **practising, practised.** Note: the verb 'practise' is spelt with an 's' at the end.

prairie *n* a great stretch of flat grassland.

praise *v* to say that someone or something is very good. **praising, praised.**

pram *n* a kind of cot on wheels, pushed by hand.

prance *v* (of a horse) to jump about on the hind legs. **prancing, pranced.**

prawn *n* a shellfish that looks like a large shrimp.

pray *v* to speak to God, silently or aloud. **praying, prayed.**

prayer *n* the words used when people pray.

preach *v* to give a sermon, usually from a church pulpit. **preaching, preached.**

precious *adj* very valuable.

precipice *n* a steep cliff.

prefect *n* a senior boy or girl at school with authority over others.

prefer *v* to like one person or thing more than another. **preferring, preferred.**

prefix *n* a part with one or two syllables put before a word to make a new word with a different meaning, as in '<u>un</u>happy' or '<u>inter</u>national'.

pregnant *adj* going to have a baby.

prehistoric *adj* living a very long time ago before history was written: *a prehistoric monster*.

prepare *v* to get ready. **preparing, prepared.**

preposition *n* a word that links two nouns, and says whether one is: *over, by, on, through,* or *under* the other: in 'Tom walked on the grass', the word 'on' is a preposition.

present[1] (prez ent) 1. *n* a gift to someone. 2. *adj* (often with **at**) attending: *Everyone is present*. **at present** now

present[2] (pree <u>zent</u>) *v* to give a prize or gift to someone. **presenting, presented.**

presently (<u>prez</u> ent li) *adv* soon.

preserve *v* to keep something safe from harm or decay. **preserving, preserved.**

president *n* the head of a country which has no king or queen.

press *v* 1. to push or squeeze. 2. to push a hot iron over. **pressing, pressed.**

pretend *v* 1. to play at being someone else. 2. to make yourself appear to be something you are not. **pretending, pretended.**

pretty *adj* attractive. **prettier, prettiest.**

prevent *v* (often with **from**) to stop something happening, or someone doing something. **preventing, prevented.**

previous *adj* coming before this one.

prey *n* a bird or animal hunted by another for food.
bird of prey a bird such as an eagle or owl that hunts and feeds on smaller creatures.

price *n* the amount of money that you pay when you buy something.

priceless *adj* too valuable to have a price.

prick *v* to make a small hole with a sharp point. **pricking, pricked.**

prickle *n* a sharp point like a thorn.

pride *n* the feeling you have when you are proud.

priest *n* a minister of religion, often in charge of a church. *fem* **priestess.**

primary *adj* earliest.

prime *adj* most important: *The Prime Minister.*

primrose *n* a pale yellow spring flower.

prince *n* the son of a king or queen.
Prince of Wales the eldest son of a British ruler.

princess *n* the daughter of a king or queen.

print *v* 1. to write using letters that are not joined together. 2. to press type or pictures on to paper using a special machine and ink. **printing, printed.**

prison *n* a building where criminals are kept.

prisoner *n* 1. a man or woman kept in prison. 2. someone who has been captured.

private *adj* not for everyone: *a private road.*

prize *n* a reward for doing well at something.

probable *adj* likely to happen, or to be true. *opp* **improbable.**

problem *n* a difficult puzzle or question.

proceed *v* to go on. **proceeding, proceeded.**

procession *n* a large number of people, horsemen, or coaches moving along in a line.

prod *v* to push something with the end of a stick or a finger. **prodding, prodded.**

produce *v* 1. to make. 2. to bring out something so that it can be seen: *Tom produced his pen.* **producing, produced.**

profession *n* a job that needs years of training, like that of a doctor or a lawyer.

professor *n* a teacher of high rank at a university.

profit *n* the money you make by selling a thing for more than it cost to buy or make.

programme *n* 1. a show, play, or talk on television or radio. 2. a list of the things to be seen or heard at a concert, play, or show.

progress *n* 1. movement forwards. 2. improvement. 3. growth: *the progress of a business.*

project *n* 1. collecting information on a particular subject and writing about it. 2. a plan.

projector *n* a machine with a lamp, for showing films or pictures on a screen.

promenade *n* a wide road along a sea-front where people can stroll.

promise *v* to say that you will be sure to do, or not to do, something. **promising, promised.**

prompt *adj* done at once or very quickly: *a prompt reply.*

prong *n* one of the spikes of a fork.

pronoun *n* a word used instead of a noun. In 'Bob said he rode his bicycle' the word 'he' is a pronoun used for the noun 'Bob'.

pronounce *v* to say the sound of a word. **pronouncing, pronounced.**

proof *n* something that shows what is the truth.

-proof a word-ending meaning 'giving protection against': *water-proof, bullet-proof.*

prop 1. *n* a support. 2. *v* (with **up**) to hold up something to prevent it from falling. **propping, propped.**

propeller *n* a shaft with blades, turning round and moving a ship or some kinds of aeroplane.

proper *adj* correct: *the proper way to saw wood.*

property *n* anything that belongs to someone, especially a house or other building.

prophet *n* someone who says what will happen in the future.

propose *v* 1. to suggest something. 2. to make an offer of marriage. **proposing, proposed.**

prosecute *v* to say in court that someone has done something against the law. **prosecuting, prosecuted.**

protect *v* to keep safe from danger. **protecting, protected.**

protest *v* to say or show that you are not happy about something. **protesting, protested.**

proud *adj* 1. feeling pleased at having done something well. 2. having too high an opinion of yourself. See **pride.**

prove *v* to show that something is true. **proving, proved.** See **proof.**

proverb *n* a saying that advises you what to do. 'Look before you leap' is a proverb.

provide *v* to give what is needed. **providing, provided.**

prowl *v* to move round silently looking for something to eat or steal. **prowling, prowled.**

prune *n* a dried plum.

pry *v* to try to find out about something that is not your business. **she pries, prying, pried.**

psalm *n* one of the hymns in the Bible.

public 1. *adj* open to, belonging to, or concerning everyone. 2. *n* all the people.

pudding *n* a soft cooked sweet food eaten at the end of a meal.

puddle *n* a small pool of water.

puff 1. *n* a quick blow of breath, smoke, steam, or wind. 2. *v* (with **out** or **up**) to swell up. **puffing, puffed.**
puffed out of breath.

puffin *n* a sea bird with a thick coloured beak.

pull *v* to take hold of something and make it come towards you. **pulling, pulled.**

pulley *n* a grooved wheel fitted with a rope, for pulling heavy weights. *pl* **pulleys.**

pullover *n* a woollen article of clothing with sleeves, that is pulled on over your head.

pulpit *n* a small raised platform in church, from which the priest can talk to the people.

pulse *n* the regular throb of blood moving through your body.

pump *n* a machine that forces air or water through a tube.

punch *v* 1. to hit with your fist. 2. to make a hole in: *to punch a ticket.* **punching, punched.**

punctual *adj* exactly on time.

punctuation *n* full-stops, commas, and other marks in writing to make it easier to read.

puncture *n* a small hole in a tyre.

punish *v* to make someone suffer for doing something wrong. **punishing, punished.**

punishment *n* something done to punish someone.

pupil *n* 1. someone taught at school or college. 2. the black centre of your eye.

puppet *n* a doll moved by strings, or by fitting it on the hand like a glove.

puppy *n* a young dog. *pl* **puppies.**

purchase *v* to buy. **purchasing, purchased.**

pure *adj* not mixed with anything else. *opp* **impure.**

purple *n* a colour made by mixing blue and red.

purpose *n* what you mean to do.
on purpose meaning to do it: *done on purpose.*

purr *n* the sound a cat makes when it is happy.

purse *n* a small bag to hold money.

pursue *v* to chase. **pursuing, pursued.**

push *v* to move something away from you. **pushing, pushed.**

put *v* to move something into a place. **putting, put.**
to put up with to have to accept.

putty n a special grey paste that sets hard, for fixing glass in a window-frame.

puzzle n a question that is hard to answer, or a problem that you work out for fun: a jigsaw puzzle.

pygmy, pigmy n one of a race of very small people living in Africa. pl **pygmies, pigmies.**

pyjamas n pl a loose jacket and trousers worn in bed.

pylon n a tall tower holding up electric cables.

pyramid n a solid shape with a square base and sloping sides meeting at a point at the top.

python n a very large snake.

Qq

quack n the noise made by a duck.

quake v to shake with fear.

quality n how good or bad a thing is.

quantity n an amount. pl **quantities.**

quarrel v to disagree and argue with angry words. **quarrelling, quarrelled.**

quarry n an opening made in a hillside, or in the earth, where stone is cut for building. pl **quarries.**

quarter n one of four equal parts.

quay n a place for loading and unloading ships.

queen n 1. a woman who is the ruler of a country. masc **king.** 2. the wife of a king. 3. a playing-card with the picture of a queen. 4. a female bee that lays eggs.

queer adj strange.

quench v 1. to put an end to: to quench your thirst. 2. to put out: to quench a fire. **quenching, quenched.**

query n a question when you think something might be wrong. pl **queries.**

question n something you ask that needs an answer.
  question mark the sign (?) put at the end of a sentence that asks a question.

queue n a line of people waiting for something.

quick adj fast. **quicker, quickest.**

quiet adj 1. without any sound. 2. not loud.

quieten v to make quiet. **quietening, quietened.**

quilt n a cover for a bed, like a large flat cushion.

quite adv 1. completely. 2. up to a certain point: Your spelling is quite good.

quiver 1. v to shake: He quivered with fear. **quivering, quivered.** 2. n a case for holding arrows.

quiz n a game in which those taking part answer a lot of questions to see who knows most. pl **quizzes.**

quote v to repeat someone's words exactly. **quoting, quoted.**

Rr

rabbi n a Jewish priest.

rabbit n a small furry animal with long ears.

race n 1. a competition to see who can go fastest. 2. living things of the same kind: the human race.

rack n a frame with bars or pegs for holding things.

racket n 1. a lot of noise. 2. a bat with a lot of strings stretched tightly, for hitting a ball.

radar n a way of finding the position of ships or aircraft by using reflected radio waves.

radiator n 1. a set of hot-water pipes or a metal container that gives out heat in a room. 2. the part inside a car that keeps the engine cool.

radio n a machine that can receive programmes and messages sent through the air and change them into sound so that people can listen to them. pl **radios.**

radish n a small red-skinned plant eaten in salads.

radius n the distance from the centre of a circle to the edge. pl **radii.**

raffia n dried strips of palm-leaves, like straw, which are woven into baskets and mats.

raffle n a way of making money for something. People buy tickets with printed numbers and some numbers win prizes.

raft n logs or planks tied together to make a floating platform.

rafter n one of the beams holding up a roof.

rag n a scrap of old cloth.

ragged adj wearing torn clothes.

rage n great anger.

raid n a sudden attack on a place.

rail n 1. a wooden or metal bar: a handrail. 2. a long metal bar that is part of a railway line.

railings n pl a fence of bars, usually of metal.

railway *n* two steel rails for trains to travel on.

rain *n* water falling in drops from the clouds.

rainbow *n* an arch in the sky, of many colours, seen when the sun shines on falling rain.

raincoat *n* a waterproof coat.

raise *v* 1. to lift up or make something higher. 2. to bring up children or animals: *to raise a family*. 3. to collect: *to raise money*. **raising, raised.**

raisin *n* a dried grape, used in cakes.

rake *n* a long-handled garden tool with a row of short spikes to scratch the soil.

rally *n* a meeting of a lot of people. *pl* **rallies.**

ram 1. *n* a male sheep. *fem* **ewe.** 2. *v* to crash into. **ramming, rammed.**

ramble *n* a long walk in the country.

ran see **run.**

ranch *n* a large cattle farm in America.

rang see **ring.**

range *n* 1. a line: *a range of hills*. 2. the distance a weapon can shoot or a rocket can travel.

rank *n* 1. a title that shows how important a position someone has: *the rank of captain in the army*. 2. a row of people.

ransom *n* money paid to set someone free.

rap *v* to knock quickly and loudly. **rapping, rapped.**

rapid *adj* very quick.

rapids *n pl* a part of a river where it flows quickly over rocks.

rare *adj* not often found.

rascal *n* 1. a mischievous child. 2. a dishonest person.

rash 1. *n* red spots or patches that appear on your skin. 2. *adj* taking risks without thinking.

raspberry *n* a soft red juicy berry. *pl* **raspberries.**

rat *n* an animal that looks like a large mouse.

rate *n* speed: *the car went at a fast rate*.

rather *adv* 1. more gladly: *I would rather go fishing*. 2. quite: *rather cold*.

rattle *n* 1. the sound made by shaking a lot of hard things together. 2. a baby's toy that makes this sound.

rave *v* to talk in a very enthusiastic way. **raving, raved.**

raven *n* a large black bird.

ravenous *adj* very hungry.

ravine *n* a deep narrow valley with steep sides.

raw *adj* not cooked: *raw meat*.

ray *n* a thin line of light.

razor *n* a sharp instrument for shaving off hair.

re- a prefix meaning 'again': *To re-write a letter*.

reach *v* 1. to put out your hand to touch or get something. 2. to arrive at. **reaching, reached.**

read (reed) *v* to look at words and understand them or say them aloud. **reading, read** (red).

ready (red i) *adj* prepared and willing.

real *adj* 1. existing: *a real person, not a ghost*. 2. not artificial: *real pearls*.

realise *v* to come to understand. **realising, realised.**

really *adv* truly: *I really mean what I say*.

realm *n* the land ruled by a king or queen.

reap *v* to cut down and gather in a harvest. **reaping, reaped.**

rear 1. *n* the back part. 2. *v* to bring up children or animals. 3. (of a horse) to stand on the hind legs. **rearing, reared.**

reason *n* anything that explains why something has happened.

reasonable *adj* 1. fair. 2. sensible. *opp* **unreasonable.**

rebel *v* to turn against those in authority and refuse to obey orders. **rebelling, rebelled.**

recall *v* to remember. **recalling, recalled.**

receive *v* to get what has been given or sent to you. **receiving, received.**

receiver *n* 1. the part of a telephone that you put to your ear. 2. a radio or television set.

recent *adj* happened or made not long ago.

reception *n* 1. a welcome: *a warm reception*. 2. a big party in honour of someone.

recipe *n* instructions for making something to eat or drink, and what to put in it.

recite *v* to say aloud a story or a poem from memory. **reciting, recited.**

reckless *adj* doing silly things and not caring about possible danger.

reckon *v* 1. to count. 2. to consider: *I reckon I can win*. **reckoning, reckoned.**

recognise *v* to know someone or something again by sight. **recognising, recognised.**

recommend *v* 1. to advise. 2. to speak well of: *I can recommend this cake*. **recommending, recommended.**

record *n* 1. a black plastic disc that produces music or other sounds when it turns round on a record-player. 2. the best yet: *a record win*. **record-player** a machine that makes music or other sounds come out of records.

recorder *n* a wooden musical instrument like a tube, that you blow into.

recover *v* 1. to get something back that you have lost. 2. to get better after an illness. **recovering, recovered.**

recreation *n* hobbies or games that people like to play.

rectangle *n* a shape with four straight sides and four corners like those of a square. Two of its sides are longer than the other two.

red 1. *n* the colour of blood. 2. *adj* having this colour.

redcurrant *n* a small round red berry.

reduce *v* to make something smaller or less. **reducing, reduced.**

reed *n* a tall grass growing by water.

reef *n* a line of rocks just below or just above the surface of the sea. *pl* **reefs.**

reel 1. *n* a round piece of wood or metal that thread or film is wound round. 2. *v* to stagger when feeling dizzy. **reeling, reeled.**

refer *v* (with **to**) to mention while talking about something else: *She referred to her dog.* **referring, referred.**

referee *n* someone who takes charge of a game and sees that the rules are obeyed.

reflect *v* 1. to show a picture of something, as a mirror does. 2. to throw back light from a shiny surface. **reflecting, reflected.**

refreshment *n* a light meal or a drink.

refrigerator *n* a special metal container for keeping food cold so that it does not go bad.

refuge *n* a place of safety or shelter.

refuse[1] (re <u>fewz</u>) *v* 1. to say you will not do what someone has asked you to do. 2. to say you do not want what someone is offering you. **refusing, refused.**

refuse[2] (<u>ref</u> yewss) *n* rubbish.

regard *v* 1. to look at. 2. to think of someone or something in a certain way. **regarding, regarded.**

regiment *n* a number of soldiers under the command of a colonel.

region *n* a part of a country or the world.

register *n* a list of names in a book.

regret *v* to be sorry about something. **regretting, regretted.**

regular *adj* 1. usual. 2. always happening at certain times: *regular sleep.*

rehearsal *n* a practice for a play or concert.

rehearse *v* to practise something, such as a play. **rehearsing, rehearsed.**

reign 1. *v* to rule as king or queen. **reigning, reigned.** 2. *n* the length of time a king or queen reigns.

rein *n* a leather strap used to guide a horse.

reindeer *n* a large deer that lives in cold northern countries. *pl* **reindeer.**

rejoice *v* to be very happy about something. **rejoicing, rejoiced.**

relate *v* to tell. **relating, related.**

relation, relative *n* someone else of the same family.

relay race *n* a race between teams with each person running only part of the way.

release *v* 1. to set someone free. 2. to let go of something. **releasing, released.**

reliable *adj* able to be trusted. *opp* **unreliable.** See **rely.**

relief *n* freedom from worry or pain.

relieve *v* 1. to end worry or pain. 2. to take over a duty from someone. **relieving, relieved.**

religion *n* belief in God or gods, and the way people worship.

religious *adj* having to do with religion.

rely (with **on**) *v* to trust. **he relies, relying, relied.** See **reliable.**

remain *v* 1. to stay behind. 2. to be left over: *some food remained.* **remaining, remained.**

remainder *n* what is left over.

remark *v* to say a few words about something you have thought or seen. **remarking, remarked.**

remarkable *adj* unusual and worth mentioning. *opp* **unremarkable.**

remedy *n* a cure. *pl* **remedies.**

remember *v* to bring something back into your mind. **remembering, remembered.**

remind *v* to make or help someone remember something. **reminding, reminded.**

remove *v* to take away. **removing, removed.**

renew *v* 1. to put something new in place of something worn: *to renew a tyre.* 2. to borrow for a further period: *to renew a library book.* **renewing, renewed.**

rent *n* I. money you pay for the use of a house, television set, or something else you do not own. 2. a tear in cloth.

repair *v* to mend. **repairing, repaired.**

repeat *v* to say or do something again. **repeating, repeated.**

repent *v* to be sorry about something you have done or said. **repenting, repented.**

replace *v* I. to put back. 2. to take the place of or put in the place of. **replacing, replaced.**

reply I. *n* an answer. *pl* **replies.** 2. *v* to answer. **he replies, replying, replied.**

report *n* I. a written or spoken account of something, such as someone's progress in school: *a school report.* 2. a loud bang.

reporter *n* someone who collects news for a newspaper, radio, or television.

represent *v* I. to be a picture or model of something. 2. to say or do something in place of someone else or a group of people. **representing, represented.**

reptile *n* an animal with cold blood, like a snake or tortoise, that lays eggs.

republic *n* a country whose head is not a king or queen, but a president who is elected.

reputation *n* what people think and say about you.

request *v* to ask politely for something. **requesting, requested.**

require *v* to need. **requiring, required.**

rescue *v* to save from danger. **rescuing, rescued.**

resemble *v* to look or sound like something or someone else. **resembling, resembled.**

reserve I. *v* to arrange for seats, library books, or something else to be kept for you until a later time. **reserving, reserved.** 2. *n* someone who will play in a game if one of the other players is hurt or unwell.

reservoir *n* a large lake or container for storing water.

resist *v* to struggle against. **resisting, resisted.**

resort *n* a place where people go for a holiday.

respect *v* to admire someone. **respecting, respected.**

respectable *adj* of good character. *opp* **unrespectable.**

responsible *adj* being in charge and taking the blame if anything goes wrong.

rest I. *n* the state of being still and quiet. 2. whoever or whatever remains: *the rest of the boys.* 3. *v* to be still and not work. **resting, rested.**

restaurant *n* a place that serves meals for payment.

restore *v* I. to make something as good as it was before: *to restore a painting.* 2. to put, bring, or give something back. **restoring, restored.**

result *n* I. the score at the end of a game. 2. the answer to a sum. 3. anything that happens because something else has happened.

retire *v* to stop working because you are too old or too ill. **retiring, retired.**

retreat *v* to go back. **retreating, retreated.**

return *v* I. to go back or come back. 2. to give back. **returning, returned.**

reveal *v* to show something that is hidden. **revealing, revealed.**

revenge *n* a wish to hurt someone who has hurt you, getting your own back.

reverse I. *v* to go backwards. **reversing, reversed.** 2. *n* the opposite side of something.

revive *v* to bring to life again. **reviving, revived.**

revolt *n* a rebellion.

revolution *n* I. a lot of people turning against the rulers of their country and overthrowing them, often with fighting and killing. 2. a complete turn of something like a wheel.

revolve *v* to turn round and round: *revolving doors.* **revolving, revolved.**

revolver *n* a pistol that fires several shots without needing to be reloaded.

reward *n* a prize given for doing a good deed.

rhinoceros *n* a large thick-skinned African or Asian animal with one or two horns on its nose. *pl* **rhinoceroses.**

rhubarb *n* a plant with long red stalks which are cooked and eaten.

rhyme *n* a word that ends with the same sound as another word. 'Blow' and 'snow' are rhymes.

rhythm n a regular beat of strong sounds in music or poetry.

rib n one of the curved bones in your chest protecting your lungs.

ribbon n a narrow strip of material used to keep long hair tidy, or for decoration: *a hair-ribbon.*

rice n white grains from a plant that grows in hot countries.

rich adj having plenty of money.

rid v to get free of something that is a nuisance: *to rid a garden of weeds.* **ridding, ridded.**

ridden see **ride.**

riddle n a puzzling question, such as: *What is black and white and red (read) all over?* (The answer is a newspaper.)

ride v to sit on (a horse or bicycle) or in (a car or train) and be carried along. **riding, rode, I have ridden.**

ridge n the top where two sloping parts meet: *the ridge of a roof.*

ridiculous adj silly.

rifle n a gun with a long barrel.

right 1. adj correct. 2. n the side or direction opposite to left. Most people use their right hand when they write. 3. adv What is good: *You did right to tell the truth.* opp **wrong.** 4. completely: *The bike went right over.*
right-handed using the right hand to write and to do most things.

rim n the edge of a cup, bowl, or wheel.

rind n the thick skin of an orange or some similar fruit, or of a slice of bacon.

ring 1. n a circle. 2. a metal band to wear on your finger. 3. v to make a bell sound. 4. to sound like a bell. 5. (often with **up**) to telephone. **ringing, rang, I have rung.**
ring-road a road built so that traffic can go round a town or city.

rink n a stretch of ice or ground for skating on.

rinse v to wash soap or dirt from something with clean water. **rinsing, rinsed.**

riot n a lot of people making a violent and noisy disturbance.

rip v to tear. **ripping, ripped.**

ripe adj (of fruit) ready to be picked and eaten. opp **unripe.**

ripple n a tiny wave on smooth water.

rise v 1. to go upwards. 2. to get up: *He rose early.* 3. to slope up: *The road rises slowly.* **rising, rose, I have risen.**

risk n a chance of harming yourself.

risky adj full of risk. **riskier, riskiest.**

rival n someone who is trying for the same prize as you.

river n a large stream of water.

road n a hard smooth way on which cars and other vehicles can travel.

roam v to travel around, going to no particular place. **roaming, roamed.**

roar v to make a low loud sound like that made by a lion. **roaring, roared.**

roast v to cook in an oven or over a fire. **roasting, roasted.**

rob v to steal from by force. **robbing, robbed.**

robber n someone who robs.

robe n a long loose dress.

robin n a small brown bird with a red breast.

robot n a machine that can move and do some things that people can do.

rock 1. n a hard substance that mountains are made of. 2. a lump of this substance. 3. a sweet, shaped like a round stick, that is sold at the seaside. 4. v to move gently backwards and forwards or from side to side. **rocking, rocked.**

rocket n 1. a firework at the end of a stick, that goes high in the air when lit. 2. a long tube-shaped machine that is shot into space by a strong jet of gases.

rod n a long round stick of wood or metal.

rode see **ride.**

rogue n a dishonest person, a cheat or swindler.

roll 1. n something made into the shape of a tube: *a roll of paper.* 2. a small round piece of bread. 3. a list of names. 4. v to turn over and over: *The ball rolled.* **rolling, rolled.**

roller n 1. a round piece of metal or plastic that rolls. 2. a tube-shaped piece of metal or plastic for making curls in the hair: *a hair-roller.* 3. a long curling wave in the sea.
roller-skate a skate with four rollers.

roof n the covering of a building or vehicle. pl **roofs.**

rook n a large black bird.

room n 1. one of the inside spaces of a house. 2. space: *There is plenty of room on the bus.*

root n the part of a plant that grows in the ground.

rope n a lot of strong fibres twisted together.

rose 1. n a beautiful flower growing on a thorny bush. 2. v see **rise.**

rosy adj having a pink colour. **rosier, rosiest.**

rot v to go bad. **rotting, rotted.**

rotten adj too bad to be eaten or used.

rough adj 1. not smooth. 2. not calm: a rough sea.

round 1. adj in the slope of a circle or ball. 2. prep and adv on all sides of something: round the house.

roundabout n 1. a circle of road where several roads meet. 2. a machine at a fair, with toy horses or cars that you ride as they go round.

rounders n pl an outside game that two teams play, using a round bat to hit a small hard ball.

rouse v to wake someone up. **rousing, roused.**

route n 1. a way of getting to a place. 2. a way that is used very often: the number 6 bus route.

row[1] (rhymes with **no**) 1. n a straight line of people or things. 2. v to make a boat move by using oars. **rowing, rowed.**

row[2] (rhymes with **now**) n 1. a quarrel. 2. a lot of noise.

royal adj having to do with a king or queen.

rub v to move one thing against another a lot of times. **rubbing, rubbed.**

rubber n 1. a substance that can stretch and bounce. It is used to make tyres, balls, and many other things. 2. a piece of soft rubber for rubbing out pencil marks.

rubbish n 1. useless things to be thrown away. 2. nonsense: Gary talks rubbish.

ruby n a red jewel. pl **rubies.**

rudder n an upright movable piece of wood or metal at the back of a ship or aeroplane, used for steering.

rude adj not polite.

rug n a small carpet to put on the floor.

rugby football n football played with an oval ball which can be handled as well as kicked.

rugged adj rough: rugged mountains.

ruin 1. n an old building that has fallen down. 2. v to spoil completely. **ruining, ruined.**

rule 1. n an order. 2. a ruler of wood or metal. 3. v to govern. **ruling, ruled.**

ruler n 1. a king, queen, or emperor. 2. a straight strip of wood, plastic, or metal for measuring or drawing lines.

rumble v to make a low rolling sound: The thunder rumbled. **rumbling, rumbled.**

rumour n a story passed round from one person to another. It may or may not be true.

run v to move quickly on your feet. **running, ran, I have run.**

rung 1. n one of the short bars of a ladder. 2. v see **ring.**

runner-up n the one next after the winner of a race or competition. pl **runners-up.**

runway n a wide long path for aeroplanes to start from and land on.

rush 1. v to move quickly. 2. to do something very quickly or too quickly. **rushing, rushed.** 3. n a plant with tall leaves growing in marshy ground.

rust n a reddish-brown coat that forms on iron and steel, caused by damp.

rustle n a soft sound like whispering.

rut n a groove made by a wheel in the ground.

Ss

Sabbath n a day in the week for rest: Saturday for Jews and Sunday for Christians.

sack n a large bag for holding things.

sacred adj very holy.

sacrifice n 1. something you value that you give up. 2. a gift to God, or a god.

sad adj unhappy. **sadder, saddest.**

saddle n a leather seat for the rider of a horse or bicycle.

safari n a journey to hunt or look at wild animals like lions and buffaloes.

safe 1. adj free from danger. 2. reliable: a safe driver. 3. n a strong box in which valuable things are locked for safety.

safety n freedom from danger.

sag v to bend low in the middle: The heavy rope sagged in the centre. **sagging, sagged.**

sage n a herb used in cooking.

said see **say.**

sail 1. n a sheet of canvas on the mast of a boat to catch the wind and make the boat move. 2. v to travel in a boat. **sailing, sailed.**

sailor n a member of a ship's crew.

saint n a man or woman who has lived a holy life.

sake n benefit: I went to the shop for your sake.

salad n a mixture of raw or cold vegetables served together and eaten.

salary n a payment every month for work done. pl **salaries.**

sale n 1. the selling of something. 2. the selling of goods at prices lower than usual, to get rid of old stock.

salmon *n* a large fish with pink flesh. *pl* **salmon.**

salt *n* a white powder used to flavour food.

salute *v* for a soldier to touch his forehead in respect to an officer. **saluting, saluted.**

same *adj* exactly alike.

sample *n* a small piece of something that shows you what the rest is like.

sand *n* tiny grains of rock that make up deserts and some beaches.

sandal *n* a light shoe fastened to your foot with straps.

sandwich *n* two slices of bread and butter with meat, jam, or some other food between.

sang see **sing.**

sank see **sink.**

sap *n* the liquid inside plants and trees.

sardine *n* a small sea-fish.

sari *n* a length of cotton or silk that an Indian woman or girl wraps round herself and wears as a dress.

sash *n* a broad ribbon, usually worn round the waist.

sat see **sit.**

satchel *n* a bag for carrying school-books.

satellite *n* 1. a planet moving round a larger planet. The moon is a satellite of the earth. 2. a man-made object that travels in space round the earth.

satin *n* a smooth shiny silk cloth.

satisfactory *adj* satisfying: *satisfactory progress at school.* *opp* **unsatisfactory.**

satisfy *v* to please someone by being good enough: *The meal satisfied him.* **satisfying, satisfied.** *opp* **dissatisfy.**

Saturday *n* the seventh day of the week.

sauce *n* a liquid with a strong flavour, added to food to make it taste better.

saucepan *n* metal pan with a handle and lid, used for cooking.

saucer *n* a round dish for a cup to stand on.

sausage *n* a tube of thin skin containing meat.

savage *adj* fierce: *a savage bull.*

save *v* 1. to free someone from danger. 2. to keep something for use later on: *to save money.* **saving, saved.**

saw 1. *n* a metal tool with sharp points along one edge for cutting wood. 2. *v* to cut with a saw. **sawing, sawed, I have sawed** or **sawn.** 3. see **see.**

sawdust *n* powdered wood from sawing.

say *v* to use your voice to make words. **saying, said.**

saying *n* wise words that are often said, such as 'Least said, soonest mended'.

scab *n* a crust that forms over a cut on your skin.

scaffolding *n* a frame of poles and planks round a building that is being built or repaired.

scald *n* a burn from boiling liquid or steam.

scale *n* 1. one of the thin flakes on the skin of many fish and reptiles. 2. a set of musical notes, like steps.

scales *n pl* a pair of pans with a weight in one pan, used for weighing things.

scalp *n* the skin and hair on top of your head.

scamper *v* to run quickly. **scampering, scampered.**

scar *n* a mark left on your skin after a cut or a burn has healed.

scarce *adj* 1. less than is needed: *In a famine food is scarce.* 2. rare.

scare *v* to frighten. **scaring, scared.**

scarecrow *n* a figure dressed like a man, set up in a field to frighten birds from a farmer's crops.

scarf *n* a length of cloth worn round the neck. *pl* **scarfs** or **scarves.**

scarlet *n* a very bright red colour.

scatter *v* 1. to throw or fall in all directions. 2. to move in all directions: *The birds scattered.* **scattering, scattered.**

scene *n* 1. a view: *a pretty scene.* 2. a part of a play. 3. a place where something happened.

scenery *n* 1. what you see out in the open air, such as hills and fields. 2. a painted cloth at the back of a stage to show where a play takes place.

scent *n* 1. a liquid with a sweet smell. 2. any sweet smell.

school *n* a place where boys and girls are taught.

schooner *n* a sailing-ship with two or more masts.

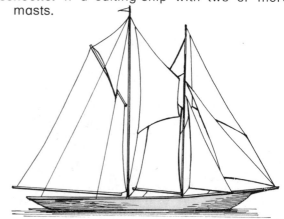

science *n* a study of some part of nature, looking for facts and doing experiments. Chemistry (the study of substances) and astronomy (the study of stars) are sciences.

scientific *adj* having to do with science. *opp* **unscientific.**

scientist *n* someone who studies a science.

scissors *n pl* a tool for cutting, with two blades fastened together and handles to move them.

scold *v* to grumble at someone angrily: *Mum scolded Nazim for being late.* **scolding, scolded.**

scone *n* a small round flat cake.

scooter *n* I. a toy with two small wheels and a handlebar. You put one foot on a board and push yourself along with the other foot. 2. a small vehicle with two wheels and a petrol engine.

scorch *v* to burn slightly. **scorching, scorched.**

score I. *n* the number of runs, points, or goals made in a game. 2. twenty: *a score of eggs.* 3. *v* in games, to make a number of runs, points, or goals. **scoring, scored.**

scorn *n* an act of showing that you think someone or something is worth very little.

scoundrel *n* a wicked person.

scour *v* I. to clean by rubbing hard. 2. to search thoroughly. **scouring, scoured.**

scout *n* a soldier sent out to spy on the enemy.

scowl *n* an angry frown.

scramble *v* I. to move quickly using hands and feet. 2. to beat up eggs with milk and butter, and cook the mixture. **scrambling, scrambled.**

scrap *n* a small piece: *a scrap of paper.*

scrape *v* to rub or smooth with something hard or sharp. **scraping, scraped.**

scratch *v* I. to make a mark on something with a sharp point. 2. to rub part of your skin that itches. **scratching, scratched.**

scrawl *n* bad writing.

scream *v* to make a loud shrill cry of pain or fear. **screaming, screamed.**

screech *n* a high shrill noise: *the screech of brakes.*

screen *n* I. the part where you see the picture on a television set or at the cinema. 2. a movable covered frame or curtain for hiding or protecting something.

screw *n* a kind of nail with a spiral groove, for fastening things together.

scribble *v* to write or draw in a quick careless way. **scribbling, scribbled.**

scripture *n* I. a sacred book such as the Bible. 2. (as a school subject) the study of the scriptures.

scroll *n* in olden times, a long sheet of paper with writing on it, that could be rolled up.

scrub *v* to clean by rubbing hard with soap and a wet brush. **scrubbing, scrubbed.**

sculptor *n* someone who carves statues or shapes, using stone, wood, metal, or clay.

sculpture *n* carving in wood, metal, or clay.

scum *n* dirty froth on the top of still water.

scurry *v* to run with little steps. **he scurries, scurrying, scurried.**

scythe *n* a long handle with a large curved blade at the end for cutting grass.

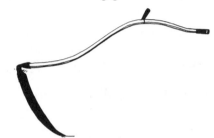

sea *n* a great stretch of salt water.

seagull *n* a sea-bird that feeds on fish.

seal I. *n* a furry animal that lives in the sea and on land. 2. *v* to fasten two things tightly together, often by using something sticky. **sealing, sealed.**

seam *n* a line where two pieces of cloth are sewn together.

search *v* I. to look everywhere for something. 2. to examine carefully: *The prisoner was searched for weapons.* **searching, searched.**

seaside *n* a place by the sea.

season I. *n* one of the four parts of the year. Their names are spring, summer, autumn, and winter. 2. a special time for something: *the football season.* 3. *v* to make food taste better by putting something like salt and pepper on it. **seasoning, seasoned.**

seat *n* something to sit on, such as a chair or bench.

seaweed *n* a plant growing in the sea.

second *n* I. a very small measure of time. There are 60 seconds in a minute. 2. the next after first: *Alec was second in the race.*

secondary *adj* next after the first: *A secondary school is the one you go to after the primary school.*

second-hand *adj* used by someone else before you.

secret *n* some news that you keep to yourself or one or two friends, and do not tell everybody.

section *n* a part: *A section of the roof is leaking.*

secure *adj* 1. safe. 2. firmly fastened.

see *v* 1. to learn something by using your eyes. 2. to understand. **seeing, saw, I have seen.**

seed *n* a small grain or nut from a plant, from which a new plant grows.

seek *v* to look for. **seeking, sought.**

seem *v* to look as if something is true or likely: *Baby seems to be asleep.* **seeming, seemed.**

seen see **see.**

seesaw *n* a plank balanced in the middle, with two people who sit one at each end and make it go up and down.

seize *v* to grab. **seizing, seized.**

seldom *adv* not often.

select *v* to choose carefully. **selecting, selected.**

self *n* one's own person: *myself (pl ourselves); yourself (pl yourselves); himself, herself, itself (pl themselves).*

selfish *adj* caring only about yourself and what you want. *opp* **unselfish.**

sell *v* to hand over something in return for money. **selling, sold.**

semi- a prefix meaning 'half': *A semicircle is half a circle.*

senate *n* a kind of parliament, as in the United States of America, Australia, and Canada.

send *v* to make something or someone go somewhere: *to send a letter.* **sending, sent.**

senior *n* and *adj* someone who is older or more important.

sensation *n* 1. a feeling. 2. great excitement.

sense *n* 1. the wisdom to know what it is best to say or do. 2. one of the five ways we get to know the world: through seeing, hearing, touching, smelling, and tasting.

sensible *adj* full of good sense.

sent see **send.**

sentence *n* 1. a number of words that make a complete statement. 2. punishment given in a court of law: *a sentence of five years in prison.*

sentry *n* a soldier on guard. *pl* **sentries.**

separate 1. *adj* not joined together. 2. *v* to put something at a distance from something else: *We separated the sheep from the goats.* **separating, separated.**

September *n* the ninth month of the year.

sergeant *n* a policeman or soldier in charge of other policemen or soldiers.

serial *n* a story told or shown in parts in a magazine or on the radio or television.

serious *adj* 1. important and requiring attention. 2. very bad: *a serious illness.*

sermon *n* a talk on religion and living a good life by a preacher in church.

serpent *n* a snake.

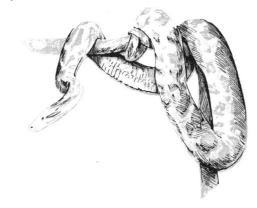

servant *n* someone who is paid to work for someone else.

serve *v* 1. to work for someone or something. 2. to bring or give out food to others at a table. 3. to sell things to people in a shop. **serving, served.**

service *n* 1. working for others. 2. duty as a soldier, sailor, or airman. 3. a religious ceremony. 4. a set of crockery: *a tea-service.*

serviette *n* a table napkin.

set 1. *n* a group of things that go together: *a set of golf clubs.* 2. a television or radio receiver. 3. *v* to put things in place: *to set the table.* 4. to go down: *The sun sets.* 5. to become solid: *A jelly sets.* **setting, set.**

settee *n* a long soft seat with a back, for two or three people.

settle *v* 1. to get comfortable and stay in a place. 2. (often with **on**) to decide something. 3. to pay a bill. **settling, settled.**

seven *n* and *adj* one more than six, 7. *adj* **seventh.**

seventeen *n* and *adj* ten more than seven, 17. *adj* **seventeenth.**

seventy *n* and *adj* ten times seven, 70. *adj* **seventieth.**

several *adj* not many, but more than two of something.

severe *adj* 1. not mild: *a severe winter.* 2. serious.

sew *v* to stitch with a needle and thread. **sewing, sewed, I have sewed** or **sewn.**
    sewing-machine a machine for sewing cloth.

sex *n* being male or female. A man, a bull, and a cock are of the male sex; a woman, a cow, and a hen are of the female sex.

shabby *adj* looking old and worn. **shabbier, shabbiest.**

shade *n* 1. a place hidden from the sun. 2. something to cut off strong light: *a lamp-shade*. 3. how light or dark a colour is: *a deep shade of blue*.

shadow *n* a patch of darkness caused by something standing in the way of a shining light.

shady *adj* full of shadows: *a shady wood*.

shaft *n* 1. a thin pole. 2. a deep hole going down into a mine. 3. a ray: *a shaft of light*.

shaggy *adj* with long untidy hair.

shake *v* to move, or make something move, quickly from side to side or up and down. **shaking, shook, I have shaken.**

shall *v* (before another verb) to say what you are going to do: *I shall read, I shall play*.

shallow *adj* not deep.

sham *adj* not real: *The ring is made of sham gold*.

shame *n* a feeling of being unhappy because you have done wrong.

shampoo *n* a liquid soap for washing hair.

shamrock *n* a plant like the three-leaved clover.

shan't short for **shall not.**

shape *n* the pattern made by a line drawn round the outside of something.

share *v* 1. to divide out. 2. to use together: *The two boys shared a bedroom*. **sharing, shared.**

shark *n* a large fish that has a lot of sharp teeth.

sharp *adj* 1. with an edge or point that can easily cut or make a hole. 2. sudden: *a sharp bend in a road*. 3. quick to notice or understand something.

sharpen *v* to make sharp. **sharpening, sharpened.**

shatter *v* to break suddenly into small pieces. **shattering, shattered.**

shave *v* to cut off hair with a razor. **shaving, shaved.**

shawl *n* a square piece of cloth folded across and worn round the shoulders or wrapped round a baby.

sheaf *n* a bundle of corn stalks tied together. *pl* **sheaves.**

shear *v* to cut the wool from a sheep. **shearing, sheared, I have shorn.**

shears *n pl* a cutting tool for trimming hedges or shearing sheep.

sheath *n* a cover for the blade of a sword or a dagger.

sheaves see **sheaf.**

shed 1. *n* a hut for storing tools or materials. 2. *v* to let fall: *to shed tears*. **shedding, shed.**

sheep *n* an animal bred for its wool, and for its meat which is called 'mutton'. *pl* **sheep.**

sheet *n* 1. a large piece of cloth used on a bed. 2. a large piece of paper, flat thin glass, or metal.

shelf *n* a board on a wall or in a cupboard for putting things on. *pl* **shelves.**

shell *n* 1. a thin hard covering round eggs, nuts, and some kinds of animals such as crabs and snails. 2. a large bullet that explodes on hitting something.

shelter *n* a place that gives protection or cover.

shelves see **shelf.**

shepherd *n* someone who looks after sheep.

sheriff *n* an important law officer of a county or district.

shield *n* 1. a large piece of armour carried in olden days by soldiers on their left arm. 2. anything that protects you.

shift *v* 1. to move something. 2. to change your position. **shifting, shifted.**

shin *n* the front of your leg between your knee and your ankle.

shine *v* 1. to give out light. **shining, shone.** 2. to polish. **shining, shined.**

shingle *n* a lot of small stones on a beach.

shiny *adj* having a surface that shines. **shinier, shiniest.**

ship *n* a large boat that sails on the sea.

shipping *n* 1. sending goods by ship. 2. all ships.

shipwreck *n* a ship that is damaged and sinks at sea.

shirt *n* a piece of clothing with a collar, sleeves, and buttons down the front.

shiver *v* to shake with fear or cold. **shivering, shivered.**

shoal *n* a large group of fish swimming together.

shock *n* 1. a sudden fright. 2. a sudden pain caused by electricity: *an electric shock*.

shocking *adj* coming as a bad surprise.

shoddy *adj* badly made, of poor quality: *a shoddy piece of work*.

shoe *n* 1. an outer covering for your foot, often made of leather. 2. a bent piece of iron nailed under a horse's hoof to protect it.

shone see **shine.**

shook see **shake.**

shoot 1. *v* to fire a bullet, shell or arrow. 2. to kick a football towards a goal. **shooting, shot.** 3. *n* a small new part growing on a plant or tree.

shop 1. *n* a building where things are sold. 2. *v* to buy from shops. **shopping, shopped.**

shore *n* land at the edge of a sea or lake.

shorn see **shear.**

short *adj* 1. not measuring a lot from end to end. 2. not taking a lot of time: *a short journey.*

shortage *n* a number or quantity of something that is smaller than that which is needed.

shorten *v* to make shorter. **shortening, shortened.**

shorts *n pl* trousers that do not cover below the knees.

shot *n* 1. the firing of a gun. 2. *pl* pellets in a cartridge that are fired from a shotgun.

shot see **shoot.**

should *v* (before another verb) ought to: *I should stay in.*

shoulder *n* the part of your body between your neck and your arm.

shout *v* to speak or call out loudly. **shouting, shouted.**

shove *v* to push hard. **shoving, shoved.**

shovel *n* a spade with a wide blade and curved-up edges, for lifting sand or coal.

show 1. *v* to let someone see something. **showing, showed, I have shown.** 2. *n* an entertainment. 3. an exhibition.

shower *n* 1. a short fall of rain or snow. 2. a wash while standing under a spray of water.

shrank see **shrink.**

shred *n* a tiny strip or scrap of something.

shriek *v* to give a piercing scream. **shrieking, shrieked.**

shrill *adj* sounding very high and loud.

shrimp *n* a small grey shellfish that turns pink when cooked.

shrink *v* to become smaller. **shrinking, shrank, it has shrunk.**

shrivel *v* to become very dry and curl up, like a dead leaf. **shrivelling, shrivelled.**

shrub *n* a bush.

shrunk see **shrink.**

shudder *v* to shake suddenly with fear or cold. **shuddering, shuddered.**

shun *v* to avoid. **shunning, shunned.**

shut *v* to move a door or lid to block up an opening. **shutting, shut.**

shy *adj* afraid to speak or to meet other people. **shyer, shyest.**

sick *adj* ill, not well.

side *n* 1. a flat surface: *the front side of a house.* 2. a team of players.

sideboard *n* a piece of dining-room furniture with drawers and cupboards.

sideways *adv* 1. with the left or right part going first. 2. moving towards the left or right.

siege *n* a time when an enemy surrounds a town or fort and stops help or food getting in.

sieve *n* a fine metal or plastic net that lets only liquids and small pieces pass through.

sigh *n* a heavy breathing out to show that you are bored, unhappy, or happy.

sight *n* 1. being able to see. 2. something that is seen: *a wonderful sight.*

sign 1. *n* a notice, drawing, or movement to tell or show people something: *road signs.* 2. *v* to write your name in your own way. **signing, signed.**

signal *n* a message sent by movement, sound, or light, when it is not possible to speak.

signature *n* your name written by yourself in your own way.

signpost *n* a post at a crossroads with arms pointing to different places.

silence *n* a time when you can hear nothing at all.

silent *adj* not making any sound.

silk *n* the fine soft thread of silkworms woven into smooth shiny cloth.

sill *n* a ledge below a window.

silly *adj* not clever or sensible. **sillier, silliest.**

silver *n* 1. a precious shiny white metal. 2. coins that are silver in colour.

similar *adj* nearly the same. *opp* **dissimilar.**

simple *adj* 1. easy. 2. plain: *a simple design.*

sin *n* an act or feeling that is very bad.

since 1. *adv* from that time until now: *I have been away since Monday.* 2. *conj* because.

sincere *adj* honest. *opp* **insincere.**

sing *v* to make a tune with your voice, using sounds or words. **singing, sang, I have sung.**

singe *v* to burn slightly. **singeing, singed.**

single *adj* I. one only. 2. unmarried: *a single man*. 3. for one only: *a single bed*. 4. for one way only: *a single railway ticket*.
to walk in single file to walk one behind another.

singular *adj* referring to one only. 'Dog' is a singular noun; 'dogs' is plural.

sink I. *n* a place in a kitchen with taps, for washing-up. 2. *v* to go under water: *The ship is sinking*. **sinking, sank, it has sunk.**

sip *v* to drink in small amounts. **sipping, sipped.**

sir *n* I. a polite way of speaking to a man. *fem* **madam.** 2. The title of a knight: *Sir John Smith*. *fem* **Lady.**

siren *n* a machine that makes a loud screaming noise to warn people about something.

sister *n* I. a girl or woman who has the same parents as someone else. *masc* **brother.** 2. a nun. 3. a senior nurse in a hospital.

sit *v* to rest on your bottom on a chair, or something similar. **sitting, sat.**

site *n* the place where something was built or will be built.

situation *n* I. position: *the situation of a building*. 2. the state of something: *What is the situation in the cricket match?*

six *n* and *adj* one more than five, 6. *adj* **sixth.**

sixteen *n* and *adj* ten more than six, 16. *adj* **sixteenth.**

sixty *n* and *adj* ten times six, 60. *adj* **sixtieth.**

size *n* how big a thing is.

sizzle *v* to make the crackling sound of something frying in a pan. **sizzling, sizzled.**

skate *n* a thin metal blade fixed under a boot for gliding on ice, or rollers worn under a shoe for gliding on the ground.

skateboard *n* a board with wheels on which you balance while it moves over the ground.

skeleton *n* the set of bones in the body of a person or an animal.

sketch *n* a quick drawing.

ski *n* one of two long pieces of wood, metal, or plastic fastened to boots for moving quickly over snow. *pl* **skis** or **ski.**

skid *n* a sudden slip on something slippery or very smooth.

skill *n* being clever at doing something: *He has great skill at football*.

skim *v* I. to take the cream off milk. 2. to glide over a surface and only just touch it. 3. (often with **through**) to read very quickly. **skimming, skimmed.**

skin *n* the outer covering of people, animals, and of some fruits and vegetables.
skin-diver a person who swims under water with a container of air to breathe but without a diving-suit.

skip *v* I. to jump lightly from one leg to the other, often over a turning rope. 2. to leave out something: *to skip the first page*. **skipping, skipped.**

skipper *n* a captain of a ship or a team.

skirt *n* a garment hanging down from the waist, worn by women and girls.

skittles *n* a game in which someone uses a ball to try to knock down pieces of wood or plastic shaped like bottles.

skull *n* the bony part of your head that holds your brain.

sky *n* the space above the earth where you can see the sun, moon, stars, and clouds. *pl* **skies.**

skylark *n* a small bird that sings in the sky.

skyscraper *n* a modern building that is very tall.

slab *n* a thick flat piece of anything.

slack *adj* I. loose: *a slack rope*. 2. lazy: *a slack worker.*

slain see **slay.**

slam *v* to close something with a loud noise: *to slam a door*. **slamming, slammed.**

slanting *adj* sloping: *a slanting roof.*

slap *v* to hit with the open hand. **slapping, slapped.**

slash *v* to make long cuts with a knife or sword. **slashing, slashed.**

slate *n* one of the small thin sheets of grey rock used to cover a roof.

slaughter *n* killing people or animals in large numbers.

slave *n* a person who is not free but is owned by a master.

slay *v* to kill. **slaying, slew, I have slain.**

sled, sledge *n* a low platform with two smooth strips on which it moves over snow.

sleep *v* to rest completely with closed eyes, as people do at night. **sleeping, slept.**

sleet *n* a mixture of rain and snow.

sleeve *n* the part of a garment that covers your arm.

sleigh *n* a sledge pulled by an animal.

slender *adj* thin: *a slender poplar tree.*

slept see **sleep.**

slew see **slay.**

slice *n* a thin flat piece cut from something: *a slice of bacon.*

slide I. *v* to glide smoothly along. **sliding, slid.** 2. *n* a small photograph or picture that is shown on a screen.

slight *adj* I. small: *a slight cold.* 2. thin: *a slight old invalid.*

slim *adj* thin: *a slim person.* **slimmer, slimmest.**

slime *n* wet slippery mud or anything else that is wet and slippery.

slimy adj covered with slime. **slimier, slimiest.**

sling I. *n* a loop of cloth wrapped round an injured arm and tied round the neck to support the arm. 2. a strip of leather used in olden days to throw stones. 3. *v* to fling. **slinging, slung.**

slink *v* to move quickly in a sly way or because you feel guilty about something. **slinking, slunk.**

slip I. *v* to slide a little way by accident. 2. (often with **away** or **off**) to move away quietly. **slipping, slipped.** 3. *n* a small mistake.

slipper *n* a soft shoe for wearing indoors.

slippery *adj* having a surface so smooth that it is difficult to walk on or get hold of.

slit *n* a long cut or narrow opening.

slope *v* to be higher at one end than the other. **sloping, sloped.**

slot *n* a narrow opening.

slovenly *adj* I. untidy. 2. careless.

slow *adj* I. taking a long time. 2. behind time: *The clock is slow.* 3. not good at learning.

slug *n* I. a kind of snail with no shell. 2. a pellet.

slunk see **slink.**

slush *n* melting snow.

sly *adj* clever at doing things in a secret way. **slyer, slyest.**

smack *v* to hit with the open hand. **smacking, smacked.**

small *adj* little.

smart I. *adj* quick to understand. 2. neat and well-dressed. 3. *v* (of a wound) to give a stinging pain. **smarting, smarted.**

smash *v* to break into pieces. **smashing, smashed.**

smear *v* I. to rub something sticky over a surface. 2. to make a dirty mark by rubbing. **smearing, smeared.**

smell I. *v* to be aware of something by breathing through your nose. 2. to give off a smell. **smelling, smelt** or **smelled.** 3. *n* anything that can be smelt. 4. one of our five senses.

smile *v* to widen your lips showing you are pleased or happy. **smiling, smiled.**

smoke I. *n* the dark cloud that floats up from something burning. 2. *v* to burn tobacco in a cigarette or pipe, take in the smoke through the mouth, and breathe it out. **smoking, smoked.**

smooth *adj* having no rough parts.

smother *v* I. to cover all over. 2. to stop someone breathing by covering the mouth and nose. **smothering, smothered.**

smoulder *v* to burn slowly without a flame but with a lot of smoke. **smouldering, smouldered.**

smudge *n* a dirty mark made by rubbing.

smuggle *v* to take goods into or out of a country secretly when it is against the law. **smuggling, smuggled.**

snack *n* a light meal that is easy to get ready.

snail *n* a small slow-moving creature with a shell on its back.

snake *n* a long smooth reptile without legs, that glides along the ground.

snap *v* I. to break suddenly. 2. to speak in a sudden angry way. **snapping, snapped.**

snare *n* a hidden loop used to trap an animal.

snarl *v* to growl and show the teeth. **snarling, snarled.**

snatch *v* to grab. **snatching, snatched.**

sneak I. *v* to move, trying not to be seen or heard. **sneaking, sneaked.** 2. *n* someone who tells tales.

sneer *v* to show a feeling of scorn. **sneering, sneered.**

sneeze *v* to make a sudden noise when air rushes out of your nose because it tickles. **sneezing, sneezed.**

sniff *v* to breathe air in quickly through your nose. **sniffing, sniffed.**

snip (often with **off**) *v* to cut a little bit off something. **snipping, snipped.**

snob *n* someone who only bothers with people that he or she thinks are important, clever, or rich.

snooker *n* a game played on a big table with long sticks, or cues, and twenty-two coloured balls.

snooze *v* to doze. **snoozing, snoozed.**

snore *v* to breathe very noisily while you are asleep. **snoring, snored.**

snorkel *n* a tube for someone to breathe through while swimming just beneath the surface of water.

snout *n* an animal's nose that sticks out like that of a pig.

snow *n* frozen water that falls from the clouds as soft white flakes.

snowdrop *n* a little white flower growing from a bulb and appearing in early spring.

snowplough *n* a machine for clearing snow from the roads.

snug *adj* cosy. **snugger, snuggest.**

snuggle *v* to lie or sit close to someone so that you become warm and comfortable. **snuggling, snuggled.**

soak *v* to make something very wet: *We were soaked by the rain.* **soaking, soaked.**

soap *n* something that is used with water for washing.

soar *v* to rise high into the sky. **soaring, soared.**

sob *v* to cry noisily. **sobbing, sobbed.**

soccer *n* a game played by two teams of eleven players with a round ball.

sociable *adj* (of a person) friendly and fond of company. *opp* **unsociable.**

sock *n* a covering for your foot and ankle, or your foot and the lower part of your leg.

socket *n* a special hole into which something fits: *a socket for an electric plug.*

sofa *n* a long soft seat with arms and a back, for two or more people.

soft *adj* 1. not hard. 2. not strong: *a soft wind.* 3. quiet: *a soft voice.*

soggy *adj* soaked with water. **soggier, soggiest.**

soil *n* ground in which plants grow.

solar *adj* having to do with the sun.

sold see **sell.**

soldier *n* someone who belongs to an army.

sole *n* the part underneath a foot, sock, or shoe.

solemn *adj* serious: *a solemn face.*

solid *adj* 1. firm and not changing its shape: *solid ice.* 2. not hollow.

solo *n* something done by one person alone: *a solo flight. pl* **solos.**

solution *n* the answer to a problem or mystery.

solve *v* to find the answer to a problem or mystery. **solving, solved.**

some *adj* 1. a few. 2. an amount of: *some money* 3. one or other: *We shall find some way out of the wood.*
　somebody, someone some person.
　something some thing.
　sometimes at some time.
　somewhere in some place.

somersault *n* a jump head over heels.

son *n* boy or man who is someone's child.

song *n* 1. words that are sung. 2. the musical sounds of a bird.

soon *adv* in a short time: *It will soon be Sunday.*

soot *n* black powder that comes from smoke.

soothe *v* to make someone who is upset feel calmer. **soothing, soothed.**

sorcerer *n* a magician who works spells.

sore *adj* painful: *a sore tooth.*

sorrow *n* sadness.

sorry *adj* feeling unhappy at something that has happened, or something you have done.

sort 1. *n* a kind: *all sorts of flowers.* 2. *v* to put things in groups of the same kind: *to sort letters.* **sorting, sorted.**

sought see **seek.**

soul *n* the part of a person that cannot be seen but is thought to go on living after the person has died.

sound 1. *n* anything that can be heard. 2. *v* to make sounds: *The music sounds lovely.* **sounding, sounded.** 3. *adj* in good condition: *These plums are sound.*

soup *n* a liquid food made by boiling meat or vegetables in water.

sour *adj* 1. with the sort of taste that lemons and vinegar have. 2. not fresh: *sour milk.*

source *n* the place where something has come from: *the source of a river.*

south *n* the direction to your left as you face the setting sun.
　South Pole the place that is furthest south in the world.

southern *adj* in or of the south.

souvenir *n* something kept because it reminds you of a place or person: *a souvenir of London.*

sovereign *n* a king, queen, emperor, or empress.

sow¹ (rhymes with **now**) *n* a female pig or hog. *masc* **boar.** *young* **piglet.**

sow² (rhymes with **go**) *v* to put seeds in the ground so that plants will grow up from them. **sowing, sowed.**

space *n* 1. the distance between things. 2. a place that is empty: *a space to sit in*. 3. all the places beyond the earth's atmosphere. **spaceship** a rocket that can carry astronauts through space.

spacious *adj* having plenty of space.

spade *n* 1. a long-handled garden tool with a blade for digging the ground. 2. one of the four kinds of playing cards.

spaghetti *n* long tubes of flour paste used for food.

span *n* the distance between the tips of the thumb and the little finger when the fingers are spread out.

spaniel *n* a dog with long hair and hanging ears.

spank *v* to hit someone on the bottom. **spanking, spanked.**

spanner *n* a tool that can turn a nut and make it tighter or looser.

spare 1. *adj* not being used but kept in case it is needed: *spare paint*. 2. *v* to give or lend something: *Can you spare me some paper?* **sparing, spared.**

spark *n* 1. a speck of something burning. 2. a tiny electric flash.

sparkle *v* to glitter. **sparkling, sparkled.**

sparrow *n* a small brown and grey bird.

spat see **spit.**

spatter *v* to splash with rain or mud: *spattered with mud.* **spattering, spattered.**

spawn *n* the eggs of fish, frogs, newts and some other water creatures.

speak *v* to say something. **speaking, spoke, I have spoken.**

spear *n* a long-handled weapon with a very sharp point.

special *adj* of a particular kind or for a particular use: *special clothing*.

speck *n* a tiny bit: *a speck of dirt or soot*.

speckled *adj* marked with small spots.

spectacles *n pl* a pair of glass or plastic lenses held in front of the eyes in a frame so that someone can see better.

spectator *n* someone who watches a game, or show.

speech *n* 1. a talk given to some people. 2. the power of speaking.

speed *n* how quickly something moves or happens.

spell 1. *v* to write or say the letters of a word. **spelling, spelt** or **spelled.** 2. *n* (in fairy tales) magic words spoken to make something happen.

spend *v* 1. to pay out money. 2. to use time: *Philip spent his time swimming*. **spending, spent.**

sphere *n* any object shaped like a ball.

spice *n* part of a plant used to flavour food, as ginger or nutmeg.

spider *n* a small creature with eight legs and no wings. Many types of spiders spin webs.

spied see **spy.**

spike *n* a long sharp point.

spill *v* to let a liquid overflow. **spilling, spilt** or **spilled.**

spin *v* 1. to turn round quickly. 2. to make threads: *to spin wool or cotton*. **spinning, spun.**

spinach *n* a kind of green vegetable.

spine *n* 1. a long set of bones that fit together down the middle of the back of people and of many animals. 2. a thorn. 3. a spike on a hedgehog.

spinster *n* an unmarried woman. *masc* **bachelor.**

spiral *n* and *adj* a curve shaped like a clock-spring or the thread of a screw: *a spiral staircase*.

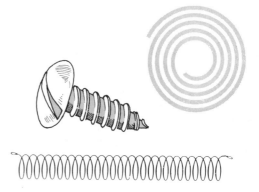

spire *n* a tall pointed part on top of a tower, often on a church.

spirit *n* 1. a person's soul. 2. a ghost. 3. courage and energy.

spit *v* to send something out of your mouth. **spitting, spat.**

spite *n* a wish to hurt someone by cruel words or behaviour: *He broke the toy out of spite*.

splash 1. *n* the noise made when someone or something heavy falls into water. 2. *v* to scatter liquid about. **splashing, splashed.**

splendid *adj* wonderful.

splinter *n* a sharp chip of wood, metal, or glass.

split *v* to crack, to break open from end to end. **splitting, split.**

spoil v 1. to make something less good or less useful. 2. to be too kind to someone, especially a child. **spoiling, spoiled** or **spoilt**.

spoke 1. n one of the rods from the hub to the rim of a wheel. 2. v see **speak**.

sponge n 1. a light soft cake. 2. a soft yellow material full of holes. It soaks up water and is used for washing.

spoon n a little bowl at the end of a handle, used for stirring and eating with.

sport n an active game that usually takes place outside. Football, hockey, and running are all sports.

spot 1. n a small mark. 2. a place. 3. v to notice. **spotting, spotted**.

spout n a short tube that is part of a container through which a liquid flows: the spout of a kettle.

sprain v to twist the wrist, ankle, or shoulder so that it becomes painful. **spraining, sprained**.

sprang see **spring**.

sprawl v to sit or lie with arms and legs spread out. **sprawling, sprawled**.

spray v to scatter fine drops of liquid all over something. **spraying, sprayed**.

spread v 1. to make something cover a surface: to spread jam on bread. 2. to open out: The eagle spread its wings. **spreading, spread**.

spring 1. n the season between winter and summer. 2. a place where water flows out of the ground. 3. a metal spiral that goes back into shape after it has been pressed or stretched. 4. v to jump up suddenly. **springing, sprang, I have sprung**.

sprinkle v to scatter powder or drops of liquid: He sprinkled salt on his food. **sprinkling, sprinkled**.

sprint v to run very quickly for a short distance. **sprinting, sprinted**.

sprout v (of a plant) to start to grow. **sprouting, sprouted**.

sprung see **spring**.

spun see **spin**.

spur n an instrument on a horse-rider's heel, to make the horse go faster.

spurt v 1. (of a liquid) to gush out suddenly in a jet. 2. to try to go faster at the end of a race. **spurting, spurted**.

spy 1. v to watch secretly. **spying, spied**. 2. n someone who tries secretly to find out things about a person or an enemy country. pl **spies**.

squabble v to quarrel over something that is not important. **squabbling, squabbled**.

square n 1. a flat shape with four equal sides and four equal angles. 2. an open space in a city or town.

squash 1. v to crush. 2. to squeeze. **squashing, squashed**. 3. n a drink made from crushed fruit: lemon squash.

squaw n a North American Indian woman.

squeak n the faint high sound that a mouse makes.

squeal n a long high cry: the squeals of pigs.

squeeze v to press something hard. **squeezing, squeezed**.

squint n a cross-eyed look.

squirm v to wriggle. **squirming, squirmed**.

squirrel n an animal with a long fluffy tail that lives in trees.

squirt v to shoot out liquid in a fine stream. **squirting, squirted**.

stab v to wound someone with a pointed weapon. **stabbing, stabbed**.

stable n a building in which horses are kept.

stack n a heap of things one on top of another: a stack of bricks.

staff n a group of people working together in a school, shop, or office.

stag n a male deer. fem **hind**. young **fawn**.

stage n 1. a platform in a theatre or hall for plays or concerts. 2. the point someone has reached in doing something. **stage-coach** a coach with horses taking people from town to town.

stagger v to walk in an unsteady way. **staggering, staggered**.

stain n 1. a spot of a different colour that has marked something. 2. a dye that changes the colour of something.

stairs n a set of steps leading from one floor of a building to another.

stake n a thick pointed post.

stale adj not fresh: stale bread.

stalk 1. n the stem of a plant. 2. v to follow an animal quietly, keeping out of sight, to watch or catch it. **stalking, stalked**.

stall n 1. a table in a market for selling things. 2. a place for a cow or horse to stand in a cattle-shed or stable.

stallion n a male horse. fem **mare**. young **foal**.

stammer v to speak nervously, repeating the sounds at the beginning of words. **stammering, stammered**.

stamp 1. n a piece of sticky printed paper, used for sending letters. 2. v to bang your foot on the ground. **stamping, stamped**.

stand l. *v* to be on your feet, or rise to your feet. 2. to bear: *I can't stand the noise.* 3. to mean: *kg stands for kilogramme.* **standing, stood.** 4. *n* rows of raised seats, often covered with a roof, from which people watch a game.

star *n* l. a very big object in space that looks like a point of bright light in the sky at night. 2. a popular actor or singer.

starboard *n* the right side of a ship looking forward towards the bow. *opp* of **port.**

stare *v* (with **at**) to watch someone or something for a long time with a steady look. **staring, stared.**

starling *n* a dark speckled bird often seen in flocks.

start *v* l. to be at the first stage of doing something. 2. to make something happen: *to start an engine.* **starting, started.**

startle *v* to make a person or animal feel surprised or frightened. **startling, startled.**

starve *v* to be very ill or die because there is not enough food to eat. **starving, starved.**

state *n* l. how someone or something is: *a bad state of health.* 2. one of the main parts of some countries: *the United States.*

statement *n* something important that is said or written.

station *n* l. a stopping-place on a railway. 2. a building used by the police or firemen.

stationery *n* writing-paper and envelopes.

statue *n* the figure of a person or animal, in wood, stone, or metal.

stay *v* l. to be in one place. 2. to live somewhere that is not your home for a short time: *We stayed in a hotel.* **staying, stayed.**

steady *adj* l. firm: *the ladder was steady. opp* **unsteady.** 2. not changing: *a steady rain.* **steadier, steadiest.**

steak *n* a thick slice of meat or fish for cooking.

steal *v* to take something that is not yours and keep it. **stealing, stole, I have stolen.**

steam *n* clouds of gas from boiling water.

steamer *n* a ship with an engine that works by the power of steam.

steel *n* a strong metal made from iron.

steel band *n* a West Indian Band, with instruments made from old oil drums.

steep *adj* sloping sharply: *a steep hill.*

steeple *n* a church tower with a spire.

steer l. *v* to make a ship or vehicle go where you want. **steering, steered.** 2. *n* a young bull.

stem *n* l. the main part of a plant. 2. the thin part of a plant that holds up a leaf, flower, or fruit.

step *n* l. a movement in one direction made by your foot. 2. the part of a stair or ladder on which you tread.

stepfather *n* your new father, if your mother married a second time. *fem* **stepmother.**

step-ladder *n* a folding pair of ladders.

stereo *n* a record-player with two loudspeakers.

stern l. *adj* strict or severe. 2. *n* the back part of a ship or boat.

stew *n* meat and vegetables cooked together in water.

stick l. *n* a long thin piece of wood. 2. a thin piece of anything: *a stick of chalk.* 3. *v* to fasten or be fastened. **sticking, stuck.**

sticky *adj* able to stick to something. **stickier, stickiest.**

stiff *adj* not easy to move or bend.

stile *n* a step or steps on each side of a fence or wall to help you get over it.

still l. *adj* quiet and with no movement: *a still day.* 2. *adv* now as before: *He is still in bed.*

stilts *n pl* two poles with a step at the side, for walking high above the ground.

sting *v* (of some animals and plants) to prick someone with a sharp point holding poison. **stinging, stung.**

stir *v* l. to mix soft or liquid things by moving them round with a spoon. 2. to start to move: *The baby stirred after a long sleep.* **stirring, stirred.**

stirrups *n pl* a rider's footrests hanging from each side of a horse's saddle.

stitch *n* l. (in sewing and knitting) a loop of thread made with a needle. 2. a sharp pain in your side.

stoat *n* a small, fierce, wild animal that kills and eats other animals such as rabbits and mice.

stock *n* a lot of things kept to be used or sold: *a stock of coal.*

stocking *n* a long close-fitting cover for the leg and foot.

stoke *v* to put solid fuel on a fire. **stoking, stoked.**

stole, stolen see **steal.**

stomach *n* a kind of bag in your body where food goes when you have eaten it. *pl* **stomachs.**

stone *n* 1. rock. 2. a small piece of rock. 3. the large hard seed of some fruits: *a plum-stone.* 4. a jewel: *a precious stone.*

stood see **stand.**

stool *n* a small seat with no back.

stoop *v* to bend forward and downward. **stooping, stooped.**

stop 1. *v* to end. 2. to bring to an end. 3. to come to rest: *The plane stopped.* **stopping, stopped.** 4. *n* a place where a bus or train stops for passengers.

store 1. *n* a large shop: *a grocery store.* 2. *v* to keep a supply of goods to use in the future. **storing, stored.**

storey *n* one floor of a building and all the rooms on it. *pl* **storeys.**

stork *n* a large bird with a long beak, neck, and legs.

storm *n* bad weather with heavy rain or snow, strong winds, and, sometimes, thunder.

story *n* words that tell you about something that has really happened or that someone has imagined. *pl* **stories.**

stout *adj* fat: *a stout old man.*

stove *n* something that provides heat for cooking or heating.

stowaway *n* someone who hides in a ship or aircraft to travel free.

straight *adj* and *adv* in one direction without a curve.
straight away at once.

straighten *v* to make straight: *He straightened his tie.* **straightening, straightened.**

strain *v* 1. to stretch, pull, push, or try too much. 2. to hurt a part of your body by trying too hard to do something. **straining, strained.**

straits *n pl* a narrow channel connecting two seas.

stranded *adj* 1. (of a ship) driven ashore. 2. (of a person) lost without money or help.

strange *adj* 1. unusual. 2. not known to you: *a strange bird.*

stranger *n* someone you have not seen before.

strap *n* a strip of leather, plastic, or cloth.

straw *n* 1. dried stems of corn. 2. a thin tube for drinking through.

strawberry *n* the juicy red fruit of a plant that grows close to the ground. *pl* **strawberries.**

stray *v* to wander and get lost. **straying, strayed.**

streak *n* a stripe: *a streak of paint.*

stream *n* 1. a small river. 2. a flow of air or people.

street *n* a road with buildings on either side.

strength *n* being strong: *A carthorse has great strength.*

stretch 1. *v* to make something longer, wider, or tighter by pulling it. 2. to go from one place to another, as a road does. **stretching, stretched.** 3. *n* an area: *a stretch of grassland.*

stretcher *n* a bed of canvas with two poles for carrying people who are sick or hurt.

strict *adj* insisting on always being obeyed.

stride *v* to walk with long steps. **striding, strode, I have stridden.**

strike *v* 1. to touch a person or a thing with a lot of force, often hurting or doing damage. 2. to stop work until changes are made and things get better. 3. (of a clock) to ring at regular intervals so that people know what time it is. **striking, struck.**
to strike a match to rub a match along a special surface so that it bursts into flame.

string *n* a thin cord for tying things.

strip 1. *n* a long narrow piece of anything. 2. *v* to take off a covering or clothes: *to strip a bed.* **stripping, stripped.**

stripe *n* a long narrow band of colour.

strode see **stride.**

stroke 1. *v* to rub gently. **stroking, stroked.** 2. *n* a hit: *a stroke with a cricket bat.*

stroll *v* to go for a slow walk. **strolling, strolled.**

strong *adj* 1. able to do things that need a lot of energy. 2. hard to break: *a strong stick.* 3. having a lot of flavour: *strong tea.*

struck see **strike.**

struggle *v* 1. to make a great effort in fighting or trying to get free. 2. to try hard to do something that you do not find easy. **struggling, struggled.**

stubborn *adj* obstinate.

stuck see **stick.**

student *n* someone who studies at a college or university.

studio *n* 1. a place where television or radio programmes or films are made. 2. a place where an artist or photographer works. *pl* **studios.**

study *v* I. to learn about something. 2. to look at carefully. **studying, studied.**

stuff *v* to fill something tightly: *a drawer stuffed with toys.* **stuffing, stuffed.**

stuffy *adj* having no fresh air: *a stuffy room.* **stuffier, stuffiest.**

stumble *v* to knock your foot against something and nearly fall. **stumbling, stumbled.**

stump *n* I. the part of a tree left in the ground after the trunk has been cut down. 2. (in cricket) one of the three sticks in the wicket.

stun *v* I. to knock someone unconscious, or nearly so. 2. to give someone shocking or very surprising news. **stunning, stunned.**

stung see **sting.**

stupid *adj* I. silly. 2. not intelligent.

sturdy *adj* strong and healthy. **sturdier, sturdiest.**

stutter *v* to stammer. **stuttering, stuttered.**

sty *n* a place where pigs are kept. *pl* **sties.**

style *n* a way of doing or making something.

subject *n* I. a matter that is being talked or written about or studied. 2. a person ruled by a king, queen, or government: *a British subject.*

submarine *n* a ship that can travel under water.

submit *v* to surrender. **submitting, submitted.**

substance *n* any material.

subtract *v* to take away: *Subtract 5 from 7 and 2 is left.* **subtracting, subtracted.**

subtraction *n* the act of taking away numbers.

subway *n* a tunnel under a busy road, for people to walk through and get to the other side.

succeed *v* I. to manage to do what you are trying to do. 2. to follow and take the place of somebody: *King George II succeeded George I.* **succeeding, succeeded.**

success *n* a person or thing that succeeds in what was attempted.

such *adj* I. so much. 2. of the same kind: *flowers such as these.*

suck *v* I. to draw something into your mouth: *to suck lemonade through a straw.* 2. to roll something in your mouth, but not chew it: *to suck a sweet.* **sucking, sucked.**

sudden *adj* quick and usually unexpected.

suffer *v* to feel pain or sorrow. **suffering, suffered.**

sufficient *adj* enough: *sufficient money.* opp **insufficient.**

sugar *n* a sweet food used in cooking and put in drinks to give a sweet taste.

suggest *v* to offer an idea to other people. **suggesting, suggested.**

suit I. *n* a matching set of clothes such as jacket and trousers. 2. *v* to fit in with someone's plans: *Your idea suits me.* 3. to look well on someone: *That dress suits you.* **suiting, suited.**

suitable *adj* right: *a suitable gift.* opp **unsuitable.**

suitcase *n* a box with a handle for carrying things on journeys.

sulk *v* not to speak to people because you are angry that you did not get what you wanted. **sulking, sulked.**

sultana *n* a small raisin containing no seeds.

sum *n* I. the total amount when you add things together. 2. a problem that has to do with numbers.

summer *n* the warmest season of the year, between spring and autumn.

summit *n* the top: *the summit of a mountain.*

sun *n* the bright star that we see during the day and which sends us heat and light.

sunbeam *n* a ray of sunshine.

sunburn *n* the burning of your skin by the sun.

Sunday *n* the first day of the week.

sundial *n* an instrument that shows the time by the position of a shadow that falls on to a dial.

sung see **sing.**

sunk see **sink.**

sunny *adj* lit up with sunshine. **sunnier, sunniest.**

sunrise *n* the time when the sun comes up.

sunset *n* the time when the sun goes down.

sunshine *n* the light of the sun when it is shining.

supermarket *n* a large shop where people take from the shelves the things that they want and pay for them as they leave.

supersonic *adj* travelling faster than sound.

superstition *n* a belief in magic, charms, and spells.

supper *n* a meal or snack eaten in the evening.

supply 1. *v* to provide what is needed. **supplying, supplied.** 2. *n* things kept ready to be used or sold: *a supply of food.* *pl* **supplies.**

support *v* 1. to hold up: *We supported the injured man.* 2. to help or encourage: *to support a football team.* **supporting, supported.**

suppose *v* 1. to think something is likely to be true or likely to happen: *I suppose he'll bring it later.* 2. to imagine: *Let's suppose that Janice is queen.* **supposing, supposed.**

sure *adj* certain that something is true or right. *opp* **unsure.**

surf *n* waves breaking in foam on the seashore.

surface *n* 1. the outside of anything: *the surface of the moon.* 2. the top of something, often a liquid: *the surface of the sea.*

surgeon *n* a doctor who does operations.

surgery *n* a room where a doctor or dentist sees patients. *pl* **surgeries.**

surname *n* a family name: *Tom Lee's surname is Lee.*

surprise 1. *n* something unexpected. 2. *v* to do something that someone does not expect: *We surprised him with our visit.* **surprising, surprised.**

surrender *v* to stop fighting and do what the enemy tells you to do. **surrendering, surrendered.**

surround *v* to be all around. **surrounding, surrounded.**

suspect *v* to think that someone has done something wrong or that something is wrong: *The police suspected him of the theft.* **suspecting, suspected.**

suspicious *adj* 1. feeling that someone has done something wrong: *I am suspicious of Tony.* 2. making you doubt something: *His behaviour is suspicious.*

swallow 1. *v* to pass food and drink down your throat. **swallowing, swallowed.** 2. *n* a blue and white bird with a forked tail.

swam see **swim.**

swamp *n* an area of soft, very wet ground.

swan *n* a large white water-bird with a long neck.

swap *v* to change one thing for another. **swapping, swapped.**

swarm *n* a large group of insects: *a swarm of bees.*

sway *v* to rock from side to side. **swaying, swayed.**

swear *v* 1. to make a solemn promise. 2. to use bad language. **swearing, swore, I have sworn.**

sweat *n* the moisture from your skin when you are very hot or ill.

sweater *n* a heavy woollen pullover.

sweep 1. *v* to clean the floor or ground with a brush or broom. **sweeping, swept.** 2. *n* someone who cleans chimneys.

sweet 1. *adj* tasting like sugar. 2. pleasant to smell. 3. *n* a piece of sweet food. 4. a pudding.

swell *v* to get bigger. **swelling, swelled, it has swollen** or **swelled.**

swept see **sweep.**

swerve *v* to change direction suddenly: *The car swerved.* **swerving, swerved.**

swift 1. *adj* fast. 2. *n* a bird with a forked tail like a swallow.

swim *v* to move through water using your arms and legs. **swimming, swam, I have swum.**

swing 1. *v* (of something fixed at the top or one side) to move from side to side, backwards and forwards, or in a curve. **swinging, swung.** 2. *n* a seat hanging on ropes or chains for you to sit on and move backwards and forwards.

switch 1. *n* a little knob or lever to turn electricity on or off. 2. *v* to change from one thing to another. **switching, switched.**

swollen see **swell.**

swoop *v* to move down quickly: *The eagle swooped on the lamb.* **swooping, swooped.**

sword *n* a long steel blade with a handle, used in olden days as a weapon.

swore, sworn see **swear.**

swum see **swim.**

swung see **swing.**

sycamore *n* a tall tree with broad leaves.

syllable *n* a part of a word. '<u>Win</u> <u>ter</u>' has two syllables.

symmetrical *adj* having two halves that are exactly alike but opposite ways round.

sympathy *n* a feeling of being sorry for someone who is ill, sad, or in trouble.

synagogue *n* a Jewish church.

syrup *n* a thick sweet sticky liquid.

Tt

table *n* 1. a piece of furniture with a flat top and legs. 2. facts set out in columns on paper: *a multiplication table.*
  table-tennis a game played on a table with round bats and a small light ball.

tablet *n* a small flat piece of medicine.

tack *v* to sew two things together using long stitches. **tacking, tacked.**

tackle 1. *v* to try to do something hard: *The boys tackled the job.* 2. (in a game like football) to try to get the ball from someone. **tackling, tackled.** 3. *n* the things you need for some kinds of sport or job: *fishing tackle.*

tadpole *n* a small creature that comes from spawn and turns into a frog or toad.

tail *n* 1. the movable end of an animal, fish, or bird. 2. the end part of an aeroplane.

tailor *n* someone who makes clothes.

take *v* 1. to get hold of and carry. 2. to lead or carry away: *I'll take you to the house.* **taking, took, I have taken.**

tale *n* a story: *a fairy-tale.*

talent *n* being able to do something very well: *Darren has a real talent for painting.*

talk *v* to say something. **talking, talked.**

talkative *adj* fond of talking.

tall *adj* higher than usual.

tambourine *n* a musical instrument that you shake or knock on gently.

tame *adj* (of an animal) not wild or dangerous: *a tame elephant.*

tamper (with **with**) *v* to make changes in something without permission: *Do not tamper with the television set or you will spoil the picture.* **tampering, tampered.**

tan 1. *n* a light brown colour. 2. *v* to make animal skins into leather. **tanning, tanned.**

tangerine *n* a small kind of orange.

tangle *v* to get something in a muddle: *to tangle a ball of wool.* **tangling, tangled.** *opp* **untangle.**

tank *n* 1. a large container, usually of metal, for holding liquid or gas. 2. a kind of large armoured car moving on two metal belts instead of wheels, and with a large gun on top.

tanker *n* 1. a large ship for carrying oil. 2. a large lorry for carrying liquids.

tap 1. *n* a small handle to let water or gas flow from a pipe. 2. *v* to knock gently. **tapping, tapped.**

tape *n* 1. a long narrow strip of cloth, gummed paper, or plastic. 2. a long narrow plastic strip used in a tape-recorder.
  tape-recorder a machine that takes down music or speech on a special plastic tape which can be played back later.

taper *v* to get thinner towards one end. **tapering, tapered.**

tar *n* a thick black sticky substance used in making roads.

target *n* something that people aim at with a gun or other weapon and try to hit.

tart *n* a pie of fruit or jam on pastry.

tartan *n* woollen cloth with a pattern of stripes and squares, often used for making kilts.

task *n* a piece of work to be done.

taste *v* to eat or drink a little of something to try its flavour. **tasting, tasted.**

tasty *adj* having a nice flavour: *a tasty pudding.* **tastier, tastiest.**

tattered *adj* badly torn: *a tattered old coat.*

taught see **teach.**

taunt *v* to make unkind remarks to someone. **taunting, taunted.**

tax *n* money which has to be paid to the government by the people. *pl* **taxes.**

taxi *n* a car that you pay to ride in. *pl* **taxis.**

tea *n* 1. a plant growing in parts of Asia whose dried leaves make a drink when boiling water is poured on them. 2. an afternoon meal with a drink of tea.

teach *v* to show people how to do things or make them able to understand something. **teaching, taught.**

teacher *n* someone whose job is to teach.

team *n* 1. a group of people playing together in a match. 2. a group of animals or people working together: *a team of workmen.*

tear¹ (rhymes with **clear**) *n* a drop of water falling from your eye.

tear² (rhymes with **pair**) *v* to pull something apart so that it is damaged. **tearing, tore, I have torn.**

tease *v* to worry or annoy someone for fun. **teasing, teased.**

teddy bear *n* a toy bear made of yellow cloth.

tedious *adj* boring, dull: *a tedious job*.

teenager *n* someone between thirteen and nineteen years of age.

teeth see **tooth.**

telegram *n* a written message that the post office sends very quickly along electric wires.

telegraph pole *n* a tall pole that holds up the telephone wires.

telephone *n* an instrument that lets you speak to anyone else who has a telephone by sending your voice along electric wires.

telescope *n* a tube with glass lenses that makes distant things look larger and nearer when you look through them.

television *n* an instrument that can receive sound and pictures sent through the air.

tell *v* to pass on information or instructions by speaking. **telling, told.**

temper *n* the mood someone is in: *a good temper*.
　to lose your temper to be very angry.

temperature *n* how hot or cold something is.

temple *n* 1. a church for prayer and worship. 2. one of the two parts at the ends of your forehead, just above your cheeks.

tempt *v* to try to get someone to do something that is enjoyable but wrong. **tempting, tempted.**

ten *n* and *adj* one more than nine, 10. *adj* **tenth.**

tender *adj* 1. not tough: *tender meat*. 2. sore. 3. gentle.

tennis *n* a game played by two or four players with rackets and a ball which is knocked over a net.

tent *n* a canvas shelter held up by poles or metal frame, and ropes.

term *n* one of the three parts of the school year between the main holidays.

terminus *n* the place at the end of a railway line or bus route. *pl* **termini.**

terrace *n* 1. a row of houses joined together. 2. a raised flat piece of land, especially in front of a large house.

terrible *adj* dreadful: *a terrible accident*.

terrier *n* one of several kinds of small dog.

terrific *adj* enormous: *a terrific bang*.

terrify *v* to make a person or animal very frightened. **terrifying, terrified.**

territory *n* a large area of land. *pl* **territories.**

terror *n* great fear.

test 1. *n* questions asked to find out how well someone has learned a certain subject. 2. *v* to give someone a test. 3. to try out: *to test a car*. **testing, tested.**

tether *v* to tie an animal to something so that it cannot walk far. **tethering, tethered.**

than *conj* compared with: *She is older than I am*.

thank *v* to tell someone that you are pleased about something that he or she has given you or done for you. **thanking, thanked.**

that 1. *adj* the one over there: *That is their house*. *pl* **those.** 2. *pron* which: *the house that we live in*.

thatch *n* straw or reeds used for making a roof.

thaw *v* (of snow and ice) to melt. **thawing, thawed.**

theatre *n* a building where plays are acted.

theft *n* stealing.

their *adj* belonging to them: *their coats*.

theirs *pron* belonging to them: *The hats are theirs*.

them *pron* those persons or things: *I like them*.

themselves *pron* they only: *They did it themselves*.

then *adv* 1. after that. 2. at that time.

there *adv* in that place or to that place: *Stay there!*

therefore *adv* for that reason.

thermometer *n* an instrument that measures temperature in degrees.

these see **this.**

thick *adj* 1. deep, fat: *a thick slice of bread*. 2. not flowing easily: *thick soup*. 3. dense: *thick fog*.

thief *n* someone who steals. *pl* **thieves.**

thigh *n* the top part of your leg above your knee.

thimble *n* a cover for the end of a finger when pushing a needle through cloth.

thin *adj* not thick or fat. **thinner, thinnest.**

thing *n* anything that can be seen or touched.

think *v* 1. to use your mind. 2. to have an opinion: *I think she's telling the truth*. **thinking, thought.**

third *adj* next after second, 3rd.

thirst *n* the wish or need to drink.

thirsty *adj* wanting a drink. **thirstier, thirstiest.**

thirteen *n* and *adj* one more than twelve, 13. *adj* **thirteenth.**

thirty *n* and *adj* ten times three, 30. *adj* **thirtieth.**

this *pron* and *adj* the one here: *this hat.* *pl* **these.**

thistle *n* a prickly plant with purple flowers.

thorn *n* a sharp point on a plant's stem.

thorough *adj* 1. done properly and carefully: *a thorough job.* 2. complete: *a thorough rest.*

those see **that.**

though *conj* although.

thought 1. *n* what is in your mind when thinking. 2. *v* see **think.**

thoughtful *adj* 1. thinking deeply. 2. thinking of others and what they would like: *Jill was very thoughtful for her pets.*

thousand *n* and *adj* ten times one hundred, 1000. *adj* **thousandth.**

thrash *v* to beat someone with a stick. **thrashing, thrashed.**

thread *n* a long thin piece of cotton, silk, or other material used in sewing.

threat *n* a warning that harm or punishment may be coming.

threaten *v* to make a threat. **threatening, threatened.**

three *n* and *adj* one more than two, 3. See **third.**

threw see **throw.**

thrill *n* a feeling of excitement.

thrilling *adj* very exciting.

throat *n* the front of your neck and the tube inside it for food, liquid, and air to pass into your body.

throb *v* to beat strongly. Your heart throbs when you have been running fast. **throbbing, throbbed.**

throne *n* a special chair for a king, queen, or bishop.

through *prep* or *adv* from one end or side to the other: *We walked through the wood.*

throw *v* to make something leave your hand and move through the air. **throwing, threw, I have thrown.**

thrush *n* a brown song-bird with a speckled breast.

thrust *v* to push hard and quickly: *He thrust his hand into his pocket.* **thrusting, thrust.**

thud *v* to make a dull heavy sound. **thudding, thudded.**

thumb *n* the short thick finger nearest each wrist.

thump *v* to hit hard with the fist. **thumping, thumped.**

thunder *n* the loud noise that follows a flash of lightning in a storm.

Thursday *n* the fifth day of the week.

thus *adv* therefore.

tick *v* 1. to keep on making clicks. Many clocks tick. 2. to make a mark like this ✓. **ticking, ticked.**

ticket *n* 1. a small piece of paper or card that you get when you pay for a seat on the bus or at a concert. 2. a label showing the price of something.

tickle *v* to touch or stroke someone very lightly to make him or her laugh. **tickling, tickled.**

tide *n* the rise and fall of the sea twice every day.

tidy *adj* with everything properly arranged. **tidier, tidiest.** *opp* **untidy.**

tie 1. *v* to fasten something with a knot or a bow. *opp* **untie.** 2. (in a game) to draw. **tying, tied.** 3. *n* a long strip of material worn under the collar of a shirt and tied at the front.

tiger *n* a striped wild animal like a very large cat, living in parts of Asia. *fem* **tigress.**

tight *adj* 1. fitting very closely: *a tight shoe.* 2. firmly stretched or fastened: *a tight rope.*

tights *n pl* a piece of clothing that fits closely over the feet, legs, and the body up to the waist. Women and girls wear tights.

tile *n* a flat piece of material, usually baked clay, for covering floors, walls, or roofs.

till 1. *conj* and *prep* until. 2. *n* a drawer for keeping money in a shop. 3. *v* to plough land. **tilling, tilled.**

tilt *v* to make something lean to one side. **tilting, tilted.**

timber *n* wood that can be used for making things.

time *n* 1. a certain moment in the day: *What time is it?* 2. a space in our lives measured in years, months, days, hours, minutes, or seconds.

timid *adj* shy.

tin *n* 1. a silvery metal. 2. a can or box made of iron and coated with tin.

tingle *v* to have a prickly feeling. **tingling, tingled.**

tinkle *n* the ringing sound of a small bell.

tinned *adj* preserved in a tin: *tinned sardines.*

tinsel *n* small strips of thin metal used for decoration.

tint *n* a shade of colour: *a greenish tint.*

tiny *adj* very small. **tinier, tiniest.**

tip 1. *n* a pointed end: *a finger-tip.* 2. a place where rubbish is left. 3. *v* to tilt something so that what is inside falls out. **tipping, tipped.**

tiptoe *v* to walk on your toes and not make any noise. **tiptoeing, tiptoed.**

tired *adj* 1. needing to rest or sleep. 2. feeling bored with something: *I'm tired of school.*

tissue *n* very thin soft paper.

tissue-paper *n* a very thin kind of paper.

title *n* 1. the name of a book or film. 2. a word before a person's name to show his or her rank. Lord, Sir, Doctor, Mrs are some titles.

to *prep* in the direction of: *He went to London.* **to and fro** backwards and forwards.

toad *n* an animal like a frog but with a rougher skin.

toadstool *n* a plant that is often shaped like a mushroom. Some toadstools are poisonous.

toast *n* bread that is made crisp and brown by heating it.

tobacco *n* a plant whose leaves are dried and used for smoking in pipes, cigars, or cigarettes.

toboggan *n* a sledge for sliding down hills covered with snow.

today 1. *n* this day. 2. *adv* on this day: *My cousin came today.*

toddle *v* to walk with short steps as a small child does. **toddling, toddled.**

toe *n* one of the five parts at the end of each foot.

toffee *n* a sweet to be chewed and eaten.

together *adv* 1. with something or someone else. 2. at the same time.

toilet *n* a lavatory.

told see **tell.**

tomahawk *n* a battle-axe used by Red Indians.

tomato *n* a plant with a round red fruit. *pl* **tomatoes.**

tomb *n* a grave.

tomorrow *n* the day after today.

tone *n* 1. a musical sound. 2. the way someone's voice sounds: *an angry tone.* 3. a shade of colour: *a tone of green.*

tongue *n* the soft movable part of your mouth that can be used for licking and tasting.

tonight *n* this evening or night coming.

tonne *n* a measure of weight equal to 1000 kilograms.

tonsils *n pl* two small lumps at the back of the mouth.

too *adv* 1. also: *Gary came too.* 2. more than enough: *too much chocolate.*

took see **take.**

tool *n* something to help you to do work. Hammers, saws, spades, and axes are tools.

tooth *n* one of the hard white parts in your mouth with which you bite and chew. *pl* **teeth.**

toothache *n* a pain in a tooth.

top *n* 1. the highest point or surface of something. 2. a toy that can be made to spin.

topic *n* some special interest that you find out about at school.

topple *v* (often with **over**) to fall down after becoming unsteady. **toppling, toppled.**

torch *n* an electric light that you can carry in your hand.

tore, torn see **tear.**

torpedo *n* a bomb shaped like a cigar that is fired from a submarine through the sea to sink a ship. *pl* **torpedoes.**

torrent *n* a very fast stream of water.

tortoise *n* a slow-moving animal with a hard shell.

torture *v* to cause horrible pain to someone. **torturing, tortured.**

toss *v* to throw up into the air. **tossing, tossed.**

total *n* the whole amount when several figures are added: *The total of $3+5+2$ is 10.*

totter *v* to walk in an unsteady way. **tottering, tottered.**

touch *v* 1. to put your fingers or another part of your body gently against something. 2. to be so near to something else that there is no space in between. **touching, touched.**

tough *adj* 1. not easily broken or bent. 2. hard to chew or cut: *tough meat.*

tour *v* to visit a number of places. **touring, toured.**

tournament *n* a competition between several players in any game: *a tennis tournament.*

tow *v* to pull something with a rope, chain or cable. **towing, towed.**

toward, towards *prep* in the direction of.

towel *n* a cloth or paper for drying something wet.

tower *n* a tall narrow building, or part of a building. Churches and castles often have towers.

town *n* a lot of houses, shops, offices, schools, and factories built near one another. A town is larger than a village.

toy *n* something to play with.

trace I. *v* to copy a picture by laying thin transparent paper over it and going over the lines with a pencil. 2. to find after following clues: *to trace a robber.* **tracing, traced.** 3. *n* a small amount: *a trace of grease.*

track *n* I. the set of metal rails a train travels along. 2. a kind of path in the country. 3. the course followed by runners in a race. 4. marks on the ground left by something moving: *the track of a wolf.*
track suit *n* a special suit worn for sport.

tractor *n* a machine with wheels and a powerful engine that is used on farms for pulling a plough or heavy loads.

trade *n* I. the business of buying and selling. 2. a job needing the use of tools: *a carpenter's trade.*

traffic *n* everything that moves by road, rail, sea, or air.

tragedy *n* something very sad that has happened. *pl* **tragedies.**

trail I. *n* marks and smells on the ground left behind by an animal. 2. a rough path. 3. *v* to pull something loosely behind you. **trailing, trailed.**

trailer *n* a kind of cart pulled along behind a car or lorry.

train I. *n* a railway-engine pulling carriages or goods wagons. 2. *v* to practise, especially for sports. **training, trained.**

trainer *n* someone who teaches or prepares you for some exercise or sport.

traitor *n* someone who works against his friends or country.

tramp I. *n* a person without a home or a job who walks from place to place. 2. *v* to walk heavily. **tramping, tramped.**

trample *v* to tread all over something and spoil it. **trampling, trampled.**

trampoline *n* a large canvas sheet fastened to a frame with springs, for people to bounce on.

transfer I. *v* to move something or somebody to another place. **transferring, transferred.** 2. *n* a picture that can be moved from paper on to something else.

transistor radio *n* a kind of radio that can be carried about easily.

transparent *adj* clear enough for you to see through it: *Glass is transparent.*

transplant *v* to dig up a plant and put it back in the ground somewhere else. **transplanting, transplanted.**

transport *n* vehicles or machines of any kind that are used for carrying goods or people.

trap I. *n* something made for catching birds or animals: *a mouse-trap.* 2. a plan for catching someone in a clever way. 3. *v* to catch in a trap. **trapping, trapped.**
trapdoor a door in a floor or ceiling.

trapeze *n* a swinging bar held by two ropes, used by acrobats in a circus.

travel *v* to make a journey. **travelling, travelled.**

trawler *n* a boat that catches fish by pulling along a large net behind it.

tray *n* a flat sheet of wood, metal, or plastic for carrying things: *a tea-tray.*

treacle *n* a thick dark sweet syrup.

tread *v* to step or walk on something. **treading, trod, I have trodden.**

treasure *n* a lot of valuable things together.

treat *v* to pay for someone else's food or drink. **treating, treated.**

tree *n* a tall plant with a wooden trunk and branches.

tremble *v* to shake with fear, excitement, or cold. **trembling, trembled.**

tremendous *adj* huge.

trench *n* a long narrow hole dug in the ground.

trespass *v* to go on someone's land without permission. **trespassing, trespassed.**

trial *n* I. trying something out to see how well it works. 2. a time when people listen to what is said in a court and decide whether or not a person is guilty of a crime.

triangle *n* I. a space or area enclosed by three straight lines whose ends meet. 2. a musical instrument made from a steel rod bent in this shape. It is played by striking with a metal rod.

tribe *n* a group of families who live together, sometimes with a chief.

trick I. *n* something clever that a person or animal has learnt to do. 2. a quick action to deceive people: *a conjuring trick.* 3. *v* to deceive. **tricking, tricked.**

trickle *n* a very thin stream of liquid.

tricycle *n* a three-wheeled bicycle.

tried see **try**.

trifle *n* a sweet of sponge-cake, jelly, and cream.

trigger *n* the small part of a gun that you pull to fire it.

trim *v* to make something tidy by cutting off the extra parts: *to trim a hedge*. **trimming, trimmed.**

trio *n* a group of three, especially three musicians.

trip 1. *n* a short journey for pleasure. 2. *v* (often with **over**) to stumble. **tripping, tripped.**

triumph *n* a great victory or success.

trod, trodden see **tread**.

trolley *n* 1. a kind of basket on wheels, as used in a supermarket. 2. a set of trays on wheels to carry dishes. *pl* **trolleys.**

trophy *n* a cup or shield won in a competition. *pl* **trophies.**

troop *n* a group of soldiers, scouts, or animals: *a troop of monkeys*.

trot *v* to run gently. **trotting, trotted.**

trouble *n* anything that worries, or disturbs you.

trough *n* a long narrow open box holding water or food for animals.

trousers *n pl* a piece of clothing that reaches from the waist to the ankles and has one part for each leg.

trout *n* a fish that lives in lakes and rivers. *pl* **trout.**

trowel *n* 1. a small garden tool with a curved blade. 2. a small tool with a flat blade for spreading mortar.

truant *n* a pupil absent from school without permission.

truck *n* an open wagon or lorry.

trudge *v* to walk in a slow heavy way. **trudging, trudged.**

true *adj* 1. correct. 2. to be relied on: *Frank is a true friend*. *opp* **untrue.**

trumpet *n* a kind of metal horn which makes sounds when you blow down it.

trunk *n* 1. the main part of a tree, or of your body. 2. the long nose of an elephant. 3. a large case for taking things on a journey or for storing things.

trunks *n pl* very short trousers worn by a swimmer.

trust *v* to believe that someone can be relied on. **trusting, trusted.** *opp* **distrust** or **mistrust.**

truth *n* what is true.

try *v* 1. to make an effort to do something. 2. to test something to see if it works well: *We will try your plan*. 3. to judge someone in a law court. **he tries, trying, tried.**

T-shirt *n* a sports shirt with short sleeves and no collar.

tub *n* a round container, often open at the top.

tube *n* 1. a long thin hollow piece of metal, plastic, rubber, glass, or wood. 2. a soft round container for something to be squeezed out at one end: *a tube of toothpaste*. 3. an underground railway.

tubing *n* a length of tube.

tuck 1. *v* to put the loose ends of something out of the way: *He tucked his shirt into his trousers*. **tucking, tucked.** 2. *n* a fold sewn in a garment.
to tuck someone up to put sheets and blankets closely around someone in bed.

Tuesday *n* the third day of the week.

tuft *n* a little bunch of grass, hair, or feathers: *a tuft of grass*.

tug 1. *v* to pull sharply. **tugging, tugged.** 2. *n* a small powerful boat used for towing ships.

tulip *n* a flower shaped like a small cup, that grows from a bulb.

tumble *v* to fall down. **tumbling, tumbled.**

tumbler *n* a drinking-glass with a flat bottom.

tune *n* a set of notes that make a piece of music.

tunic *n* the jacket part of a uniform.

tunnel *n* a covered passage cut through the ground.

turban *n* a long sash wound round the head and worn as a hat.

turf *n* grass cut short and the soil it is growing in. *pl* **turves** or **turfs.**

turkey *n* a large bird grown for food. *pl* **turkeys.**

turn 1. *v* to move round: *The wheels are turning*. 2. to change direction, colour, or appearance: *to turn left, to turn black*. **turning, turned.** 3. *n* a time for you to do something after other people have done it or are still waiting to do it: *It's your turn*.

turnip *n* a vegetable with a large round white root.

turquoise *n* a bright colour between blue and green.

turret *n* a little tower on a building.

turtle *n* a large sea-animal that looks like a tortoise.

tusk *n* one of two very long teeth sticking out from the mouth of an elephant or wild boar.

tweed *n* a rough woollen cloth.

tweezers *n pl* a small metal tool for picking up small objects carefully.

twelve *n* and *adj* one more than eleven, 12. *adj* **twelfth**.

twenty *n* and *adj* one more than nineteen, 20. *adj* **twentieth**.

twice *adv* two times.

twig *n* a very small branch on a tree or bush.

twilight *n* the faint light before sunrise or after sunset.

twin *n* one of two babies born at the same time to the same mother.

twine *v* to twist round something: *The ivy twined round the post.* **twining, twined.**

twinkle *v* to sparkle with small flashes: *Stars twinkle at night.* **twinkling, twinkled.**

twirl *v* to spin round quickly. **twirling, twirled.**

twist *v* 1. to wind things round each other. *opp* **untwist**. 2. to curve: *the road twisted.* **twisting, twisted.**

two *n* and *adj* one added to one, 2. See **second**.

tying see **tie**.

type 1. *n* a kind: *a type of car*. 2. letters used to print books. 3. *v* to write with a typewriter. **typing, typed.**

typewriter *n* a machine with keys that are pressed to print letters and numbers on paper by using type.

typhoon *n* a storm with very strong winds.

tyre *n* a rubber ring, usually filled with air, round the wheel of a car, lorry, or bicycle.

Uu

ugly *adj* not pretty or nice to look at. **uglier, ugliest.**

umbrella *n* a round folding frame of thin steel ribs covered with cloth, held to keep the rain off.

umpire *n* someone in charge of a game of tennis or cricket who sees the rules are obeyed.

un- a prefix that can mean: 1. not. Unable means 'not able to'. 2. to do the opposite. Unfold means 'to open out'.

uncanny *adj* strange, mysterious.

uncertain *adj* not sure.

uncle *n* 1. a brother of your father or mother. 2. your aunt's husband.

unconscious *adj* not awake and not aware of anything around you.

uncover *v* to take a cover or wrapping off. **uncovering, uncovered.**

undecided *adj* not sure.

under, underneath *prep* or *adv* 1. beneath: *under(neath) the table*. 2. less than: *under £3*.

underground 1. *adj* or *adv* under the ground. 2. *n* a railway that runs through underground tunnels.

undergrowth *n* bushes or small trees growing under larger ones.

underhand *adj* sly.

underline *v* to draw a line underneath some writing. **underlining, underlined.**

underneath see **under**.

understand *v* to know the meaning of something or how it works. **understanding, understood.**

undertake *v* to agree to do something. **undertaking, undertook, I have undertaken.**

underwear *n* clothes like vests and pants that you wear under other clothes.

undo *v* to unfasten or untie something: *Jimmy undid the buttons of his coat.* **undoing, undid, I have undone.**

undress *v* to take off your clothes. **undressing, undressed.**

uneasy *adj* worried.

uneven *adj* not level or smooth: *uneven ground*.

unexpected *adj* coming as a surprise: *an unexpected present*.

unfair *adj* not just: *an unfair game*.

unfasten *v* to open: *to unfasten a gate*. **unfastening, unfastened.**

unfit *adj* 1. not in a fit condition. 2. not suitable.

unfold *v* to open something folded: *to unfold a roll of cloth*. **unfolding, unfolded.**

ungrateful *adj* not grateful.

unhappy *adj* not happy. **unhappier, unhappiest.**

unhealthy *adj* not healthy. **unhealthier, unhealthiest.**

unicorn *n* an imaginary animal like a horse with a horn on its forehead.

uniform *n* special clothes worn to show that people belong to the same group or go to the same school.

union *n* 1. a joining together. 2. a group of workers in the same trade or occupation who have joined together to make sure that they are all treated fairly by the people in charge of them.

Union Jack the flag of the United Kingdom.

unit *n* 1. a single thing. 2. an amount used for measuring. The metre is a unit of length and the second is a unit of time. 3. Any number under 10.

unite *v* to join together. **uniting, united.**

universe *n* the earth, all the planets, and all the stars and everything in or on them.

university *n* a place for those who have left school to carry on their education. *pl* **universities.**

unkind *adj* not kind.

unless *conj* except if: *I shall not go unless you do.*

unlikely *adj* probably not going to happen.

unload *v* 1. to take off a load: *to unload a lorry.* 2. to take the bullets out of a gun. **unloading, unloaded.**

unlock *v* to open a lock by using a key. **unlocking, unlocked.**

unlucky *adj* having bad luck. **unluckier, unluckiest.**

unnecessary *adj* not necessary.

unpack *v* to take clothing out of a case. **unpacking, unpacked.**

unpleasant *adj* not pleasant.

unroll *v* to open out something that has been rolled up. **unrolling, unrolled.**

untidy *adj* not tidy. **untidier, untidiest.**

untie *v* to undo something that has been tied. **untying, untied.**

until *conj* up to the time when: *Wait until I come.*

unusual *adj* not usual: *an unusual name.*

unwell *adj* ill.

unwrap *v* to take the wrapping off: *to unwrap a parcel.* **unwrapping, unwrapped.**

up *prep* or *adv* 1. to a higher place. 2. along: *up the road.*
up-to-date recent.

upon *prep* on or on top of.

upper *adj* higher: *the upper jaw.*

upright *adj* straight up: *She sat upright.*

uproar *n* a lot of noise and shouting made by people who are angry or excited.

upset *v* 1. to make someone very sad. 2. to knock over. **upsetting, upset.**

upside-down *adv* with the top part at the bottom.

upstairs *adv* 1. on a higher floor. 2. up the stairs: *Eileen ran upstairs.*

urge 1. *v* to try to get someone to do something: *They urged her to enter the competition.* **urging, urged.** 2. *n* a sudden strong wish to do something.

urgent *adj* needing something to be done at once: *an urgent message for help.*

us *pron* having to do with me and others.

use[1] (yooz) *v* to make something help you: *We use a knife to eat.* **using, used.**

use[2] (yooss) *n* 1. the power of using. 2. value: *This old knife is of no use.*

useful *adj* helpful: *a useful idea, a useful tool.*

useless *adj* not useful: *These scissors are useless.*

usual *adj* as happens most often: *We made our usual journey by bus.* *opp* **unusual.**

utmost *adj* greatest.

utter 1. *v* to speak. **uttering, uttered.** 2. *adj* complete: *That is utter nonsense!*

Vv

vacant *adj* empty: *The house is vacant.*

vaccination *n* an injection to prevent someone from catching a disease.

vacuum *n* an empty space with no air or gas in it. **vacuum cleaner** an electric machine that sucks up dust from carpets and floors.

vain *adj* having too high an opinion of yourself. **in vain** without success.

valley *n* low land between hills or mountains. *pl* **valleys.**

valuable *adj* worth a lot of money: *a valuable ring.*

value *n* 1. the amount of money something could be sold for. 2. how important something is.

valve *n* a part of a machine that lets air or a liquid flow in one direction only.

van *n* a light covered vehicle or a railway wagon for carrying goods, parcels, or luggage.

vanilla *n* a flavouring for food, often put in ice-cream.

vanish *v* to disappear. **vanishing, vanished.**

vanity *n* being vain.

variable *adj* changeable, not staying the same: *a variable wind.*

variety *n* 1. a collection of different things: *a great variety of shops.* 2. a certain kind. *pl* **varieties.**

various *adj* different: *Various schools took part.*

varnish *n* a sticky liquid that is painted on to wood or metal to make it shiny.

vary *v* to make something different: *She varies the meals each day.* **she varies, varying, varied.**

vase *n* a pretty jar for holding flowers.

vast *adj* huge: *a vast desert.*

vault *v* to jump over something using your hands or a special pole. **vaulting, vaulted.**

veal *n* meat from a calf used as food.

vegetable *n* part of a plant (but not fruit) used for food.

vehicle *n* something built to be pulled by an engine or an animal, and to carry people or things over land.

veil *n* a net or thin piece of cloth worn to hide the face or protect it from the sun.

vein *n* one of the thin long tubes in your body carrying blood to your heart.

velvet *n* a kind of cloth that is soft and smooth on one side.

ventilator *n* a kind of opening for letting air into or out of a room.

venture *v* to dare to take a risk: *Jim ventured into the cave.* **venturing, ventured.**

veranda, verandah *n* a platform with a roof built on to the outside of a house.

verb *n* a word in a sentence that says what someone or something is doing. In the sentence 'Kate walked to the shop', the word 'walked' is a verb.

verdict *n* the decision of a jury or a magistrate at the end of a trial: *a verdict of 'not guilty'.*

verge *n* an edge often of grass beside a road.

vermin *n* a small animal or insect that does damage. Rats and cockroaches are vermin. *pl* **vermin.**

verse *n* 1. a group of lines in a poem or a song. 2. poetry.

version *n* one person's story about something that has happened.

vertical *adj* upright.

very *adv* extremely.

vessel *n* 1. a ship or boat. 2. a container for liquids.

vest *n* a garment worn next to the skin on the top half of the body.

vet *n* someone who looks after animals that are ill or hurt.

viaduct *n* a long bridge with a lot of arches, that carries a road or railway over a valley.

vibrate *v* to shake: *The bridge vibrated as the train went over it.* **vibrating, vibrated.**

vicar *n* a clergyman.

vicious *adj* cruel.

victim *n* someone who has been killed, hurt, or robbed.

victor *n* a winner of a contest.

victorious *adj* winning.

victory *n* a win in a battle or match. *pl* **victories.**

videotape *n* a special tape used for television, that shows pictures and produces sounds when it is played through a special machine.

view *n* 1. everything that you can see from one place: *a good view of the match.* 2. an opinion.

viewpoint *n* a place giving a good view.

vigour *n* strength: *to be full of vigour.*

Vikings *n pl* in olden times, pirates from northern Europe who raided the coasts of many countries.

vile *adj* horrible: *a vile taste.*

village *n* a group of houses and shops in the country, smaller than a town.

villain *n* a bad person.

vine *n* a long climbing plant on which grapes grow.

vinegar *n* a sour liquid used to flavour food.

vineyard *n* a large piece of ground where vines grow.

violence *n* great force, often causing damage.

violent *adj* very rough, and often causing damage: *a violent storm.*

violet *n* 1. a small wild plant with a blue, purple, or white flower. 2. a bluish-purple colour.

violin *n* a musical instrument with four strings, played with a bow.

virtue *n* something good: *Patience is a virtue.*

vision *n* 1. being able to see. 2. something seen in your imagination.

visit *v* to go to see a person or a place. **visiting, visited.**

visor *n* the movable part at the front of a helmet protecting the face and eyes.

vitamin *n* one of a group of substances found in some foods, that are necessary for good health.

vivid *adj* 1. bright and clear: *a vivid sunset*. 2. so clear that it seems real: *a vivid dream*.

vixen *n* a female fox.

vocabulary *n* 1. a list of words in the order of the alphabet and with their meaning. 2. all the words you know. *pl* **vocabularies.**

voice *n* the sound from your mouth when you are speaking or singing.

volcano *n* a mountain with an opening at the top from which molten rock, hot gases, and ash sometimes rush out. *pl* **volcanoes.**

volley *n* a number of bullets or stones shot or thrown at the same time. *pl* **volleys.**

volume *n* 1. the amount of space something fills. 2. how loud a sound is: *high volume*. 3. one of a set of books.

volunteer *v* to offer to do something although you do not have to do it. **volunteering, volunteered.**

vote *v* to say who you would choose. **voting, voted.**

vow *n* a solemn promise.

vowel *n* any one of the five letters 'a', 'e', 'i', 'o', or 'u'.

voyage *n* a long journey by sea.

vulture *n* a large bird of prey that eats dead animals.

Ww

waddle *v* to walk swaying from side to side like a duck. **waddling, waddled.**

wade *v* to walk through water. **wading, waded.**

wafer *n* a thin biscuit often eaten with ice-cream.

wag *v* to move quickly from side to side: *The dog wagged his tail*. **wagging, wagged.**

wage *n* or **wages** *n pl* money people get for doing work, often in weekly payments.

wagon, waggon *n* 1. a cart with four wheels for carrying heavy loads. 2. a railway truck for carrying goods.

wail *n* a long sad cry.

waist *n* the part of your body between your ribs and your hips.

wait *v* (sometimes with **for**) to stay in one place until something happens or someone comes. **waiting, waited.**

waiter *n* someone who serves meals in a restaurant, café, or hotel. *fem* **waitress.**

wake 1. *v* to stop someone sleeping. 2. to stop sleeping. **waking, woke** or **waked, I have waked** or **woken.** 3. *n* the smooth or foamy part of the sea behind a moving ship.

walk *v* to go on foot. **walking, walked.**

walkie-talkie *n* a portable radio for sending and receiving messages.

wall *n* 1. a barrier made of bricks, stones, or concrete. 2. the side of a building or room.

wallet *n* a small folding leather case for bank notes and papers that is carried in a pocket.

walnut *n* a kind of nut with a round hard shell.

walrus *n* a kind of large seal with two long tusks.

waltz *n* a smooth graceful dance in which the dancers twirl round.

wand *n* a thin rod: *a fairy's magic wand*.

wander *v* to roam about. **wandering, wandered.**

wane *v* to grow smaller: *The full moon started to wane*. **waning, waned.**

want *v* 1. to wish for. 2. to need. **wanting, wanted.**

war *n* a long fight between countries or between groups of people in the same country.

warble *v* to sing like a bird. **warbling, warbled.**

ward *n* a large bedroom for patients in a hospital.

warder *n* a prison officer who guards prisoners.

wardrobe *n* a tall cupboard for hanging clothes in.

warehouse *n* a building where goods are stored.

warm *adj* 1. fairly hot. 2. enthusiastic: *a warm welcome*.

warn *v* to tell someone about possible danger or difficulty. **warning, warned.**

warren *n* a place where rabbits live, with several holes leading underground.

warrior *n* (in olden times) a soldier.

warship *n* a ship carrying guns and built for fighting.

wart *n* a small hard lump on the skin.

wash *v* to make something clean with water. **washing, washed.**

washing-machine *n* a machine that washes clothes.

wasp *n* a black and yellow flying insect that stings.

waste 1. *v* to use more of something than you need. **wasting, wasted.** 2. *n* anything that you do not need any more.

watch 1. *v* to look at. 2. (sometimes with **over**) to keep someone or something safe from other people. **watching, watched.** 3. *n* a small clock usually worn on the wrist.

water *n* the liquid that falls as rain.

waterfall *n* a stream of water falling down a cliff or steep slope.

waterproof *adj* not letting water pass through.

wave 1. *n* a raised line of water moving on the surface of the sea. 2. *v* to move your hand and arm as a way of saying hello or goodbye to someone. 3. to move up and down or from side to side: *flags waving in the wind.* **waving, waved.**

wavy *adj* with curves in it: *David has wavy hair.*

wax *n* a soft material that melts very easily. It is used to make candles and crayons.

way *n* 1. a road or direction: *the way to town.* 2. how to do something: *the way to bake a cake.*

we *pron* the word used to refer to yourself and one or more other people.

weak *adj* not strong: *a weak animal, a weak light.*

wealth *n* a lot of money or valuable things.

weapon *n* anything used for fighting or hunting. Guns, swords, and spears are weapons.

wear *v* 1. to be dressed in something: *Sarah wore a dress.* 2. (often with **out** or **away**) to become weak or damaged because it has been used so much: *to wear away a carpet.* **wearing, wore, I have worn.**
to wear someone out to make someone very tired.

weary *adj* very tired. **wearier, weariest.**

weasel *n* a small wild animal that kills and eats smaller animals such as birds and mice.

weather *n* what it is like outside. Weather is usually sunny, cloudy, hot, cold, fine, or wet.

weave *v* to make cloth by moving threads under and over one another. **weaving, wove, I have woven.**

web *n* a net of sticky threads spun by a spider to trap flying insects.
web-foot a foot with skin between the toes. Birds and animals such as ducks and otters have web-feet.

wedding *n* the time when a man and woman become husband and wife.

wedge *n* a piece of wood or metal that is very thin at one end and wider at the other.

Wednesday *n* the fourth day of the week.

weed *n* any wild plant that grows in places where it is not wanted.

week *n* seven days. The first day of the week is Sunday.

weekday *n* any day except Sunday.

weekend *n* Saturday and Sunday.

weekly *adv* once a week: *a weekly paper.*

weep *v* to let tears fall from the eyes. **weeping, wept.**

weigh *v* to find how heavy a thing is by putting it on scales. **weighing, weighed.**

weight *n* 1. how heavy something is. 2. one of a set of metal pieces used for weighing things.

weird *adj* very strange.

welcome *v* to say you are very pleased when someone has come to see you. **welcoming, welcomed.**

well 1. *adv* in a good way. 2. *adj* healthy: *I feel very well. opp* **unwell. better, best.** 3. *n* a deep hole in the ground with water or oil at the bottom.

wellingtons *n pl* rubber boots usually nearly reaching the knees.

went see **go.**

wept see **weep.**

west *n* the direction of the setting sun.

western 1. *adj* in or of the west. 2. *n* a cowboy film.

wet *adj* full of a liquid or covered with a liquid. **wetter, wettest.**

whale *n* the largest sea animal. It looks like a fish.

what 1. *adj* which: *What car is that?* 2. *pron* the thing which: *I don't know what to do.*

whatever *pron* anything that: *I will do whatever I can.*

wheat *n* a plant like tall grass. Its seeds are ground to make flour.

wheel 1. *n* a ring or disc of wood or metal that can keep turning round an axle. 2. *v* to push something on wheels. **wheeling, wheeled.**

wheelbarrow *n* a little cart with two handles and one wheel.

when *adv* 1. at what time. 2. at the time that: *It was two o'clock when they started.*

whenever *adv* at any time: *We will go whenever you are ready.*

where *adv* 1. in what place. 2. in the place that: *We will stop where we can rest.*

wherever *adv* in any place: *I will search for him wherever he is.*

whether *conj* if: *Carole did not know whether she could go.*

which 1. *adj* what person or thing. 2. *pron* (a word showing the one you are talking about): *the coat which I wore.*

whiff *n* a faint smell: *a whiff of scent.*

while 1. *conj* during the time that: *I watched television while dinner was cooking.* 2. *n* a space of time: *Mark slept for a short while.*

whimper *v* to make a soft crying sound of fear or pain. **whimpering, whimpered.**

whine *v* (of a dog) to make a long sad cry. **whining, whined.**

whip 1. *n* a long piece of cord or thin leather fastened to a handle and used for hitting things. 2. *v* to hit with a whip. 3. to stir a liquid so hard that you make froth on it. **whipping, whipped.**

whirl *v* to spin round quickly. **whirling, whirled.**

whiskers *n pl* the long stiff hairs that grow on the upper lip of some animals, such as a cat.

whisper *v* to speak very softly. **whispering, whispered.**

whistle 1. *v* to make a shrill sound by blowing through your lips or through a small pipe. **whistling, whistled.** 2. *n* a small pipe that makes a shrill sound when blown.

white *n* 1. the colour of snow. 2. the part of an egg round the yolk.

Whitsun *adj* to do with Whitsuntide, the period of seven weeks after Easter.

who *pron* 1. what person or persons. 2. the person that: *the woman who came.*

whoever *pron* the person not known who: *Whoever came left no note.*

whole *adj* all of something: *the whole school.* **on the whole** mostly.

whooping-cough *n* an illness that makes you cough a lot.

whose *pron* belonging to what person: *I know whose hat this is.*

why *adv* for what reason: *Why did you do it?*

wick *n* the thin string in a candle or oil lamp.

wicked *adj* very bad: *a wicked crime.*

wicket *n* (in cricket) three stumps at each end of the pitch.

wide 1. *adj* measuring a long way from one side to the other: *a wide river.* 2. *adv* completely: *wide open.*

widow *n* a woman whose husband is dead.

widower *n* a man whose wife is dead.

width *n* how wide something is: *the width of a road.*

wife *n* a married woman. *pl* **wives.**

wig *n* false hair worn on the head, often over someone's own hair.

wigwam *n* a tent that Red Indians used to live in.

wild *adj* 1. not controlled: *a wild animal.* 2. growing freely and not looked after: *a wild rose.* 3. stormy: *a wild night.*

wilderness *n* an open desert place where no one lives.

wilful *adj* 1. doing only what you want to do. 2. done on purpose: *wilful damage.*

will 1. *n* a written paper saying who is to have someone's money and things when he or she is dead. 2. the power of your mind to choose what to do. 3. *v* (before another verb, to say what you are determined to do): *I will not let her beat me.*

willing *adj* glad and ready to do what is wanted. *opp* **unwilling.**

willow *n* a tree that has thin drooping branches.

wilt *v* to droop: *The plant wilted.* **wilting, wilted.**

wily *adj* sly: *a wily old fox.* **wilier, wiliest.**

win *v* to beat someone else in a game or fight. **winning, won.**

wince *v* to move slightly because you suddenly feel a pain. **wincing, winced.**

wind¹ (rhymes with **tinned**) *n* air moving past quickly.

wind² (rhymes with **find**) *v* 1. to wrap tightly round. *opp* **unwind.** 2. to turn a key to make a machine work. 3. to twist and turn: *The river wound through the forest.* **winding, wound.**

windmill *n* a mill like a tower with four sails turned by the wind, used to grind corn into flour.

window *n* an opening in the wall of a building, filled with glass, to let in light.

wine *n* a strong drink made from the juice of grapes or other fruit.

wing n 1. one of the parts of a bird, bat, or insect used for flying. 2. a flat stretch of metal on either side of an aeroplane to hold it in the air while flying.

wink v to close and open one eye quickly. **winking, winked.**

winter n the coldest season of the year, between autumn and spring.

wipe v to rub something with a cloth to make it clean or dry. **wiping, wiped.**

wire n a long metal thread.

wireless n a radio.

wisdom n being wise.

wise adj able to make good use of knowledge.

wish v to say what you would like to happen. **wishing, wished.**

witch n in fairy tales, a bad woman with magic powers.

with prep 1. in the company of: *Joyce walked with Karen.* 2. having: *the girl with dark hair.* 3. using: *He hit it with his bat.* 4. because of: *Neil shouted with joy.*

wither v to become dry, paler, and smaller. **withering, withered.**

within prep inside.

without prep not having.

witness n someone who saw something happen.

witty adj clever and amusing. **wittier, wittiest.**

wives see **wife.**

wizard n in fairy tales, a man with magic powers.

wobble v to move unsteadily from side to side. **wobbling, wobbled.**

woke, woken see **wake.**

wolf n a grey wild animal like a dog. pl **wolves.**

woman n a grown-up female human being. (masc **man**). pl **women.**

won see **win.**

wonder 1. v to want to know: *I wonder where he is?* 2. to doubt: *I began to wonder if he would come.* **wondering, wondered.** 3. n amazement.

wonderful adj giving you a lot of pleasure.

won't short for **will not.**

wood n 1. the hard part of a tree under the bark. 2. a large number of trees growing together, but smaller than a forest.

wooden adj made of wood: *a wooden chair.*

woodpecker n a bird that makes holes in wood with its beak to get at the insects which live under the bark.

wool n 1. the thick hair of sheep. 2. the thread made from wool.

woollen adj made of wool: *a woollen scarf.*

word n a sound or group of sounds that means something when it is spoken, written, or read.

wore see **wear.**

work 1. n something that you have to do. 2. something that people do regularly to earn money. 3. v to do a job. **working, worked.**

worker n someone who works, usually with his or her hands.

works, workshop n a place, such as a factory, where people make or mend things.

world n the earth or any other planet.

worm n a small thin creature without legs that wriggles and lives in the ground.

worn see **wear.**

worn-out adj 1. used up by wear: *a worn-out carpet.* 2. very tired after hard work.

worry v to feel unhappy about something bad that may happen or may have happened. **she worries, worrying, worried.**

worse adj and adv more than bad.

worship v to show love for God or a god. **worshipping, worshipped.**

worst adj most bad.

worth adj 1. equal in value to: *worth several pounds.* 2. deserving: *a film worth seeing.*

would v (before another verb, meaning 'shall' or 'will' if something is possible or if things were different): *I would go if my parents let me.*

wound[1] (woond) n an injury such as a cut.

wound[2] (rhymes with **found**) see **wind**[2].

wove, woven see **weave.**

wrap v to put paper or cloth round something: *to wrap a present.* **wrapping, wrapped.**

wreath n a large ring of flowers or leaves twisted together.

wreck n anything destroyed, as a ship on rocks or a crashed aeroplane.

wren n a very small brown bird with an upright tail.

wrench v to twist or pull suddenly. **wrenching, wrenched.**

wrestle v to struggle with someone and try to force him or her to the ground. **wrestling, wrestled.**

wretched adj miserable.

wriggle v to twist and turn the body. **wriggling, wriggled.**

wring v to twist something wet so that water is squeezed out of it. **wringing, wrung.**

wrinkle *n* a crease in the skin.

wrist *n* the joint between your hand and arm.

write *v* 1. to put words or signs on paper or a board so that people can read them. 2. to send a letter. **writing, wrote. I have written.**

wrong *adj* 1. not correct. 2. not good.

wrote see **write.**

wrung see **wring.**

Xx

Xmas *n* a short way of writing 'Christmas'.

X-rays *n pl* special rays that are used to take a photograph of the inside of your body.

xylophone *n* a musical instrument made of wooden bars of different lengths that are hit with small hammers.

Yy

yacht *n* a light boat with tall sails, for racing or pleasure.

yard *n* 1. a measurement of 3 feet or $91\frac{1}{2}$ centimetres. 2. a small space behind a building and with a wall round it.

yawn *v* to take a deep breath through the mouth and then breathe out because you are tired. **yawning, yawned.**

year *n* a measure of time lasting 365 days, 52 weeks, or 12 months.

yeast *n* a substance used to make the dough rise when making bread.

yell *v* to shout very loudly. **yelling, yelled.**

yellow *n* the colour of a lemon, grapefruit, or buttercup.

yelp *n* (of a dog) a sharp bark of pain or excitement.

yes *adv* a word meaning you agree to something.

yesterday *n* the day before today.

yet 1. *adv* up to now: *I have not seen the postman yet.* 2. at some time that is coming: *He may arrive yet.* 3. *conj* but.

yew *n* an evergreen tree that grows very slowly.

yield 1. *v* to give in. **yielding, yielded.** 2. *n* the amount produced: *a good yield of fruit.*

yogurt, yoghurt *n* a thick creamy food made from milk, sometimes mixed with fruit to give it flavour.

yoke *n* a wooden bar fastened over the necks of oxen working together.

yolk *n* the yellow part of an egg.

young *adj* in the early part of life.

your *adj* belonging to you.

yours *pron* belonging to you.

yourself *pron* you alone. *pl* **yourselves.**
    by yourself, by yourselves on your own.

youth *n* 1. a young man. *pl* **youths.** 2. the time when you are young.

Zz

zebra *n* an African wild animal like a horse with black and white stripes.
    zebra crossing a street-crossing with black and white stripes.

zero *n* the number nothing, 0.

zigzag *n* a line full of sharp turns from side to side.

zinc *n* a bluish-white metal.

zip, zip-fastener *n* a metal or plastic fastener with a sliding part, for joining together two edges of material or for closing a purse.

zoo *n* a place where wild animals are kept for people to look at them.

zoom *v* to move very fast. **zooming, zoomed.**

USEFUL INFORMATION

Days, Months, Dates and Holidays

Days
Sunday
Monday
Tuesday
Wednesday
Thursday
Friday
Saturday

Months
Months	Number of days
January	31
February	28*
March	31
April	30
May	31
June	30
July	31
August	31
September	30
October	31
November	30
December	31

There are 365 days in a year, but every fourth year, which is called a leap year, has 366 days. The extra day is added to February. Here is a rhyme to help you to remember the number of days in each month:

Thirty days has September,
April, June, and November;
All the rest have thirty-one,
Excepting February alone,
And that has twenty-eight days clear
And twenty-nine in each leap year.

Holidays and Special Days
New Year's Day	January 1
Chinese New Year	During the first moon (Jan 20–Feb 19) for one week
St. Valentine's Day	February 14
St. David's Day	March 1
St. Patrick's Day	March 17
April Fool's Day	April 1
Good Friday	Friday before Easter Sunday
Easter Sunday	March or April
Passover	Eight day celebration in March or April
St. George's Day	April 23
Rosh Hashanah (Jewish New Year)	September or October
Yom Kippur	Tenth day of the first month of the Jewish year
Diwali (Hindu Festival of Light)	During October or November for 5 days
Halloween	October 31
Guy Fawkes' Day	November 5
Remembrance Day	The nearest Sunday to November 11
St. Andrew's Day	November 30
Hanukkah (Chanukah)	Eight day Jewish festival in December
Christmas Day	December 25
Boxing Day	December 26
Hogmanay (New Year's Eve)	December 31

Mathematical Information

Plane shapes

square

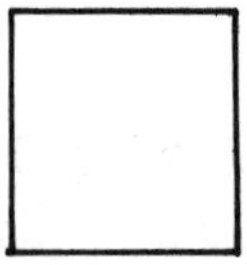

rectangle

triangle

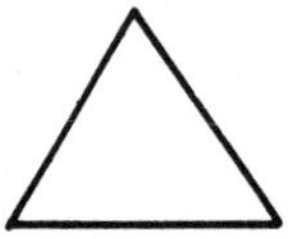

pentagon

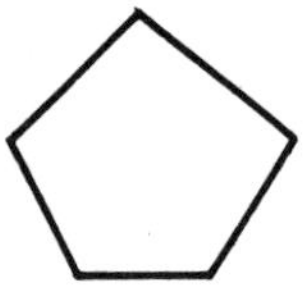

hexagon

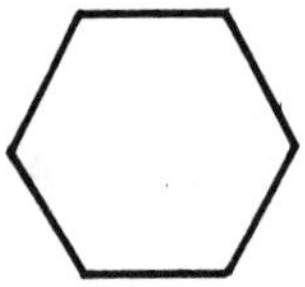

octagon

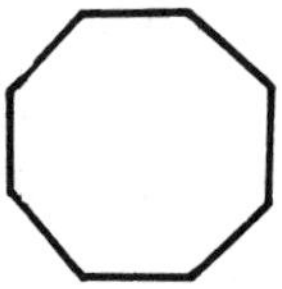

circle

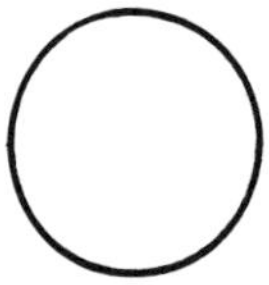

semicircle

oval

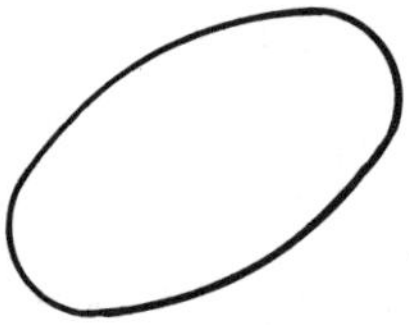

spiral

Solid shapes

cube

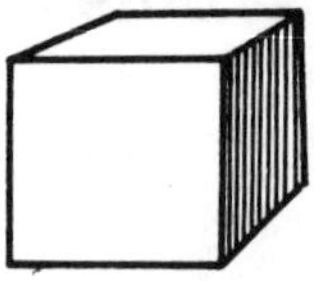

cuboid

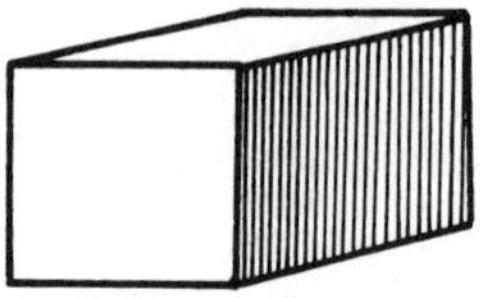

pyramid

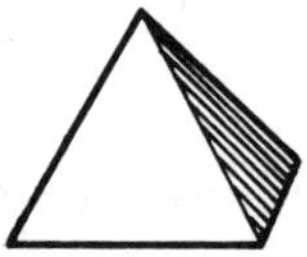

prism

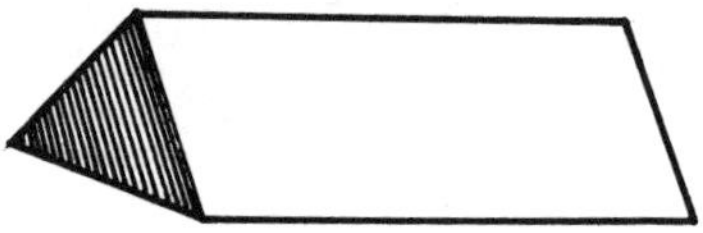

cone

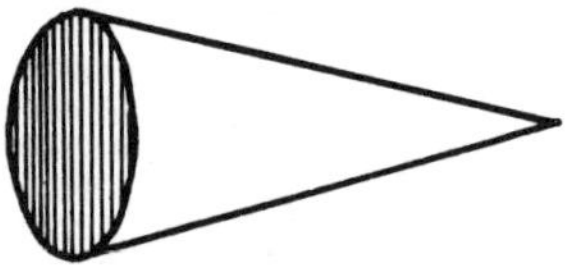

sphere

hemisphere

cylinder

spiral

Fractions

1	one whole	$\frac{1}{3}$	a third
$\frac{1}{2}$	a half	$\frac{2}{3}$	two-thirds
$\frac{1}{4}$	a quarter	$\frac{1}{8}$	an eighth
$\frac{3}{4}$	three-quarters		

THE WORLD

KEY

Continent boundaries
Country boundary
Name of country
(see index below)

70
70 CHINA

Pacific Ocean

Indian Ocean

Atlantic Ocean

Atlantic Ocean

Pacific Ocean

F

E

E

C

C

D

A

B

G

85

78
77

84

83

81
82

80
79

74
73
72
71

75
76
77

69

70

67

68

66

65

64

63

62

54

61
60

59

58

57
56
55

24

29

60

39

38

44

43

45

48

53

51

47

50

52

23

28

37

42

46

49

22

27

35

36

40
41

21

26

34

33
32

25

31

30

20

19

18

17

16

1

2

2

3

9

10

11

12

13

14

6

5

7

8

4

15

EUROPE

KEY

──────── Country boundary

⊙ Capital cities

ICELAND

• Reykjavik

Atlantic Ocean

SWEDEN   FINLAND

NORWAY

Helsinki ⊙

Oslo ⊙

Stockholm ⊙

Moscow ⊙

North Sea

DENMARK

Baltic Sea

UNION OF SOVIET

SOCIALIST REPUBLICS

UNITED
KINGDOM

IRISH
REPUBLIC

Dublin ⊙

Copenhagen ⊙

NETHERLANDS

The Hague ⊙

London ⊙

Brussels ⊙

English Channel

BELGIUM

LUXEMBOURG

Paris ⊙

Berlin ⊙

FEDERAL
REPUBLIC OF
GERMANY

Warsaw ⊙

POLAND

CZECH
REP

Prague ⊙

Bratislava ⊙

SLOVAK
REP

Vienna ⊙

Budapest ⊙

FRANCE

Bay of Biscay

Berne ⊙

SWITZERLAND

AUSTRIA   HUNGARY

ROMANIA

SLOVENIA

SERBIA

Bucharest ⊙

Black Sea

ITALY

CROATIA

BOSNIA

MONTENEGRO

MACEDONIA

BULGARIA

Sofia ⊙

PORTUGAL

SPAIN

Madrid ⊙

CORSICA

Rome ⊙

ALBANIA

GREECE

TURKEY

Lisbon ⊙

SARDINIA

BALEARIC
ISLANDS

Mediterranean Sea

SICILY

MALTA

Athens ⊙

CRETE